HOMAGE *to* AMERICANS

HOMAGE *to* AMERICANS

Mile-High Meditations, Close Readings, and Time-Spanning Speculations

Eva Brann

PAUL DRY BOOKS
Philadelphia 2010

First Paul Dry Books Edition, 2010

Paul Dry Books, Inc.
Philadelphia, Pennsylvania
www.pauldrybooks.com

Text type: Sabon MT Pro
Display type: Mrs. Eaves and TheSans
Designed and composed by P. M. Gordon Associates

Printed in the United States of America

Library of Congress Cataloging-in-Publication Data
Brann, Eva T. H.
  Homage to Americans : mile-high meditations, close readings, and
time-spanning speculations / Eva Brann. — 1st Paul Dry Books ed.
    p. cm.
  Includes bibliographical references.
  ISBN 978-1-58988-062-7 (alk. paper)
  1. Civil society—United States. 2. Toleration—United States.
3. Church and state—United States. 4. Madison, James,
1751–1836—Political and social views. 5. Lincoln, Abraham,
1809–1865. Gettysburg address. 6. Civil-military relations—
United States. 7. Civil supremacy over the military—United
States. 8. Mexico—History—Conquest, 1519–1540. I. Title.
  E183.B826 2010
  322'.50973—dc22
                                                    2010031150

To Vanni Lowdenslager in Gunnison
and to the Palisade clan,
especially Mike and Blakely, Jack and Duna—
my Colorado connection

Contents

PART ONE

MILE-HIGH MEDITATION

MILE-HIGH MEDITATION

My Take on How to Think
and How to Be

I. Denver Airport: Observations
JULY 1, 2008; 1:30 TO 5:37 P.M.

When fortune flummoxes you, take revenge by thinking things out, especially when she provides four forcibly vacant hours for coming to.

Tolerance is not my favorite virtue. It underwrites a group of behaviors preached by some well-meaning but not very keen-minded folks. It means to be humanly fine, but it can't be much more genuine than customer-relations-mandated courtesy or that yeasty expansion of our soul-dough, raised awareness. I balk, though not altogether unappreciatively. Why, I ask myself?

Because, though much better than hate-rampant bigotry, tolerance is excessive on the other side: flabbily self-indulgent intellectually (I can live with that) and culpably helpless in the face of evil (we may die from that).

For infrequent fliers: Denver Airport is, they claim, exactly 5280 feet above sea level and calls itself the Mile High Airport.

Yet it is folly to knock tolerance when a better mode is so unlikely to prevail—folly to subvert a preachable public way to behave for a not so easily articulable and uneasily sustained way to be, to swap attained decency for desirable subtlety. (I'll attempt its articulation to myself soon.) That would be a shameful result—to have to hold your head and say to yourself: "How could I have been so idiotically pure as to let unlikely 'perfect' drive out attainable 'tolerable'?"

This country, which has the most workable public ways I know of from life or from reading, is founded on practicable mediocrity, even mediocracy, the rule of the tolerable middle way, the achievable mean—not only in going fact but even in, or rather, by reason of, its founding theory. This way is laid down in our rarely read founding scripture and expressed in our incessant rights talk: of privacy and entitlement, of individuality and—curiously its opposite—"identity." Its social realization, which turns formal assertions into concrete ways of life, is suffused with tolerance (and of course with its curdled complement, righteous outrage) for everything from life-enhancing variety up to life-souring misbehavior. In fact, *the* feature that distinguishes the social tone of aristocracies from mediocracies is, it seems to me, that in the former the nays have it—good breeding is understood to be what you *don't* do, and what impinges disagreeably isn't done (or only done with malice aforethought)—while in our democracy it's "yes" to everything, until morality-mongers, insurance companies or health professionals mount anti-campaigns. So by and large whatever isn't proscribed is permitted, expansively: outrageous self-adornment, splayed occupation of personal space, emanating environing noise. (The English used to accept—no, appreciate—eccentricity; Americans have made it into a trendy commodity.) Here is a man at the table next to the one at which I've ensconced myself, suddenly moved to whistle an inherently flabby-tuned song, off-key to boot. He isn't exactly entitled, but he'd be mighty surprised to be glared at for his innocent invasion of my auditory space. As I said, all this broad behavior is periodically inhibited by a mildly or fiercely zealous citizenry as being publicly offensive or dangerous: demeaning speech, smoking, polygamy, cell phones. But what is repressed in one way comes back and is tolerated in another medium—inevitably, it seems.

For by and large, the American public, uninhibited in dress, sloppy in speech, spread-out in body, attains tolerance. Moreover, although not so many of its members are what the Old Continent would recognize as well-bred or even carefully brought up, they are for the most part good-natured and sensible—and surprising in their considerateness. Here comes a young man who doesn't look like the scion of an old family, slurping his huge drink—and then turns out of his way to deposit his cup in the trash can. (Incidentally, when as a multi-inhibited child with a bourgeois European upbringing I landed in Brooklyn, I was abashed by an evident prohibition unknown even to me: People never ate in the streets. There's another inhibition gone—that's not to say that freedom grows with permissiveness. On the contrary, there is no "permission" with impunity; it is always paid for by regulation, and as much is regulated now as was in the Brooklyn of 1941—only not by social custom but by governmental agency.)

"To tolerate" means literally "to bear" with the connotation of "to put up with." (In *Macbeth*, the word "portable" glosses "tolerable.") In life it means training ourselves to ignore things until we don't notice them—an inverted sort of self-discipline, that of being obtuse to each other. Yet one of the agreeable features of American public life is how often, as we walk forbearingly by each other, we manage to have agreeable, often comic, encounters with each other. There is in many of us an available smidgen of slantwise appreciation, of ready fellow-feeling. That is just what the isolated or commandeered crowds of totalitarian regimes with murderous governments and failed economies lack: passing friendly recognition enabled by the security of having landed on a blessedly rich continent with a sound civic constitution. It is the same friendliness in adults that children who are secure in their families show—glancing and easy, passing but satisfying. This scene comes to mind, for example: I'm taking my very moderately paced constitutional in my neighbor's Yard, the Naval Academy. At me comes an upright (and apparently uptight) senior naval officer and says in passing, "Don't exceed the speed limit"; he's by me before I can tell whether he's even cracked a smile. I've had pleasant meetings in Europe, but not so light and, to use an un-American word—though Whitman likes it—so comradely. It is a minuscule example of that American encounter the love of which (potentiated, to be sure, by eroticism) Walt works himself into—a sort of passion for the whole bubbling mess, a love-transmogrified tolerance, a little of which goes a long way with me, but that little goes deep.

> Witness of us . . . one side a balance and the antipodal side a balance. (*Leaves of Grass*)

For it is really a wonderful people, full of surprises that impeach every prejudice. Here, at a nearby table, sits a rhinoceros-backed couple with four (by my count) empty boxes once full of medium-size pizzas, plus bread sticks. (I'm on a diet so my sensitivity is raised.) The niggling European would think (and say): "Gross Americans." Well, she gets up, to get more, I guess. And what are they now revealed to be doing? They are studying a book of classic chess moves and practicing on a travel-set of chessmen. Gross, my eye.

II. Airborne: Musing

I began by casting aspersions on toleration and seem to have written myself into an encomium. So now to moderate it back into suspicion and finally even rejection, for tolerance as a psychic condition turns out to have three already intimated drawbacks discernible to me, here listed in ascending order of severity: Tolerance masks dislike; it indulges vagueness; it is helpless before reality.

The first two items are the vices of its virtues. Masking dislike, fettering frankness, is the condition for living and letting live; but it also turns souls into seething pressure-cookers given to untimely explosions, unless it dissolves that capacity for repulsion which is the toner of individuality. Similarly, schooling oneself in suppressing a too critically accurate, too acutely refined sense of the other is a condition of amiable association—but it also diminishes the taste for skewering truth-telling. (I mean making penetrating judgments intra-psychically; truth is not always the better for being told.)

The third flaw of tolerance results from its averted eyes and unfocused vision, its blindness to badness. When push comes to shove, tolerance turns out to be a contingent mode—contingent on lives lapped in civic peace, on willing mutuality. When they meet with intolerance, groups that live by tolerance are at a loss, sometimes fatal. (For each of these defects, I'm thinking of situations in my lifetime, some from my own life, which I will not tell here, because in musings of this sort this seems to me a good rule: Don't retail what you can't detail.)

In short, tolerance is a psychically strenuous but intellectually relaxed mode, when the sound human ought to be, so I think, just oppositely conditioned: serene in soul, taut in thought.

Oddly enough, devotees of toleration seem not to have thought through the other side. Some people are intolerant from a terminal clotting of the soul's flux. (In fact, the inexpressiveness of the badly schooled—co-opted into some faction's sloppy, trendy language—seems to me the bane of our social existence.) But others, both our fellow-citizens and our engaged enemies, are intolerant because they are seriously preoccupied by first and last things, to which they are more devoted than to the middle, the mediocre things. (Even Aristotle, who wrote the text for the West's adherence to the goodness of the middle, admits that the great virtues are extremes.) To those who care with consuming passion for ultimates—salvation, ancestral ways, God's bidding—tolerance seems what it indeed is: light-minded. That tolerance is light-minded seems to me not the construal of bigotry but the truth of analysis.

By light-mindedness I mean a disposition that includes all these facets, good and defective: It is intellectually the unwillingness to think to the bitter end (if so it be), and practically the willingness to live with compromises destructive of communal ultimates (as if there were others). Tolerance is the chief locus of the truth of experience: For life to be livable you have to curtail thinking. (Socrates, to be sure, says—literally—the opposite: "The unexamined life is *not* livable." That is true too, and thereby hangs my tale, I suspect.) But some human beings, decent and deep of soul, care less about the livability of life than its consecration. The party of tolerance rarely comes to grips with the party of faith—or rather, "coming to grips" probably isn't the right mode to begin with. (I want to think all that out when I'm down on earth again.) This seems to be the difficulty: to entertain the two notions that freedom might be of less value than orthodoxy—first, that being right with God comes long before living as you like, and second, that no salvation of soul is achievable individually, that humans are first and last (not just in daily public life) communal. God cares infinitely. We must care desperately—in communion.

I come to the bearing of tolerance on religion first because it is there that our notion of tolerance has its inception—in respect to religious speech and practice. Actually I didn't come to it first, and not even to political tolerance, but to that contemporary phenomenon, the "lifestyle." (Let me interject that I would rather live a chosen life in the Plutarchan sense—one that I've shaped into a sense-making narrative—than have a preferred lifestyle in our sense—one that I've let express "who

I am"—but let that be.) That order of interest is reinforced by airports with their dreary high-end offerings—the less said the better.

Three deep-thinking initiators of our tradition of tolerance, Milton, Spinoza, Locke, even they, who dealt with that most urgent need, that for religious tolerance, seem to me not to have thought through—or at least not to have admitted scruples about—the eventual dilemma. With respect to lifestyles, where tolerance at worst degrades the culture a little, and politics, where it induces some self-correcting chaos, the dilemma may be preferable to its suppression, because life has levels: There is "quality-of-life," which has to do with amenities. Amenities are anything but inessential. A daily life of private un-pleasure, of quiet or unquiet desperation, life in a confining carapace of self-protection or with a Philoctetes-wound of recurring agony, or even in the dead space of an endemic boredom, is not human; reliably recurrent pleasure is the lubricant of daily performance. That is true notwithstanding the recognition shared by the most pleasure-supplied and the most pleasure-deprived people: that there is a stratum of life where happiness fails though life is pleasure-lapped—and may reside though it is misery-burdened.

To come down some: Most quality-of-life "issues" (funny Americanism that states the problem as its solution, for "issue" derives from "outcome") are indeed neutralizable—by accommodation, avoidance, composition, withdrawal, and if worst comes to worst, regulation.

It is similar with politics, our most public level of life, in which the soul is, be it as engaged spectator or involved player, turned all outward, preoccupied by the worldly conditions of happiness—though sometimes finding inner fulfillment in that turning inside-out, that expenditure of spirit in the world of action. It is the case, especially in a successful, real democracy, that politics is mostly mundane: policy and the power to make it. It is in ancient city-states and modern totalitarianisms, that is, in the most and least communal of communities, that politics is about high things: the fulfillment of life and the fate of man. In any case, in our politics, which are so blessedly compromised in principle, and which work to "split the difference," tolerance is not a bad thing, but a good one, because its fundamental defects are "in word, not in deed," intellectual rather than practical. Actually, that proverbial Greek distinction doesn't quite do it. The weakness of the notion of tolerance shows up where soul-adherence means to infuse daily life.

The problem is less living with fuzzy reasons or contradictions than with curtailing the fullness of the spirit. This is what the founders of the nation either haven't worked through or are unwilling to enunciate: how the tolerant meet the "convinced," literally those who have been conquered by, who have surrendered to, truth.

Who are the tolerant? Some will, some won't dispute it, but I think they are, perforce, the unconvinced. Let me rehearse who, it seems to me, can be tolerant: First, the radically atomic, the ultimate individualists, who, no longer "divisible" themselves, cut themselves off from their fellows, whose opinions are therefore only of the most brutely practical interest to them; here tolerance is indifference. Second, the permissively comfortable or anxiously discomfited agnostics, who, unfixed themselves, allow for all sorts of possibilities. However, some dogmatic agnostics (by no means a contradiction in terms) are intolerant as hell, since they look down on any fixation of spirit as false in principle. They make not-knowing into an ultimate dogma.

Third, the terminally flabby, who can't get themselves coagulated enough to shape any opinion; at most they dignify their malleable soul-dough by invoking a righteous pedagogical principle, that of permissiveness. Fourth, the ironists, for whom indecision is a superior stance. These are the perennial romantics, whose avatars are the German Romantics, the inventors of ironic disengagement, that too-good-for-the-world hovering above the sides, absolved from the risks of choosing the truer truth. Of them Gottfried Keller says:

Wer über den Parteien sich wähnt mit stolzen Mienen,
Der steht zumeist vielmehr beträchtlich unter ihnen.

Who imagines himself above the parties with a proud air,
He stands most often rather considerably below them.

The ironists are democratically tolerant from proud stand-offishness.

Fifth are the seriously worldly, those who actually believe that the peaceful pursuit of prosperity is a far greater good than any orthodoxy (literally "right thinking"), because this world is all the world we have and its sensory deliverance is all we receive and its pleasures are the stuff of happiness. For them it is only sensible that we should publicly rub off the rough corners of each other's beliefs and live by some public consensus of tolerance; they are the disestablishmentarians of orthodox opinion. Some of them have lived in the anti-clerical hope that rationality would then replace sectarianism—Jefferson. Others have acted in the open-minded expectation that religions in all varieties would flourish—Madison: In public, practicable compromise underwritten by religious compromise; in private, the full faith-spectrum from atheism through agnosticism to orthodoxy, from denial through indifference to enthusiasm— this fifth way, he thought, is our way. Madison's expectation has been spectacularly realized; our country is the most religious of the Judeo-Christian West (though not if you include the Judeo-Islamic, that is, the whole Bible-based Near East).

I think that even Madison's notion of religious freedom, which requires a tolerant citizenry, is not altogether lucid. I venerate it, but its basis is obscure.

Here is a beginning: Tolerance requires letting others be, letting them alone, either from intrinsic or from cultivated indifference. Knowing your fellow humans also requires letting them be, but letting them alone is not letting them fully *be*. It is a maxim of learning: To learn anything requires letting it be, but not letting it alone. Is there a way, a mode of engagement, of *not* letting things or people alone that yet lets them be—not tolerably, not as bearable, but really *be*?

A spectacularly ill-judged case of not letting be comes to my sky-borne mind: A young, religiously gifted Jew conceives the notion that he is more the Son of God than the other Children of Israel and that to believe him, and so *in* him, is more needful than to obey the Law of the Father. The Jewish parties collude in denouncing him to the Roman occupation, and their leaders demand his execution. The instrument of his execution, the cross, becomes a symbol of a world religion and brings two thousand years of grief to his people.

Why did they not let him be—in both senses—not from underestimation of his power or indifference to his dangerous refractoriness, but to learn what self-antitheses their own people had within it? What a mistake, it seems to me up here, it was to curtail the whole by cutting off one of its inner possibilities!

There is, I hope, nothing nutty in a Jew with some of the mental habits of twenty-first-century America and some of the refractoriness of a twenty-six centuries' tradition trying to think out what would have worked, not so much to defang as to do justice to Jewish otherness. "What should I have done?" is ever the question posed to regardful participants—in history as in fiction. I'll wait till I have my feet on the ground.

III. Gunnison: *Zeroing In*

How hard it is to focus on the problem, or better, to get the problem in focus—to shape mental unease into "soluble" shape, that is, to turn it into forgettable run-off. Perhaps tolerance isn't a problem but a question, not a knot to be untied but the stigma of an uneasy basic truth. In any case, I think that the intellect is charged with getting things as straight as possible, which may end in quite a ligature after all. (Whether the caste of intellectuals is capable of using our faculty for insight is a question I mustn't go off on—that's the sliding off-topic I mean.)

It occurs to me (once again) that in the discipline of interpretation ("hermeneutics") there is a principle of charity that seems at first as weakish as tolerance: Why should human understanding be an eleemosynary endeavor? Why should the willingness to hear what others say, so as to attribute maximum sense to it, be a charitable enterprise? But then, charity was not first alms-giving but grace, and next it was giving as opposed to desiring love, such as is supposed to characterize a Christian. And isn't Thomas the faithful also Thomas the fair, in whose *Sum of All Theology* the opposition is always presented with generous care? This original principle of charity seems to me crucially good—a pointer to a more demanding private way to parallel public tolerance. Is there more to it than "taking things seriously"? Yes, that's too clunky. Perhaps "willing receptivity," "imaginative sympathy" puts it more gracefully.

But that's description, the description of a frame of mind—"psychological," as we say. The principle of charity is a working principle, not a firm first, not a prime, a ruling power of thought. The intellect wants not only clarity but all the ultimacy it can get to.

What is insufficient here, not close enough to finality? Tolerance involves putting judgment on hold, charity construing things for the best. Friendly indifference, provisional approval—it leaves me uneasy; no, as we used to say in Brooklyn, it "makes me crazy." For it suppresses right and wrong—well-judged approval and disapproval.

We are told to be non-judgmental, the mad notion being that every adverse judgment about others is a pre-judgment, a prejudice, meaning a judgment before the fact—never mind the fact that the facts may happen to support it.

A-judgmentalism does not permit retreat. It is not permissive enough to permit us to take refuge in the law, to declare for obedience to our law, and our ready willingness to accord to all the rights to which they are entitled (which in our country are pretty broad). For the non-judgmental folks know in their bones that people crave more, something for which no Title X can be written into law; they crave tolerance plus. I have the feeling that they demand whole-hearted tolerance because they really want something beyond. What is that additive that makes tolerance more potent? *It is respect.*

But surely respect is incompatible with disengaged judgment. The inclusiveness of respect is not, I hope, akin to what it seems to resemble: Romantic irony, Thomas Mann's notorious mode, in his words, "that irony which glances at both sides, which plays slyly and irresponsibly—yet not without benevolence—among opposites, and is in no great haste to take sides and come to decisions." I'm, to be sure, in no great haste—I reserve haste for the hateful business of life, and at "the sessions of sweet silent thought," futzing is my middle name. But I do think that making up my mind (as I do my bed) is a duty of good psychic housekeeping. Nor, on the other hand, can I think of all this as what the English once took to calling "doing philosophy" (sounds like the commission of a high crime). So: neither indeterminate Kierkegaardian "hovering" nor positivistic fact-finding, but an attempt to come to terms with otherness, to supplement "Know Thyself" with "Know Thy Other." What might be called tolerance-mongering precisely forestalls mutual respect, for the latter depends on criteria; it is as judgmental as can be. And these judgments are defensible. Human beings do right and wrong, well or badly, are helpful or harmful to each other, meet their obligations or default on them, sweeten the ambient air or sour the mood, think clearly or confusedly, and, perhaps most vexatiously, are lovable or not so lovable—and we can and *do* judge. (A former president of my college tells this story: He was teaching an ethics course at

a police academy. In the first class, a general discussion, ajudg-
mentalism was rampant: No one can tell another what's good
or bad. Then he, the teacher, announced his grading policy:
Every name from A to M would get an A, from N to Z an F.
Within the blink of an eye, there wasn't a non-judger left.)

There is, though, a human respect which is, on the face of
it, quite supererogatory, that is, beyond the call of criteria, and
it is, strangely, the most obligatory of all. It is a true and excellent prejudice—that for human being as such. This respect
(I don't yet know what to call it, sense, sentiment, affirming
thought) does not, to be sure, value human life absolutely, since
we have respectable and even especially honorable professions
that not only require their members to risk dying (firefighters,
rescue workers), but that command their members also to take
life (the armed services). It rather values the human being itself—not its life, which is a passing condition, but its being,
which is its steady essence—what it always did, now does, and
ever will mean to be genuinely human, in life and out.

Why must I respect human beings, and whom among them?
That it is a pre-judgment tells me that this respect I'm trying
to think out reaches *all* humanity before the judgment of wor-
thiness. It does not prevent, though it complicates, contempt
for the contemptible. There seems to be a required universal
respect and a permitted particular contempt; one is an open
posture or attitude, an aptness or disposition (perhaps all of
these), the other a closed determination; one springs from wide
judgment and inferred principles, the other from close discrimination of experienced cases. One fellow human can be the
object both of principled respect and of heartfelt contempt—
and equally, of course, of warm admiration, for we are all at
once humanity and human, universal and contingent. Here it
occurs to me that I would think it a shame in me were I incapable of entertaining—no, affirming—both sides of a thought-
duality at a time. That's not a problem to solve but a project
to construe.

IV. Santa Fe: Thinking It Out

So "whom?" is answered, but not "why?" Just why must I have noncontingent respect for human beings as such? I live in a land in which the articulate righteous (and self-righteous) see no inconsistency in declaring against prejudice as bigotry (that is, by one dictionary, "intolerant devotion to one's party") or even against the notion that anything might deserve disdain (that is, an inegalitarian sense of being better than that). We've gone so far as to make expressed hate illegal. Good sense tells me that's absurd, this *mere prejudice* against bigotry and contempt. If we indeed have the other rights we ascribe to ourselves, then the right to be a hate-filled idiot (in the original Greek sense of a perfectly private person) must surely be among them. Thus I'm a little more squeamish about the expansive holier-than-thou do-gooder than, say, the contractive, hounded-feeling anti-Semite. It should be acts and acts only that are proscribed, and fancy linguists' theory notwithstanding, speaking is not acting except in very restricted cases (such as that famous legal example of falsely shouting "fire" in a crowded theater. Auden the poet, who ought to know, says in his farewell to Yeats, "Poetry makes nothing happen." His unsaid sense is surely "and that is why it matters most: If prose sometimes causes us to act, poetry often causes us to be").

I find in myself a First Amendment freak; democratic salvation is in letting it reign. What then is wrong with prejudice except its unloveliness in the possessor and its inconvenience to the object? It is the question of the "why?" of respect gone at from the other side. If it takes me time and concentration to think it out, surely it will take the same for others, so experience tells me that bigots won't often cure themselves by sessions of thought. In the interests of the right to privacy and free speech, we'd better let them be.

So seriously, why accord respect? I declare myself to myself a disciple of Socrates, first and last in this: what? before why?

What, then, *is* respect? I'm in the habit of looking first to the earlier but now occulted meaning of words, not because I'm an unconditional believer in the final wisdom of language, but because etymology is often suggestive of connotations that are still distantly resonant. "Respect" comes from a Latin noun *respectus* formed from the verb *respicere*, "to look back on, regard, consider." We speak of holding people in high or low regard (as in "guarding, watching closely"). "Regard!" means "Pay attention!" "Respect!" means "Pay esteem-laden attention!" The looking of respect has over time absorbed a high valuation, so to speak. *Proverbs* says fairly neutrally: "It is not good to have respect of persons in judgment." We would say, with less dignity but more currency: "In judging people, don't be prejudiced by status." We do still say "in respect to . . . ," meaning merely "looking toward. . . ." But "to have respect for" means "to think well of"—not to like or prefer, but to *esteem* highly.

That's the point gained, then: "Respect" involves keen watching, attentive looking, *but* with a favorable disposition—not, to be sure, going as far as Auden's overheated opposite of intolerance: "We must love one another or die" (I'd rather die is my smart-alecky reaction). No, I mean a knowledge-able favoritism, open-eyed prejudice *for* persons and for the most revealing expression of their personhood, namely, their individual humanity: their opinions. My presumption here, left mostly inexplicit, is that human beings are by their specific nature somewhat theoretical: incapable of acting without having first opined—a view that runs plainly opposite to modern pragmatism, be it of the plain American or obscure German style. The latter especially espouses the notion that we are "always already" involved in our world of purposeful work and that standing off and just looking is a derived and second-ary mode. However (I hasten to counsel myself), this odd new attempt of the philosopher, the theorizer, the spectator and speculator *par excellence* (*theoria* being Greek for viewing, looking, beholding, as in the theater), this pragmatist's theory that asserts the primacy of the life antithetical to his own, deserves well-disposed attention too—though it's hard.

Well, finally, why respect our fellow humans, indiscriminately, so to speak, without subjecting them to criteria of deserving?

First, because of our terminal ignorance. Our cognitive finitude has, to be sure, its compensations: those attractive nuisances of the soul, insoluble problems, are re-apprehended as wonder-full mysteries. For example, the longer and the more intimately we've known specimens of our species, the more ultimately opaque they seem, the more so—here I'm driven to paradox—the more lucidly canonical the species as a whole seems. Appearances, once more, have the rambunctious habit of sometimes telling all and sometimes mis-telling all. I recall at that mile-high table in Denver seeing a female walk by, ill-looking in the older sense of "unattractive": a spongy, unwashed-looking face with a complexion like day-old porridge and an expression of pure put-upon inexpressiveness. As she passed she gave me the sweetest smile, as if we might happily know each other. That'll learn me to take untuned airport faces for psychic indices! These interpretative signs are scored so deeply in our judgment that we develop a subconscious typology, which often works well and sometimes fails spectacularly: "There's no art／To find the mind's construction in the face" (*Macbeth*, I.iv.11).

That's for casual soul-detection. When it comes to friends of a lifetime, those whose sayings and counter-sayings, whose actions and re-actions, whose expressions and withdrawals are indeed predictable (and equally lovable and infuriating, just for that), the impenetrability of the inner sanctum—holy or unholy—has fixed itself as a given: The more familiar are your appearances, willed and unregulated, the less transparent is your being, what it is to be you. The density of observed exterior and the accumulation of temporal incident seems to occlude the inner center, which is perhaps best known when surprised in the yet unjaded, highly sensitive first encounter.

So where ultimate ignorance of the other belongs to the essence of their being a person, of having an inside, respect is the best option. (Again I am permitting myself an assumption, this time not against certain philosophers but against the scientists whose consciously adopted program is to translate mind into brain and physiology, that is, to transmute what is invisibly internal into what is observably external.)

There is a discombobulating inconsistency in this, my most heartfelt reason for universally applied respect, arising from our severely limited ability to judge others' souls. How will I get back to our common humanity if my thinking rests on our ultimately inaccessible and probably disparate humanity? We should be as alike as eggs (well, in one carton) if respect is to be simply universal. That must be thought out later, but the egg simile brings on a monitory thought: By a grandly loose version of the principle of entropy, you can break eggs but not put them back together, wreak havoc readily but not recover order easily, if at all. So, if contempt can cause breakage, be preemptively respectful. Assume a virtue, if you have it not. It is a second argument for respect: from the power of its failure.

Here is a third one, mingy but effective: the tit-for-tat argument. It is not so much wise as cunning, a low version of "Do unto others. . . ." Since, I've figured, there seem to be few sayings or doings more potent than esteeming and disesteeming, it's wise to esteem to the limit. It's the wisdom of the human marketplace where status is bartered, and in psychic exchange, as in that of commodities, equilibrium seems safest. It's a reason that has the dignity of commerce—which is not none.

A fourth reason to accord respect is, as intimated, our species-nature, an argument from the class very opposite to that from the crypt of our internality: We should respect each other for being so unhiddenly patent, so uncryptically articulable to each other. Be we first as essences, beings with natural essential qualities, or first as existences, whose being is their own achievement (the two fundamental aspects under which philosophers have viewed us), we are alike, whether defined by a best steady state or a set of possibilities. We seem to have a common biological ancestry and to be, one way or another, spiritual siblings or intellectual alter egos, be we fathered by one Creator, or joined by a common attraction to Being—or even strangely united by our shared radical subjectivity (the going word for individual particularity). From this point of view, other-respect is self-respect. This respect is a sort of species-patriotism: the honor we accord ourselves, and so our fellows, as members of the only congenitally sapient, naturally speaking species on the planet. And like all fine patriotism this respect has room for all species and our shared natural world. Thereby, I begin to suspect, hangs a tale, or better, *the* question: What is the true compass of respect?

But first, which of these reasons for practicing respect counts most? They are all negative or defensive. I'm most devoted to the first one: human finitude, cognitive limitation, especially in matters human. As Heraclitus says:

> You would never find out—even if you went, passing over every which road—the boundaries of the soul. So deep a ground (*logos*) does it have.

But we are also enjoined by the example of our founding document to show "a decent respect to the opinions of mankind" ("to," incidentally, shows the "looking toward" meaning of "respect"). If my earlier defense of respect rested on our ignorance of each other's inwardness, Jefferson's citing of it depends on our ability to apprehend others' opinion, to take in each other's rationally meant speech. Presumably this ability extends, indeed most crucially, to speech we think mistaken, speech that opposes us. So I must figure out why we owe a decent respect even to the opinions that we think are wrong.

And to people whom we regard as a mediocre. To me those Whitmanesque paeans to mediocrity and its mediocracy seem at once a little absurd and very right. These Americanisms make me reflect on degrees of human quality. I think I'm entitled to those thoughts because we are, every last one of us and me too, *mirabile dictu*, somewhere in that middle range (or even above it, as in that fractured epitome of Midwesternness, Lake Wobegon in Minnesota (pop. 942), where "all the children are above average").

Universal humanity—how else could it be universal?—is ordinary. The extraordinary, the "outstanding" of the species are rightly suspect, marginal, on the verge of beyond—*and thus essential*. That paradox is shaping up to be what needs thinking out: that the outer edges that delimit and so define things are reflected into their content, imbue their matter.

V. *Annapolis: Down to Brass Tacks*

AUGUST 2008

Home, and to the hard things, ontological brass tacks—since this question is, I can see, about the status of falsity in the scheme of things. For if respect is to be accorded pretty nearly universally and for colorable cause, and if it pertains primarily to opinion, then all sorts of fall-offs from truth and devotion to wrongheadedness must have a respectable *raison d'être*.

What makes me want to say that respect pertains primarily to opinion—and derivatively to the people who hold them? Isn't it first and last for mere human life, as indiscriminately valuable, that is to say, invaluable? That can't be quite so; at least, once again, no community that expects human beings to give their lives in the line of duty (aside from the agitated question of the death penalty for capital crimes) and honors them for it can be said to respect organic human life unlimitedly. In any case, the origin of what has now shaped up into an inquiry was a sense that tolerance was a deficient way of being with each other, and tolerance does pertain primarily to opinion. Now I have come to want to say: Respect is (1) an alternative to tolerance and (2) the better one.

It is an alternative because it concerns the same issue: how to live with fellow humans who appear to be identically constituted in their need to formulate opinions and to assert them in speech (not always in that order) but disparately developed in their capacity for making sense. I put it to myself so invidiously because I want to hold onto this distinction: that some opinions are more nearly right and others wrong, that between opposite opinions one is the better. Were it not so, life would be stymied, decision frustrated, determinacy dissolved. This appeal to the practical needs of living and thinking is, I recognize, an insufficient grounding for the ontological necessity of truth. (The fancy word "ontology," incidentally, is a part of the way I talk to myself: Greek shorthand for an "account of the way things are.") I'll let myself get away with this pre-judgment for now.

Respect is better than tolerance (1) for the very reason that it discriminates, applies criteria, finds fault and functions despite that. No, better: I'll have to think out an intimation I have that I respect the mistaken opposition not in spite of but *because* of its error. (Curious, obscure coruscations—that my tent stays up and taut, tugged by the guys, the stays of opposition. Reminds me of that most beautiful Frost sonnet, "The Silken Tent," all whose ropes relent,

> So that in guys it gently sways at ease,
> And its supporting central cedar pole,
> That is its pinnacle to heavenward
> signifies the sureness of the soul.

That's the way to be!) But in any case, the flabby forbearance, the implied indifference to the way things are that tolerance falls into has far less dignity for me than the tensed, staunch judgmentalism that accords aware respect.

Respect is better than tolerance (2) for the very obverse and complement of its sternness: It does not just "bear" the others, nor just forbear to judge them. It takes them seriously, for respect is engaged regard, even appreciative receptivity. Tolerance permits, even finds, convenient slanting glances, averted eyes; respect looks the others full in the face, hears their words.

So now the question has really shaped up: How in the face of the opposition's falsity can respect be all-inclusive? Do I really mean "all-inclusive," up to the extreme of evil? Is Shakespeare right to cry:

O benefit of ill: now I find true
That better is by evil still made better? (Sonnet 119)

Yes, I think I do, by means of a distinction. In my lifetime (or anyone's) there have been fellow humans so bad that the world was out of kilter until they were made to vacate it. I've never known an evil person personally (though I know in some detail of their existence). So I've never personally known someone from whom I was forced to withdraw ultimate respect. I have often wondered how I would find a way to bear myself before such a one and imagined that I would be saved from enduring the sight of that apparently human form by getting sick. Thus in the realm of deeds, respect can fail. Indeed the most withering contempt follows disappointed respect. But even for the utterly evil, there is a realm of the spirit for which regard is possible: "God, God, forgive us all!" cries the good doctor after seeing into Lady Macbeth's nightmarish soul.

A whole slew of other reasons crowds in for substituting respect for tolerance in our way of talking. (And isn't that what I'm after?) There's, as I've thought, no doing more potent for good than esteeming and disesteeming; reputation is in fact the public business of respect. There's no power for fellowship like the mutuality of sentiment; true respect is not a one-way story; most often it elicits reciprocity of regard: jointly and severally we respect *each other*. Respect is, for all its discrimination, an equalizer, since I mustn't say: Your opinion derives from your psychological, socio-economic, what-have-you background— mine is the consequence of being well-ensconced in the way things are. Respect lives in the air of Sophocles' saying:

> Many things are awesome (*deina*), but nothing walks the world more awesome than man.

Here's a concomitant thought: Is contempt, then, perhaps contemptible? It seems I've talked myself out of an answer and into an attitude: I wish I, we, wouldn't.

Respect derives its ground in modesty from that acknowledged, awed ignorance which has a deeper dignity than the "you never know" of daily tolerance that I began with. It is the dignity of having tried to follow that subsidiary of the Socratic injunction "Know Thyself," "Know Thy Other," and having honorably failed. And finally, respect is Siamese twin to self-respect, for they are each other's other, each being an appreciatively inquiring relation to an other, another or one's own self. Moreover, the high-toned affect behind respect is reverence, the joyful affirmation of an other's grander being.

A practical addendum: I think substituting respect for tolerance is advantageous especially in our semi-public functions, such as teaching. Instead of the smarmily laborious egalitarianism, the skewing strain of coaxing slackness that democracy's teachers sometimes labor under in their relations with their students, there will be *interest*, which is the working form of respect and which obviates the embarrassments of authority. For where there is three-cornered interest—mutually in each other's thinking and together in the object of learning— discriminating respect shapes up quite naturally. So, one last time, before I bid tolerance goodbye: It's often the most viable mode in a busy democratic life that can't always be on the *qui vive*, though it's only a tolerable second-best: tolerance for the shallows, respect for the depths. Or said otherwise: tolerance for the business days, respect for the sabbaths of our lives. For all that, tolerance is a thousand times better than its opposite, hatefulness—which, in turn, has a certain, if hazardous, value.

For there's at least this to be said about hate: It might actually be a human necessity, which it is perilous to suppress. (I mean, of course, the passion, not its action.) Perhaps, then, to digest hate is a—difficult—virtue. But to criminalize it is political folly, for sure.

VI. *Into the Fall Semester: Notions*

Am I procrastinating, putting off the hard inquiry? Yes, but I've always liked (no, been driven) to traverse the approaches, establish the base camp, square away the gear and then attempt an ascent. Oddly enough, this ascent will be lateral—to the edges rather than the top, I suspect. Well, it's now or never.

What was the question? How to think of respect as universally to be accorded without fudging notions of good and bad (or evil, which is badness of soul), right and wrong, true and false.

I've already convinced myself that in the realm of actions respect should sometimes give way to contempt. The French saying that *tout comprendre, c'est tout pardonner* (or however it goes) is sometimes flabbily false, when the matter to be pardoned is harm done, at least by us humans.

I think I've also bracketed the psychological aspect of the question (by which trite term I mean not the speculative account of our common constitution as conscious beings, but an empirical acquaintance with the general habits and particular aberrations to be encountered among people). It occurs to me that there is one more strong motive to add for respectful receptivity, for "charitable," that is, well-disposed, listening—even when what we hear runs the gamut from vague through confused to recalcitrant down to malignant. It is the most "psychological" one of all: the opportunity to gain experience of human mental behavior, to learn what, discriminated as carefully as possible from the plausible persuasion of truth, humans deem believable and why.

But perhaps there's something finer than mere charity (which is a somewhat warmer sort of tolerance). Heraclitus, once more: He prefaces the request for agreement with the truth he knows by the participial phrase: "Having listened not to me but to my *Logos*. . . ." By "me" I take him to mean his "psychological" self—his motives and emotions, his past background and present foreground. By his *Logos* he means the source of his own speech, the speaking Truth. Teachers know that distinction and its temptations: to attribute students' words to their unconscious psychology or constraining circumstances, and so, with the kindest intention, to deny them the respect reserved for efforts at selfless truth-telling; students in turn don't really want to be held harmless, they want to be heard—and taken up—on what they say. The psychology game—and that of class, gender, race, and all the conditional attributes of human beings—can, of course, also be played for pure disparagement. It is a hostile intellectual ploy for evaporating the human center into circumstantiality. I think therein will lie a problem: how expressive of our universal human constitution our particular conditions really are and whence respect properly derives. In any case, I mean to listen to Heraclitus in this: to take opinions as meant to tell first and last not about the speaker's circumstances and motives but about the way things are or should or might be. In brief, the hypothesis for taking people seriously runs: They say it because they think it. Sometimes, to be sure, it takes some devotion to discover what they mean, but almost always people are grateful for that interest in their center of gravity. Always, listening shouldn't be a social charade but a focused hearing.

So to it. I believe as a condition of profitability for inquiry that some thoughts are true and others false, and I know that inquiring speech would cease if people didn't believe that; verity-seeking would cease. It follows that when we really think something to be true, thinking with all the passion of the intellect's interest and all damping of the will's self-interest, then we must think, unabashedly and *sans phrase*, that its opposite is false. That is called *conviction*, the conquest of our judgment by what is the case.

Alice's friends in Wonderland—and Wittgenstein, who wants to squelch wonder—are at skewed odds here: *They* believe six impossible things before breakfast, and *he* says that you can't assert that something is the case and not believe it. I think it depends on the soul's level for the day: When its waters run high and boisterously, belief is borne beyond itself, but when the soul's sea is calmly reflective, taking something to be so carries conviction, implies exclusivity.

But hold it. The faith that some thoughts are true and their opposites false is attended by this unease: It is not itself a truth, meaning a mode of the intellect in which it is through and through lucid and—or rather *because* it is—about something through and through genuine. It is rather an opinion, even a prejudice. The remedy is the thought that to believe in the possibility of truths is not to assert any one of these. It is rather to have a vivid and variegated notion about the catastrophic consequences of seriously held radical skepticism, meaning not the for-instance talking points of argufiers but the possible practical applications by true unbelievers. This prejudicial opinion is, in other words, one of those circumambient convictions that arise not from looking a matter straight in the face but from glancing at it askance—in fact at its non-being rather than its being: the import of its absence rather than the nature of its substance.

Is this unsceptical faith a mere needful hypothesis, necessary for our psychological ease and our practical life? I don't think so, since skeptics have been both at ease and practical. They have the negative ability to stop asking when the quest seems to turn futile. It may thus be that the ability to live with skepticism, the opinion that truth is unattainable and that terminal doubt is humanly sustainable, is a human disposition. Then so might be the whole spectrum of propensities: from not caring about the underpinnings to not ceasing to care, however apparently impassable the way. Though, *Est nulla via invia virtuti*, "No way is impassable to virtue," says the old seal of my college. It may indeed be that ultimately all is temperament—saturnine or sanguine psychology. I don't believe it.

It becomes more and more urgent to think about belief, which is our first and last mental element. Here's a way to get at it: Prejudice and opinion both seem to be species of belief. Is every prejudice an opinion? No, not insofar as an opinion seems to be an articulated belief, and prejudice can be a mere gut feeling. Is every opinion a prejudice? No, for the same reason. Yet, yes as well, insofar as every opinion is but partially thought out. Is every human assertion only an opinion? Yes, for three reasons beautifully displayed in word history. Greek for "opinion" is *doxa*, related to *dechesthai*, "to receive." Latin *opinio* is related to *optare*, "to choose or opt for." German for opinion is *Meinung*, related by a false but accepted etymology to *mein*, "mine." Opinion is often *received*, that is, we derive it from the tradition or the pervasive public or a persuasive personal influence. It is usually an option or a preference, that is, we are receptively disposed toward it rather than seized by a truth even against our inclination. And opinion is eminently mine, that is, I cling to it as expressive of my "subjectivity." We might well say that opinion is articulate prejudice. That, to be sure, lets prejudice off the hook. We do, however, generally attach a morally negative sense to the word, and so did the ancients. When Socrates, in his *Apology*, speaks of an "old prejudice" against him he uses the word *diabole*; *diabolos*, an injurious one, a slanderer, morphs into our word "devil." But we also think, ungrammatically but agreeably, that "everyone has a right to their opinion," and if so, they also have a right to their prejudices. Which indeed I think they do. It's discriminatory *action* that's unlawful. We *will* love or hate whomever we like, whatever the public preachment. As Chaucer's unbiddable Wife of Bath says: "But counseillyng is no commandement."

But that isn't altogether right. Opinions run the gamut from wrong to right. They are, precisely, not like tastes, for *de gustibus non est disputandum*, while we dispute, incessantly argue, about opinions. So we have opinions about opinions, but these second-level opinions, these judgments of others' views, may well be a little more deliberate, more reflective: "It might seem so to someone because . . ."—less legacy, inclination, proprietorship. And so for our own opinions. Their reviewing and revising is, after all, one experience that underwrites the faith in truth: There seem to be possible approaches to truth, though they are, to be sure, asymptotic. Distances of that sort, however, which steadily diminish as you go and get as small as you please without going to zero, do appear as pointing to closure at the end of time. Opinions, then, being generally understood to be articulate, can be beliefs progressing toward their own confirmation, just as faith is belief that overleaps the distance from here to infinity, that outjumps cognitive finitude.

Belief itself seems to be positively signed skepticism. Both are modes of self-limitation, and the reasons are alike: the finitude of our lifetime (the *ars longa, vita brevis* principle), which is a mere circumstance that is nonetheless rigidly uncircumventable; the limitations of our intellect, which are irreparable since we cannot even conceive what we lack; the defiance of our world, which sometimes mutely signs to us that it is massively withholding itself from our senses without pointing to any apprehensible Beyond. The skeptic rests content (or reposes in discontent) on terminal ignorance, the believer proudly turns it into a starting point: "I know myself as knowing nothing," says Socrates, and he goes on confidently to make huge hypotheses of intelligibility.

What then is belief, be it apprehended as prejudice, opinion, faith, or un-belief? It is a capability of our thinking power—so much seems obvious. An old tradition distinguishes between the thought itself and its acceptance or rejection: We may entertain a thought without asserting it or its negation. Logicians still have one term for the articulated thought: *proposition*, a "putting forth," and another for an asserted proposition: *statement*, a "fixing in place."

Belief seems to me to be such a fixing-in-place of a thought. Its place is intellectually in the whole economy of the soul, which it influences, tints or taints, as the case may be, and its place is temporally in memory, whence it can emerge when called on unchanged in gist though perhaps clothed in varying language. Belief is halted yet untethered thought; its formulation is fairly steady through time though it is not much bound by argument. One reason our store of meditations consists so largely of beliefs is surely that we forget arguments and remember conclusions, but a more important one is that belief has several sources and its strongest reasons are not lucid argument-sequences. Of course, I have been persuading myself that all our intellectual acquisitions are in any case beliefs of the opining sort and that this condition of ours is no bar to the belief in truth. I won't deny that we often draw conclusions from stretches of valid inferences, and that we base these "logical" reasonings on self-evident truths. But the trouble is that I haven't met a weighty axiom yet whose self-evidence wasn't impugned by its perfectly sensible, if apparently repugnant or *prima facie* counterintuitive, negation. For example: It is the self-evident axiom of our Founding that "all men are created equal," whose denial is arguably undemocratic but not stark nonsense, and it is a postulate of our first geometry that "the whole is greater than the part," whose denial is involved in the definition of an infinite set, which is an off-putting notion but not nonsense either.

Our ability to believe, then, seems to be backed by our propensity for holding on to thought-gist and discarding thought-circumstance, by our good memory for conclusions and our faulty memory for proofs, by our need for a position of repose and our capacity for being temperamentally charged by what we have credentially fixed on. For belief (root: *loubh*) is, way back, related to "love" and praise (*Lob* in German), and so, finally, belief is passionate toward its object; in it our affective and reflective capacities meet. Could I put it this way? Belief, especially as faith, feels the more for knowing its object less. Knowledge, where it is possible, would love its object the more for knowing it to be knowable.

Prejudice, opinion—all that needed to be broached for tackling the problem. Here it is again: The winning candidate in our—for once—spectacular presidential campaign asks, "Why can't we disagree and still remain respectful of each other?" It's a fair question, since both candidates are personally seriously respectable. But it's a rhetorical question, really an encouragement for over-heated followers to behave. Take it in the privacies of thought (never in public) as a real, an open question. If the other is dead wrong, dangerously wrong— what's to respect, except as a personal courtesy?

I'm now driven to my main point, which I suspected would push through the mush all along: It must be that somehow truth is dependent on? a condition for? a function of? falsity and even badness, and that these play *necessary* parts in the way things are and perform their roles in our accounts. There is a witty little Goethean devil, Mephistopheles, who says of his function (the grand Miltonian Satan wouldn't demean himself): "I am a part of that power/That ever seeks the evil and works the good." Although he's a frivolous spook, he seems to have it right. Since I firmly believe—because life confirms it continually—that right and wrong in deeds and good and bad in souls are closely related to true and false in thoughts, that means that *all* the right-hand rubric in that famous Pythagorean Table of Opposites is equally necessary to the whole, as indeed its originators thought. (The left is the positive side in such tables, only, I think, because they are recorded in post-

archaic Greek writing which is *from* left to right; in general
the left side is "sinister," the Latin word for "left"—perhaps
because most of us are right-handed.) I'll collect my own table for this meditation, somewhat helter-skelter (though rec-
tified in hindsight) and mixed nominally and adjectivally (as
comes naturally):

Being—Nonbeing	Deep—Shallow
True—False	Faith—Unbelief
Insight—Reason	Simplicity—Lying
Positive—Negative	Acute—Obtuse
Good—Bad	One—Many

Why or how might all these terms of clear approbation
(and questionable disapprobation) be related both by *column*
and *rank*? I can't think that out now, so I'll take as an article of faith, perhaps the principal—double-faced—prejudice of
thought in the West: It is (1) that thinking most naturally "ac-
cesses" (as we say so inelegantly) what is genuine, sound, and
excellent in ourselves and the world and that truth is thought
fulfilled by its content—"thought made adequate to its object,"
as the tradition delivers its dictum. But these clauses, it occurs
to me, are really converses; and it is the former that seems to
me first: It is the adequate matter that finds and fills thought.
Put less contortedly: We think best about what is good, "true"
in the sense of genuine, "sound" in the sense of least defective—and beautiful withal. And put more summarily: Being is
more accessible to thought than Nonbeing. Of course, this pre-
judgment is endlessly and fascinatingly contested; the opponents (not all, but think, for example, of Hobbes or Nietzsche)
tend to write with more handsome succinctness (thereby partly
undermining themselves). To me the original Western position seems to work best. It *is* a prejudice, and on days of pierc-
ing suspicion I suspect that it depends on a sound digestion—a
good ontological gut. Add in, moreover, the other face of our

first prejudice, which is (2) that each member of the column of Being marches next to its opposite, nearly equal in rank.

The last thing I mean in so suspicioning the purity of truth, both as a prejudice and as a near-coequal of falsity, is some sort of relativistic nonsense, namely that "true" means "true for me" but perhaps not for you, that truth flops about from person to person, that I live in some capsule of solipsistic ("myself alone") discourse. It's scarcely worth using up the lead of my retractable pencil on: To whom could I be writing that and to what purpose?

No, when I say "true," I mean "just true" for you and me. My insuperable finitude as a member of a mortal species and my particular deficiency as this specimen must give me pause, but not about the truth being not mine but ours and pursuable—I love this legalism—jointly and severally, in turn in conversation and in seclusion. My chief reason for thinking so is what I've just put down: The seal of truth is in the thing thought about. Christians are very used to thinking about the Being they believe in as truth incarnate, *the* Truth, so contemporary nonbelievers have at least heard such language, which signifies that "believing in," that is, placing trust, is also "believing that," that is, discerning genuine existence. (Trust and truth are conveniently related in verbal origin.)

I'm ready now to put it this way: *The way things are not is integral to the way things are.* I'm not, the gods forfend, creating novelties here. For one thing, innovation and truth-telling are incompatible, but in any case all writers I've read think it— they rejoice in it or subvert it, marvel at it or despair over it. I found this quotation from the Sanskrit *Brahmana of a Hundred Paths* in a book by Martin Buber. I have no idea what the ancient original actually says or what the modern writer meant by quoting it, but it seemed found fodder:

Since the gods speak only truth, they become weaker and poorer. Therefore, whoever speaks only truth always becomes weaker and poorer. But in the end he endures, and in the end the gods endure.

The passage seems to say, with that imperturbable Eastern paradoxicalness, what I feel myself pushed into: that truth is everything and not enough. That notion could lead to global mush, so what is called for is stretches of reasoning rationality (whose limitation is precisely that it always comes in stretches, that it is always interstitial between terminals otherwise gotten) and moments of distinction-making (which is hazardous since the world, being pervasively double-jointed, can be bent in many ways).[1]

So I'll first try sensible common sense with an ontological overtone. Thus one reason to respect the opposition is that worn-out fudge (which turns out sometimes to be freshly true) about all roads leading to Rome—meaning the Capitol, the one-time capital of the world, not the Vatican. We come from different, opposing quarters of the life-world and find the same capital city of the intellect, there to meet others or the Other. No matter where we start, we find ourselves eventually in the same metropolis, congregating in the mother city of oppositions we must regard.

Or, to change the figure: Since we are, perforce, uni-perspectival, insofar as we carry ourselves and so *our* viewpoint around in the world, an appreciation—and what I mean by respect includes appreciation, some "prizing" of the opposition—is essential to our becoming, if not omni-, then at least multi-perspectival. That's essential to seeing things in the round. So Kepler, the great first really modern Copernican, taught that even the tiny parallax granted to us as living on the orbiting earth, that newly designated planet (which means "wanderer" in Greek), made us better knowers of the true world. As for the heavens, so for ideas; they have their roundness, their backside, to speak wickedly. That is what the opposition can tell us about: the other side, the dark side of the moon—on the supposition that the things which ideas intend are so constituted: roundly. That needs thinking out, later maybe.

Second, whatever (yes, unrestrictedly *whatever*) issues from human lips has interest—except perhaps intentional entertainment—and interest is the respect one intellect pays to the utterances of another intellect. Even the most thoughtless speech is of interest—for a teacher diagnostically, but I'm not thinking of pedagogical psychology. The interest is generic, and pertains not only to the philosophical knowledge of souls, what laxness or vagueness or recalcitrant wrongheadedness or, sometimes, near-pathological originality they are capable of, but yet more to the nature of things that even passing comment might catch: what forms our moon has to present, multiform face and occulted back. (I mean the old mystery-moon, unwalked of man and uncircled by bags of piss.)

A last, but really first, reason to have respect for the opposition is our finitude. I'm not talking here of tolerance-inspiring modesty, a very decent civic frame of mind, to be sure, but of that serious openness to the hitherto unthought or unthinkable which seems to me characteristic of a philosophic disposition. We need each other to advance even by a smidgen within our limits, but we need our naysayers most to exceed the limits themselves. That's the sort of notion called an intuition, by which is meant commonly a vague but haunting sense of the way things are, but philosophically that insight which goes directly to the surest truths. My notion is in the middle: not vague but inexplicit to myself.

This inclusiveness I'm delineating—is it, albeit hidden, among what Aristotle calls "intellectual virtues," maybe one old *Ipse Dixit* himself prefigured when he appreciatively reports his predecessors' views? Or perhaps the way certain inquiries are *at once* methods (ways) to truth *and* essays (efforts) in excellence, meaning that being wrong but on the path is already being right at the destination? It occurs to me that Plato's *Meno* is the scripture of that coincidence. Its question is

"What is excellence and is it teachable?" The answer, withheld
as a formulation, is implicit in the inquiry that follows; more
accurately, it is displayed in that inquiry: Human excellence
is the readiness to learn, and it is learnable but not teachable,
though some teachers are its catalysts—with all that means for
the high vocation of teaching, which is to listen, not so as to
correct but to apprehend—and if there is something to apprehend, then there has been some epiphany of truth.

It has always seemed to me fitting that wisdom was born in
the pellucid Mediterranean and matured in the murky North.
So also the heart-expanding panoramas and the aromatic dry-
ness of the Southwest are well backstopped by this muggy little city scrunched up by creek, river, bay—as dual venues for
marshaling one's thoughts. My question, too, seems to live in
both of these scenes. In its large sweet pungency: Why are we
bidden to the maximal intellectual expansiveness? In its contracted hard kernel: Why is the false necessary to the true?
Moods attach to each version. The first can be asked by a sane,
sober, and satisfied inquirer who feels well rooted in life, teth-
ered to it in dozens of trusted stays, by anchors well dug in and
holding. The asker of the second version might be buffeted by
unease, perhaps from experiences of unexpected opposition,
the kind one feels to be false but not answerable on conceded
common ground. This version shakes my convictions not at
all, but something deeper shudders: my sense of the environment in which my beliefs are situated. Small communities are
great producers of such—not existential, but essential—anxiety, since there the conviction of a personally known opponent
informs the intellectual dissonance: What is so ardently believed by my vis-à-vis has weight; it cannot be just nonrational,
since it is expressed in words, nor altogether irrational, since
a functioning member of my community is confronting me: It
seems falsely conceived but truly important.

I have averred that some thoughts are true and therefore
their opposites false. Therefore? What makes me think it's a

"yes or no" world? To be sure, that's our tradition, but when push comes to shove (as of right now), so what? There is that famous Law of (Non-) Contradiction first laid down by Aristotle as an axiom of thinking—though its earliest mentioner, Parmenides, actually proscribes it, since he thinks, unanswerably, that no one *can* think or *should* say that anything *is not*. This law of logic says that you cannot affirm and deny, either in thought or in speech (for *logos* means both), the same matter at the same time. If you do, it's thought-confusion and speech-chaos. (It is left, as lazy textbook writers like to say, to the reader to figure out why simultaneous positing and negating makes everything true and false at once.) Aristotle goes beyond the logical law; he posits an ontological law: What holds of thinking and speaking also holds of things and their qualities and activities.

As so often, I've come on something assuredly necessary to the conduct of daily life, but maybe not on clarity about it. We can't have people baldly asserting contradictory facts or opinions: "Give a straight answer, yes or no," is the reasonable parent's request, "Did you or did you not . . . ?" the standard interrogator's demand, and even teachers conducting a conversation will press for consistency: "Didn't you just say . . . ?" Above all, the law of contradiction reaches into the moral realm: "My tongue has sworn but my mind is forsworn" is a thought (from a play by Euripides) which is simply wicked; it is iniquitous seriously to say one thing and intend another— its opposite.

"Another"—thereby hangs a tale. Parmenides had said that Nothing is not (for what could it be?), that it is unthinkable (for what is it the thought of?), and that it is unspeakable (for what is the speech about?). Anyone actually listening to him hears right away: He uses negatives and negations *a lot* in his poem. So something is awry: If it makes both deep and plain sense that Nothing can't be something, then where does our speech—indeed all human languages I've ever read of—get its "not," its negations? Are the world's oppositions that speech *seems* to be delivering back to us in truth just *our* doing, a schism introduced by *our* intellect into a world well and hale before coming to our notice, or is it, perhaps, that our yet-integral thought is polarized in verbal utterance? Are we the aboriginal negators?

But perhaps it is terminally inconvenient to believe that Nonbeing is not and we must find a way around that thought. In Plato's most philosophically positive dialogue, the *Sophist*, an intellectual parricide (there so-called) is mounted: "Father" Parmenides, the progenitor of that more-then-half of our West's philosophy, the remainder of which begins with Heraclitus, is killed. Nonbeing is *not* impossible to speak of because it has a perfectly intelligible and sayable other name: It is Otherness—diversity. In our world, to say that something is not this is not to say that it is a nonbeing, but that it is something else, *another* thing. The world is full of antitheses that are really varieties. "Not" is indeed a functioning word of human speech, and it does not bring unspeakable nullities into the world. Instead it gives utterance to the bonds of diversity: Things differ, but "being different" is their common bond—*both* the "being" (their basic condition of self-sameness) and the "different" (their modifying self-differentiation, their otherness).

This picture appeals to me. It leaves the *world* both whole and variegated when left to itself. When taken up into *speech*, it allows for degrees of genuineness. For, while "not" can mean look elsewhere, "non-" can mean the absence of something, and "un-" can mean the removal of something, all quite innocently, this adverb and these prefixes also have disparaging connotations. Not all otherness is coordinate; sometimes, to be other is to be a lesser being of a similar sort. Thus an image is *not* as real as its original and a *non*-citizen as advantaged as a citizen and an un-believer as positively endowed as a believer. Our negating language allows us to express otherness as derogation—to judge degrees of truth, presence, and repleteness.

It can also—this is a Romantic addiction—lever negativity into an advantage: the "negative faith" Coleridge names in his *Biographia Literaria*, which is a suspension of existence-judgment that permits images to work their effect on us unhindered by their unreality, and the "negative capabilities" Keats names in a letter, which is the human ability to abide in uncertainty. Neither of these attitudes appeals much to me. For the enchantment of images comes, I think, not from their deficient reality but from their reality-exceeding actuality, and sustaining uncertainty seems to me less virtuous than making it the incitement to a more soul-satisfying supposition. The negativity that preoccupies me is, in any case, not a mental mode but a way of Being.

What all these world-schemes spectacularly (though tacitly) eject is pure Nothing. All the other-negations of speech don't name, and its world seems not to contain, the state of nothingness, sheer nihility (there *is* such a word), but only, so to speak, relational negativities: other beings. So where, surely not in, but out of the world, is Nothing simply? It's easy to be misled by its name, in two ways. In an oddly charming little medieval dialogue on the confounding fact that an angel could fall and become "Satan" (meaning the "Adversary," the disloyal opposition), Anselm, the teacher, argues that as evil, the Devil is unreal, a Nothing. But the young student can't see how what has a name can be simply nothing, nor can I. So just the fact of Satan having a name is problematic, and having the name No-thing is doubly problematic, as if pure Nothing were a kind of thing, one of the "no-kind." Anselm is wonderful: The name "Not-something," or nothing, "signifies by removing, not establishing." That seems to me very observant. I "all but" get hold of pure Nothing; I do it, so to speak, by evacuating something, voiding it by exhaustion. I can't reach "real" nothing this way, any more than the limit-approach procedures of mathematics can reach zero or infinity, but at least I'm going there, without affirming, "establishing," any *thing*. Anselm just manages to preserve the nauseating thereness of evil without granting it positivity.

This limit-notion of Nothing, then, sends me where? It turns out: from the bottom to the top and all around the world of nature and thought. In the huge tradition, Nothing is the cellar of all that is, where pure dank stuff is kept: "matter not mastered by form," as says Plotinus the Neoplatonist, a latter-day (but not a lesser) philosopher, who made the conjectural inquiries of Plato's Socrates into an ontological system—whether thereby maturing or denaturing philosophy is a great question for me. In his articles on matter and on evil, Plotinus has much to say about basic materiality, the aboriginal privative state, whose shapelessness, whose formlessness, whose "un-ness" (to coin a term) he understands as pure badness, just as Anselm, conversely, takes evil to be nothingness. This notion— that the void, vacancy, is bad, even horrible (the *horror vacui*, it is called), and that its badness is in its lack of form, because form is what imparts goodness, so that even deformity is better than formlessness—is an aspect of the chief maxim of Western philosophy: the positivism, the affirmativism, so to speak, that I ventured to state before. Plotinus goes on to distinguish Nonbeing as Otherness from the "wholly non-being," which is just the Nothing.

From the basement to the top: Nothing also turns up at the pinnacle. Once again, it begins with Plato, whose Socrates speaks, in the dialogue *Republic*, of a principle called the Good that at once (1) brings into being, (2) nourishes, and (3) illuminates all there is, and he says of it that it is "beyond Being." And that means it is neither what there is, Being, nor the Non-being that functions in the world as the Other of that Being, and so—although that realization is a while in coming—it is Nothing. And therefore in Plato is the origin of what will be called "negative theology," which denies that any quality we know can pertain to God. God is, in the words of the mystic Master Eckhart, "a being-exceeding nullity," the No to all our thought-attempts, a No-thing. (Here, too, it is Plotinus, Anselm's and Eckhart's master, who shows how to creep up on unthinkable ultimates by way of negation and subtraction.)

And there is also an all-pervasive Nothing, the Void or vacant space of the Epicureans, a grim sect who call on pleasure to mitigate their harsh philosophy. The ugliest visions of the world, I keep noticing, tend to induce the most beautiful writing, and Lucretius wrote a glorious poem in which he sets out the vacuum that underlies the impenetrable little atoms; together with it they make up all that is. This void is, of course, without qualities except for one, spectacularly irrational and correspondingly revealing: It is an *abyss* into which the atoms fall—something in them knows the way down, though what could down mean? They have hell within; it is their gravity.

But the most interesting (pseudo-) location of a fourth Nothing is circumambience; Shakespeare's Prospero, a self-declared nihilist, speaks of the coming dissolution of our world, and we ourselves are but "such stuff/As dreams are made on, and our little life/Is rounded with a sleep." So also Valéry has the Serpent say in a poem: "The universe is nothing but a defect/ In the purity of non-being." For the devil, the creation is a blot on the white-out of Nothingness. The most serious version of the nihilistic circumscription of the world and its beings, however, is set out by Heidegger in an essay whose title is the question "What is Metaphysics?" and whose answer is not so much to say what it is, as to show how it is even possible—possible, namely, to study what Being is and what beings there are. We live engrossed in daily existence, but sometimes there comes upon—some of—us a mood called anxiety. In real anxiety, when we are asked what we are anxious about, we say "nothing" (in particular). That is the breaking in upon us of the Nothing that encompasses our human world. This anxiety opens us to the Beyond of our being, draws us into it, and from this outside we get a perspective on the way our world is, its Being and beings. This is Nothing as our Outer Space, as if we were ontological astronauts seeing Planet Earth, whole, for the first time.

All this thinking about Nothing pure and simple was occasioned by the question: Do we live in a yes and no world and is the world itself a Yes to a more absolute No? All I've got to is that there is a vivid sub-tradition that thinks so. But does it merit respect? Clearly more than that: awe—once our philosophical limit-thinking has made it plausible to us. Awe is respect for what is no longer subject to our "looking at," at least in the way we regard people and things. It is our feeling toward what is unattainable by thought but approachable by imagination. Pascal has this thought: Man is "equally incapable of seeing the nothingness from which he emerges and the infinity in which he is engulfed." To see it even a little can be, in one mood, to feel terror-tinged awe, but in another to feel reverential awe. It seems to me that to open my eyes even for a second every decade on these vast voids that encompass me, not really to look into directly but to glance at askance, to summon the semi-vision that attends a semi-thought and to test whether dread or reverence is the feel of them—that moment of awe, however qualified, does predispose us to respect our little atoll and our fellow castaways.

But my present business with myself was to gain clarity about the intramural, not the transcendent disposition: not awe but respect, not any respect but that owed to opponents. So I asked myself about oppositions built into the world. The inter-worldly oppositions are nothing like as pure of those so absolutely conceived: Being here and Nothing beyond. Within the world, every other is an other's other; mutuality, that is, simultaneous reciprocity, prevails. Socrates says for the benefit of a young would-be reformer: "But it's not possible to destroy bad things. . . . For there's a necessity that something always be opposite to the good." He doesn't explain the necessity, but engenders the question: Why should it take at least a modicum of bad to make a good? So much seems to follow, however: If it takes some bad for good to be, then badness has some sort of respectability. How to make that cute paradox into a piece of plain reason? How to make negativity respectable to thinking?[2]

It was enunciated in our tradition first that "all determination is negation" (Spinoza) and then that "all negation is determination" (Hegel); thus the propositions are convertible. The meaning of this piece of technical philosophy is this: Whenever I "define." that is, put *finis*, to the extent of something, set its boundaries, so that it becomes "definite," I must be doing it with one (mental) foot planted outside, straddling the border, so as to delimit it from the outside in, by saying not only "not that" *to* its beyond, but also "not this" *from* its beyond. And so also whenever I say no to something, deny something to or of it, I am giving it its inside shape, setting the terms of its being *from* within for its inside. Negating is determining seen from the borders, determining is negating seen from the center—different perspectives on one activity. Whenever we say something definite we are connoting, taking implicit note, of a rejection, without or within.

Someone once said to me: "I don't like digital watches; I prefer an analog face because it tells me not only what time it is, but also what time it isn't." She was so right; the twelve-hour face with its hands puts us somewhere definite in the earth's daily rotation, makes us temporal world-dwellers; it locates our human now in the cosmic day. As with time, so with space, or even more so. Shapes are seen in a double way, indeed can be made to flip: from the inside out, as intrinsically this or that, and from the outside in, as being thus or so contained by their boundaries. Psychologists love to construct examples, such as a goblet with a complexly turned stand that looks like two faces when seen from the outside. And that's another nice fact, much to my point about this example: It shows that every boundary has two aspects, mine on this side and yours on the other; what gives good unitary inside shape to my cocoon is just what makes it an unshapely hole to your outside view; my concavity is your convexity.

Come to think of it, that must be why we like to represent logical inclusions by shapes like intersecting circles: because whatever doesn't belong is the outside, and what does is well encapsulated within, and whatever belongs in two ways is patent to the eye by the lens-shaped overlap of two circles: It is yes and no in space. Of course—it is in space that we early on and memorably run into otherness, bang into it.

There are other othernesses, some of which have the badness not of opposing inanimate objects but of ensouled adversaries, whom we run into early—from an other, perhaps, but surely from ourselves. For we are indeed capable of being bad from our aboriginal mentational beginning (which is called in religious language original sin, our internal adversarial self-otherness). One of these we call lying—or as those naturally disingenuous houyhnhnming horses of Swift's *Gulliver* style it in their holier-than-thou disdain of us yahoos: We "say the thing which is not" with ill intent. They are only horses and don't understand that lying is just a corrupt aberration of our greatest and most redemptive capability: to try saying the thing that is not by way of venturing into the territory of the opposition. We are able to speak of otherness, to grasp and to deny it, both in one "not."

Here is the pertinent consequence of all this notioning: Everything is edged by its opposite. Everything definite I say "yes" to, others could say "no" to because it is or could or should be, in their opinion, otherwise—or because it is in their hearts to play the adversary. My being-centered world is perhaps on the verge of no-thing, and certainly internally shot through with non-being (as Socrates says, Nonbeing is "all cut up into small change") that is just variegated otherness at best and deteriorated being at worst; our world is not only one of never-cloying infinite variety but also of bad and worse variations. And this latter is just that against which tolerance is helpless and for which respect seems indefensible. And yet!

Often—everyone knows this—an event that looks like brutely bad perversion from one side of the divide looks like unavoidable human necessity on the other: variously deformed mirror-images reaching from the view of the "respectable" side of the tracks into the infamous other neighborhood. There is a great scene in the classic German movie *M* (1931), where a convention of professional criminals undertakes to anticipate the police in hunting down a psychopath on these wonderful grounds: *"Der ruiniert uns ja unser Renommé,"* "But he's ruining our reputation!" The police here are mirrored by the underworld, and the fugitive child murderer mirrors them in turn, each a little deeper into darkness. The murderer, cornered by the unforgiving thieves, convincingly if repulsively pleads his inability to stop himself; a sort of humanizing pathos attaches to the monster. Come to think of it, that's true as well of Shakespeare's Caliban, that sentient monster who hears *his* island's secret music:

Sounds and sweet airs, that give delight, and hurt not.
(*Tempest*, III.ii.137)

Points of view have to enter here. They are "points" because I, you, occupy a tiny place in the space of vision—privileged, to be sure, by the fact that a soul has its seat there, but negligible in purview. Its opposite is the God's-eye view, attributed by literary critics to novelists and by theological physicists to God—Newton calls space "God's sensorium," meaning that God's view is simultaneously omni-perspectival. So is ours, only we have to take a turn, a walk in time through space, to gain different perspectives.

Philosophers like to lever into novel ontology notions that are old hat to lay people, and perspectivalism is one such notion. It seems to me that the fact that I'm bound to myself in each position can't mean that the world is perspective-ridden, hopelessly de-centered, ungrounded, de-leveled. Just the opposite: It means that there are many takes on an *it* that stays put and invites my wandering around it. In painting, "viewpoints" imply a set scene, and to me that is a plausible method for forming opinions: to look at something closely from various standpoints and to discern as much of its set solidity as my mental eye can construe. What a loss it would be if my thinking weren't perspectival and there weren't one world willing to host it with many "views"! (The same as holds for objects goes for events. Any discernibly crucial happening has many lines leading to and from it. It is a matter of salience: Some developments are life-lines—veins or arteries. Others are more like tributary capillaries, feeding the event, even necessary to it, but negligible when the perspectival intention is to articulate live significance.)

For among other profits, our perspectival view is the condition of taking another's position—which they don't even need to vacate: We can both occupy the same standpoint (like all those angels on a pinhead), you being at home and I a guest (unless I move in). Adam Smith, a great psychologist, is wonderful on the affective capacity that underlies getting into another's place. It is not empathy (the absurd claim that *I* feel *your* pain, for only you can feel *your* feelings), but something far more subtle, which he calls "sympathy": my ability to *imagine* myself in your situation and then to *observe* what *my* feelings are.

When the aim is to take your oppositional position in thought, then the analogue to sympathy or fellow-feeling is dialectic or antithetical thinking. I mean an activity of the live intellect (humanly dramatized by Plato and abstractly presented by Hegel) that stands by as the receptive watcher, while one *position* flips on its own in its *negation*—because it has it in it, because an opposite is inherent in any original position of living thought.

Here is a very human example. (Hegel's own dialectical logic is, as I said, relentlessly abstract and its human incarnation—necessarily—abstruse.) For an optimist, whose physical and metaphysical digestive system is in indefeasibly good order (the Germans have a splendid term specific to this condition: *unverwüstlich*, "undevastatable"—however that's spelled), the world is by and large, for the most part, in the long run, quite good. For the pessimist, the past is a diary of bad days, the future a cloud of foreboding, the present a mere juncture of these. Now let the optimist go out to (or take in) the opposing point of view. The jocundity of the well-tempered constitution will be modified by a realization of the baselessness on which it is based: luck lasting, health holding, relish ever-reviving—a small icy wind, a smidgen of appalled vulnerability, a little levigation of wisdom, and on top the spice of smugness disturbed.

That is how our daily imaginative dialectic in fact works: The positive position actually gains from the negative (it's rarer the other way around), and its darkening cloud has the proverbial silver lining; the coalescence makes the edges brighter, crisper. So it works, it seems to me, throughout life. Unless the soft center grows a healthy exoskeleton under the pressure of opposition, it turns into mush, moldy liquescence. Kindness, charity, generosity degrade, turn squishy unless given hard-edged shape by otherness.

The same holds for interiority itself. We must be internally antithetical, qualify gentleness by backbone, peaceableness by spirit, unpretentiousness by pride, compromisingness by courage, and openness by an ultimate *noli me tangere*. You can't pluck a plangent note from a string that isn't fastened.

Where did that spout of metaphors come from? Well, if I ask myself what life is like, likenesses will well up. But enough. There are more thought-tethered examples of the rightness of looking respectfully at the others. (That's actually redundant, for really to look at *is*, so I've thought, to have respect.)

I have genuine friends who are fundamentalist Christians. They believe without the scruple of a doubt in the inerrancy of the Bible and in the salvation of their souls only through Jesus Christ (that is, Joshua the Anointed), the same Jesus who seems to me just a remarkable young man who prematurely anointed himself as the Messiah—and in whose second coming I consequently have no faith. As for inerrancy, it is purely wonderful, for it includes the most radical, American do-it-yourself hermeneutics; everyone must decide, without benefit of clergy, what a given scriptural text actually says. And in working that out, my friends show no gullible simplicity but keenness of mind. To be sure, their readings have limits, and what seems incredible to me is certain belief to them.

Is it wise to set them aside? Isn't it a better hypothesis that they might have a *gift*, a capacity for faith that I am without? I mean not just "for instance," but as a possible truth. I believe that they truly believe what is false, but that hypothesis makes me have, or rather, *is* my respect for them—and they in turn respect me for respecting them. To them I must be damned, but they let me affectionately be. Why? Because they must think, if only implicitly, that unbelievers belong in the world not only in fact but somehow in the scheme of things. As true believers they cannot be tolerantly indifferent, I know that. But they seem to be appreciatively open. It is a human possibility that can be lived out inexplicitly, and I long to know how it can be thought out well-groundedly.

That longing does, of course, have much to do with circumstance. I live in a country that surrounds me with opinions that are held each by people of every degree of mental endowment: sophisticated researchers who think that the soul is a neurological event and think it with modest thoughtfulness or with mind-boggling obtuseness, and the aforesaid simple folk who believe that soul's salvation depends on faith in a dogma and believe it with steadfast humility or with hysterical bigotry. I live a personal life one of whose great intimacies (not, to be

sure, a very knowledgeable one) is with a composer who super-
scribed his music "to the glory of the only God." It is, consequently, a question my like-devoted friends and I keep asking
ourselves: Where in the sphere of influence of faith does being
Bach-drenched put us?

What seems to me at the moment indicated for myself in
the religious direction is a real, a meant agnosticism. By that I
mean that the agnostics I know are really crypto-skeptics. Real
agnosticism would be a sense of *really* not knowing, neither of
God above or Life Beyond, *really* taking in the inaccessibility
of that "undiscovered country from whose bourn/No travel-
ler returns," with consequent *real* openness. With respect to
other destinations, I'm not so uncommitted, perhaps because
if there's divinity then there's eternity to learn the truth about
it, but lesser matters need to be decided sooner. I do know that
Pascal's way of securing my engagement is repulsive to me. I
mean his famous wager, the bet on God, a riskless option, as
he himself says, in a theological futures market in which the
commodity is faith. I choose knowing that I don't know. It is
next best to that energized repose that the capability for faith
seems to bestow. And, of course, if faith turns out to be misplaced, it will have been the safer position.

I think I must begin, and have begun, with believing in the
believers and interesting myself in the adversaries. I've piled up
reasons: lately, the escape from a fideistic business transaction;
before, the expansion of the imagination; earlier, a proper esti-
mation of my finitude.

Perhaps I should stop also to collect the kinds of otherness
that it is against the grain but nonetheless right to respect: since
religion was on my mind, the religious pretenders, a broadcast-
ing band, the professionals of faith, whose inner devotion has
been exhausted by too much utterance; the camp followers of
trends who say what one says; the stagnant invalids from some
one, traumatic, long-ago battle; the wrong-headed, willful
self-isolates; even the torturedly clever adherents of notional

evil (with which Russian novels teem)—but never practical badness.

Looking at this very incomplete enumeration, I see that it lies on a spectrum, the spectrum of psychic depth. No metaphor of the soul—and all speech about it is somatically figurative—seems stranger and more necessary to me than this one, the depth figure, that makes a containing solid of our immaterial part. I have thought about levels before, but now, seriously, what does it mean to be shallow, and why are the human shallows to be respected?

"Being shallow" means, I think, that a person's opinions drift on the surface of the way things are, as if he had thrown out an anchor with too short a line. These metaphors suppose that what we have opinions about has itself levels, that we can get "deeper" into matters or stay superficial. That seems to be true. One can have more intimate knowledge of people, inside knowledge of communities, a more penetrating reading of a book, more profound learning. On the other hand, a merely wide acquaintance, say with the current real world or the research about it, guarantees no wisdom at all. Heraclitus, my current hero, says:

Much-learning does not teach one to have insight.

I won't think out now how the world comes to seem layered, and what the everlastingly interesting relation of surface to depth is. Depth of soul is the notion answering to a penetrable world. It shows itself first in the fact that any intimacy is progressive, and next in the fact that it is when the surprise of revelation has ceased that the interest, say of a friendship, begins to solidify; the steadiness of long-lasting, well-anchored concern actually promotes the search for a bottom that might hold even better. I have often wondered whether the very few people I know who seem hopelessly shallow, unable to get beneath anything, in fact have no depths, or whether they have run themselves aground in their own shallows. Only their creator (if we have one) can know that for sure; they themselves probably don't. I, for one, can't believe that the human soul of which Heraclitus said that we lose our way in it is ever terminally contracted.

Is "deep" truer or better or even more interesting than "shallow"? No for all three. As for "interesting," deep people are of course one by one more inspirited, but as a recognizable class the shallows are more fascinating, because it's in its swatchways that most of us sail most of the time and perhaps some all the time. It's called worldliness, and the phenomena of this form of existence have received much hypocritical analysis: ostensibly neutral and palpably derogatory (as in Heidegger's existential analysis of the "They"). As for "better," it is a strange and terrible fact that deep souls can be evil, a fact that complicates the reasoning of those who think that evil is nothingness. But then, why shouldn't joylessly boundless lust and willfully unassuageable resentment churn up and pervert the depths in which they can find no grappling-bottom; perhaps evil souls are those whose depths are an abyss. Perhaps badness even takes a power of mind expansive enough to dare to enter darkness, though not sound enough to shed light on it. Not so the soul of shallows, whose roilings are easily raised and easily calmed.

As for "true," a lot of the most operative truths—the kind that make the world workable and viable—are to be found on the surface. These are the folk-platitudes of the ages, the Unwritten Teachings of the non-philosophers (for instance, the speech of the wonderfully named Platon Karataev—Plato of the Blank Page—the peasant who is at the center of *War and Peace*).[3] They are also the buzzwords of the moment, which always have some, if not wisdom, at least relevance to the situation.

Those who get to thinking about these things are not going to proclaim themselves shallow, so we're perforce speaking of the Other. I say, then (with some misgivings): Human superficiality is deeply interesting, and for that, as well as for the breadth of its appearance, it is to be respected.

Probably the hardest to defend, for fear of falling into cleverness, that perversion to which thinking is most vulnerable, is the respectableness (as distinct from respectability, that is, social standing) of human badness, namely evil. I can't say it often enough: There is no argument for respecting the doer and his deed, who might at most be pitied. I'm speaking of the affected soul. I have good warrant in a theological tradition that has, so to speak, hellish respect for Satan, the Opposer. It is expressed most poignantly in poetry: Milton endows his Satan with a deep intelligence (which is, not always plausibly, presented as cunning devising) and a grand pathos (which is, in a similar vein, always ineffectively countermanded in the next line).

Most deeply engaging to me is the thought that falsity demands respect. I have set out for myself my faith in truth, or at least approaches to truth; perhaps it is time to consider what kind of thinking will set me on the way of error.

First, I think one must get past a contemporary notion: In budding adolescence and again in regressing middle age, we are bidden to establish our "identity" (Latin for "self-sameness"). I'm all for that. But we are also encouraged to "find ourselves." No advice could be less helpful to the first injunction and so to us, teenagers or mid-lifers of any age: We should lose ourselves, lose ourselves in a work and in thinking. Work tires the body but shows products; thinking strains the mind but consoles the soul. The I that is at work and in thought is—this is a borrowed platitude on the deep side—an ego-less I, all there *because* all-absorbed. To put it simply: Thinking for truth is myself *not* being "personal" with myself. Example: Recognize with crystalline clarity and circumvent with indulgent derision your—I'm talking to myself—childish distractibility, adolescent ambition, middle-aged self-importance, elderly authority. Don't suppress anything, just laugh; it's not so noble or well-grounded a mode—in fact a form of that tolerance I only half respect: self-tolerance—but just as service-able and less sappy than humility.

So much for the mood. But for the mode of thinking itself, I'll choose conjecture, and have indeed all along. Conjecture yields *likelihood*. That word and way has two aspects: (1) what is most *likely*, meaning that, considering all the sides I'm able to take in, I settle, on the whole, on what is most probable; and (2) what is most *like*, meaning that similes and metaphors should be (cautiously) welcomed by the conjecturing mind.

There is a little tract by Nicholas of Cusa—an ardent student of the Neoplatonists—called *On Conjecture* (1440 C.E.), about just my term. He works, of course, in the framework of faith. For the faithful, insight is a participation in, an approximating approach to, the actuality of God's intellect. But this participation of the human spirit has, in its otherness from God's intellect, only a divergent, an unfulfilled mode—that of possibility. Our grades of participation in truth are measured by the smaller or greater distance of our possibility, of our capability, for insight, from its never-to-be-reached actualization:

> The approximation can, however, never be raised to attainment. And so the doctrines of the wise remain conjectures. Conjecture is a positive assertion which participates in truth but in the mode of otherness.

In the light of the insight of the divine other-being, Cusanus says, our reason recognizes and accepts its deficiency in exactitude in its practice of conjecture. Moreover,

> [j]ust as in the viewing of an object, the same aspect offers itself to several viewers in different ways, so the multiplicity of the object viewed is united in the unity of viewing, and even the difference of the viewers is contained in the unity of the viewing.

So what I have in mind, even up to a certain comparison with a divine mode of seeing, is here—what a find!—collected as "conjecture": unifying perspectivity, ineradicable inexactitude, approximating approach, truth-finding possibility, and even a respectful sense of otherness—though perhaps "respectful" is too weak and "reverential" would be better, since the other of my otherness is a deity. It all adds up to finding probabilities and telling myself a likely story (*eikos mythos*)—as it's called in the Platonic dialogue *Timaeus*, which tells the tale of the world—at once a likelihood and a likeness. Note: Conjecture as I think of it is not flip-floppy ambiguity, both-at-once-and-so-neither-ness. For all those too cherished intellectual's ambiguities can usually be resolved by clearing the ground a little to discern the common root.[4]

VII. *Nearly Thanksgiving: Cases*

This conjecturing has—and that's what I like—just the give and the verve, the flexibility and the firmness, that fits my notion of respect. I'll try to turn this watercolor into an ink drawing, to figure it for myself as a thinking-out of cases that I've lived with. "There's always two sides to every story" is one of those sayings that's a platitude because it's a fact as trite as it is obstreperous. Usually we mean that there are two (or more) perspectives on the issue. But that's a fact extrinsic to the matter. I want to see if those two sides might be *intrinsic*, if matters that matter to us might be, so to speak, internally aspectual.

My first example is not so much a case as a part of the human condition: stupidity. To be sure, it is, in my experience, a rare condition, rarer than ordinary rationality—not just in my particular world, a college community, which is of course not the most likely venue for dumbness, but in the world at large. I mean the healthy, natural inability to get it, not cases of mental retardation. People who have spent even a day with a person who has Down's syndrome, for example, will have experienced an intelligence which, though hindered by defects of the subservient brain from putting two and two together, still has a weird and poignant gift of salient sayings, a sporadic wisdom that zeroes in on human being. Stupidity is totally unpoignant, at once enragingly comical and discouragingly dull. Yet if you listen, you learn. For one thing, what speaks is not stupidity, for it is indeed a stupor, a numbness before any slight complexity; who speaks is a human being on the defensive. Though he means to say, "Listen not to me but to my thought," here thought is curtailed and the kindest thing is to listen to "me" instead—to begin by letting that preventive respect issuing from your humanity prevail ("preventive" in the old sense of "going before" all rationalization and in the present sense of averting harm).

Bureaucracies whose rule has become autonomous, administrations whose ministry is to themselves, are venues for natural, or what may be the same, willingly practiced stupidity, self-stupification. (For I really can't tell: Is stupidity ultimately a discretionary inability?) But here's my point: Those who are more easily struck down by the being that brutely confronts them, dumbly reflect on the world. They wordlessly raise for us the question: What is it in the world that calls up in most of us some adequacy—an "adequacy of intellect and thing" (*adaequatio intellectus et rei*), which is the old definition of truth, while consigning others to insufficiency? This question is a "reflection" on the way things are, in both senses of the word—as they invite thought and repel it. We usually raise this issue from the point of view of differential human abilities, but why not let it reflect uninvidiously and constructively on the beings we live with, whether by way of confrontation or receptivity? If *we* were all equally up to things, would the differential penetrability of *them* by us or the varying occupation of us by them ever show up? Would that crucial thought-inciting distinction between appearances and what it is they show or screen ever have come forth? Isn't, for example, the angelic intelligence that permits no individual obtuseness thereby both privileged and condemned to be unaware of mere this-worldly phenomena? And isn't the complexity of this, our world, partly mastered by seeing through appearances to a common ground? And isn't inadequacy, particularly official inadequacy, revelatory of a fascinating fact about that world: that its surface, so shiningly manifest (for that is the meaning of *phainomena*) along with being so evanescent (for that is what the usual qualifier of appearance, "mere," betokens) and also so opaquely dark (for it seems unbudgingly, solidly solid) while yet indefinitely penetrable (for our instrumentally aided sense can pierce its immediacies)—that this treacherous non-ground is where the inquiry begins? That in this shifting topsoil are, to use an upside-down metaphor, the roots of our questions, but that it is the office of stupidity to stomp it into impermeability?

I'm speaking from experience here: seven years on a governmental commission with a "facilitating" official whose duty it was first to turn our candid reports into tolerant mush and then to compact our honest ambiguities into guideline-regulated rubrics. He was fired, being too good a man to do his job well, but by watching him operate under his bureaucrat's hat, I learned about the means that sub-personal, hyper-individual institutions employ for turning the world's squishy surface into a safe, efficient, and publicly accessible pavement. They enforced a solid stupidity which was, after all, a defense against the world's chaotic recalcitrance (by "world" I mean people in their externalities and things in their physicality). It's always a study just begun, for no sooner does it seem contemptible than it seems practically necessary.

A second, tauter example of an intrinsic fracturedness of thought comes up often through life's quandaries and is of old a problem for philosophy: Thinking things out, establishing for myself some truth about them—that is what the old understanding, most definitively enunciated by Thomas Aquinas in *On Truth* (1250's), calls "making thought and thing equal [or ad-equate] to each other." Which more to which? (Thomas quotes another version, which speaks not of adequating "intellect *and* thing" but "intellect *to* thing.") He himself seems to think that there is mutuality: As a thing has being, so it can become adequate to thought; the truth comes from the genuineness of the thing, and truth-telling depends on its truly being: The thing *causes* truth. But it is in the cognition of the intellect that this truth *comes about*: Truth *is in* thought. There is also a way of speaking, already found both in ancient philosophy and early Christianity, that identifies Truth with Being itself—a being that is true to itself, truth-revealing, and a trustworthy (trust:true) terminus of belief. ("God as Truth" is in Thomas too, but not so much to my point.) If this definition be scholasticism, more power to it. It feels right— "feels" in the sense in which a thought clicks when well seated in the mind—for it takes account of all this: It seems to be an "I," me, that's making the thinking effort; and it seems to be an "it," a thing or situation, that I'm thinking about. (That much might well have been in the experience of the caveman who could put his world before himself to contemplate, as the painters of Lascaux so luminously did.) But what encapsulates the great next step in our tradition is the notion that my adequacy, my degree of getting "it," depends crucially on its, the thing's, being adequate: being genuine ("well-begotten"), being real ("thing-ly"), being discernible (distinguishable by mental sight), and other ways of fully being I don't want to assemble now.

(Incidentally, why all the etymology? That can become a cognitive cop-out: making the language speak rather than be spoken. It must be because it's internal speech, me with myself; language doesn't fly out—as Homer says: "pass the barrier of my teeth"—to be batted back, but words linger and do, indeed, seem themselves to speak to me.)

The rub here is in Thomas's notion of truth. Things aren't all I think about. There are also situations, issues (as we now say, "I have issues," lots of them), but above all non-things:

confusions, illusions, mistakes, etc., etc. That's why conjectural truth, inadequacy, and approximation, which mirror the inner fracture of being, are dearer to me than that very rare equalization or conformity of thought and thing—as our daily wonts and haunts are dearer than the idyllic rarities of our excursions.

These were two questions about the cracks of thinking that came on me in musing about the need for falsity in truth: human deficiency, mismatch of thought and thing. They're nowhere near worked out, when a third comes up. It is an old philosophical perplexity that turns out to have real practical consequences, and it comes home to me acutely in thinking about race-relations in my own community. So, let the concrete occasion for thinking about respect for the false now be *race*, the issue whether it is of the human essence, the question how somatic and psychic constitution are related—the open sur-face to the hidden depths. In less than two weeks my country will make history. That new turn will damp the passionate issue, but the reflective question won't disappear, for as questions, such topics have less urgency and more staying power; they cease to be agonizing and become interesting.

The question to meditate on presents itself to me as a problem to clue out within the sphere of respect: My notion of respect is that it goes naturally to the human essence in its universality and derivatively to its accidental qualifications—even, I've figured, stupidity. "Accidental" means—I've simply got this from books, and they got it from Aristotle—what befalls a being unnecessarily (though, oddly enough, often inevitably). If you're *born* Jewish, *participating* in Jewish fate is inevitable; you can avoid it only by curtailed memory or suppressed identity. But *being* Jewish is a choice, and so accidental in the sense of non-necessary. Being man or woman is an "essential accident"; you are necessarily one of these as a human being. But which befalls you is genetic, that is, by accident as far as you are concerned (and evidently sometimes against your sense of yourself). Having *logos*—meaning a thinking power and the speech that articulates thoughts—in inward-ness and in utterance is essentially, and so universally, human (always excepting "privations," accidental deprivations and de-fects). Here fact and reason seem to coincide—as they should, for can we even imagine what it would mean for a speechless but genetically human tribe to be discovered? And if it were discovered, how would we ever recover ourselves? Let those who want to deny that *logos* is of our essence live out that fan-tasy in their minds.

Then where does race, black race at the moment, fall? The old liberal mode was color-blindness, the new post-liberal one is race-consciousness, whose not always explicit hypoth-esis says that race so modifies human essence that there are variously specified but insuperable, non-accidental, ways of being mentally and affectively, sensorily and sensually, physi-cally and behaviorally of one's race. Thus the idea of universal humanity is thought of as an often oppressive and hypocritical construct: "What you all see first is a *black* face."

This view seems to me undeniable as a simple fact and false for multiple reasons. First of all, unlike species, races mix and propagate; how are the offspring to place themselves? Second, in all but color, the races assimilate. Assimilation was a great issue for Jews when I was a child in Germany, where the claim was made by the Nazis that Jewish faces bore racially identifi-able marks (ridiculously undermined by the mandated mark of the yellow star). Now the issue is dissimilation, since America resolved the assimilation issue all too well in a beautifully boil-ing, pungent melting pot. If we can all become similar to one another in ways of life, the argument for essential otherness gets pragmatically weak. Third, the principled race-conscious argument itself is made in rational terms. The question "Is there a racially based rationality?" can be and has, of course, been asked seriously, but it suffers from this built-in bias: that it requires an answer in a universally accessible mode of rea-son; the very fact of its being answered for my understanding will cast a "Yes" into the abyss of self-contradiction. (To be sure, I'm never proud of using mere logic to defeat a felt position: The charge of self-contradiction is the reason-scoundrel's last resort; as Hume so nicely says, it compels agreement without producing conviction—or something to that effect.)

So here is a false argument to be respected in my sense: not merely because it comes from a fellow human being (which, by its own say-so, it doesn't even exactly), but because its very claim becomes, just by being made, an intrinsic part of the way things are, and most basically because I suspect, conjecture, that the false is a constituent of the true. And that, in turn, can only be so if things contain some falloff from being in their very being, some strain of otherness in their very nature—for inner definition.

With that thought, the occasion, race, has brought me back to that perennial underpinning: I realize that this is really a case of the old appearance-and-being, one-and-many, universal-and-particular complex—one never-ceasing preoccupation with many aspects.[5]

Take that face, any face. (1) It shows, displays, makes appear, and by the same token hides. But what? I would like to say: the true being "behind" its sur-face, the soul. One might well say that "only in the detail can we understand the essential, as books and life have taught me" (Sandor Márai, *Embers*); one might claim that a unique individual implies, even displays, a universal ground, since individuation requires a prior commonality. But one could as well say that the impenetrably dense variety and elusive particularity of the facial phenomenon more than masks, indeed disowns, the invisible essence of the soul within. As good Duncan said: There is no expertise for reading faces:

> There's no art
> To find the mind's construction in the face.
> (*Macbeth* I.iv.11)

(All along I've used that word, "soul," well knowing that it's now in disrepute among the scientists, those who know, who have *scientia*, "knowledge." It always comes out, though, that there's a little something we either don't talk about or give a higher-grade, more restricted name to, such as mind or consciousness, plus whatever might be identical with them or explain their workings or make them arise. These auxiliary concepts might be matter, electrical activity, or emergence—notions so sublimated in exposition that they come perilously near to that ideality they were intended to replace. As a reflective question, this fight, anciently called "The Battle between the Gods and the Giants," is never-ending; as a part of an eristic argument it's tiresome, and easily resolved to everyone's satisfaction: I'll hang on to my soul and leave you to your soullessness.)

That face is (2) *one* face, so being two-faced is a defective mode—one face too many. A face is basically one, and so can usually be *identified*, "made the same" with its former appearances. Nonetheless, it is also *many* in many ways: We make faces to express ourselves, and then, over time, these expressions make our faces. Our face shapes our lives for decades, and then life begins to remodel it. But at any one time, too, a face is a multiplicity of features capable of minute variations; it is too insouciant a lover who has never wondered whether a nose an eighth of an inch longer wouldn't put paid to the enchantment.

And finally each face is (3) after all universal in its species-normality. Look at children's first drawings of a human face: the cup-mouth, goggle-eyes, potato-nose, and always the circle-head with the periwig—your basic, generic human. But each real face is also, once again, indefinitely detailed. No one word can capture its unique peculiarity, no multitude of words can collect its infinite variety. Even the memorious imagination holds more readily the fugitive fragrance than the dense picture. We get to know each other's invisible center, if at all, by thought-bearing speech, but we first and last meet, face each other, by appearance-delivering looks. The wonder—and lifelong study—is making the phenomena signify, *mean*, that is, speak.

Which face do I see? It now occurs to me how indicative the verb "to specify" is. We are, when all is said and done, of the same species. But we are specifiable—oddly enough we've come to use that word to mean that our species-nature is particularized. Thus we become, as we go on our observed and observing way, increasingly individual until we're too used to each other, when we relapse into seeing each other as half-noticed schemata; the end reverts to the beginning. It's with faces as with places:

> Despise not, gentle reader, first impressions. . . . If a sharp, well defined outline is drawn . . . it must be done . . . when the sense of contrast is fresh upon the mind. . . . The man who has dwelled a score of years in a place, has forgotten every feeling with which he first sighted it.

So says that great explorer, Richard Burton, in his *Wanderings*.

That's ultimately and intermediately. But what that member of my community said to me across the table may be true: What you see *first* is a black face. My answer—"How do you know I don't like it?"—wasn't to her point. She was saying that the simply unavoidable ought to figure. From her perspective, color-blindness is willful overlooking of a primary fact. (In the days when color-blindness was the most liberal position, it might indeed mean imposed assimilationism, but in fairness, more often public non-discrimination was intended.)

Ultimate, intermediate, first—how does all that work? Aristotle, who thought the most about logical opposition (as Plato thought about ontological otherness), makes use of an old notion, a version of which I made up for myself above. It is that famous Table of Opposites (*Metaphysics* XII 7). One side of this primal table lists Being, Thinghood, Actuality, Unity, Simplicity—and Good. The "other co-list" contains each opposite, the corresponding "non-", Multiplicity and Complexity among them. Why are these no-good? Once again, because thought is moved (just as in Thomas's definition of truth) by thinkable items, those that are actual, are meaningfully there, stay put and don't evanesce into multiplicity and variety under thinking.

There is a bias here for the thinkable, *the* bias of our West; as I've often said to myself: I share it. Mere human essence is ultimate not only because I can really think about it, but also because it seems to be the source of my and others' thinking. When I listen, wholly intent on what people mean to tell me as a fellow human being, I find myself discounting circumstances, among which I reckon the most internal, namely psychological states, and the most external, namely socio-economic status, and everything in between or beyond (depending where those affected place their condition), including race. Why? Because, as I thought it out before, it's demeaning to listen around the meant speech to the unwitted (I need that word) condition. That holds, wonderfully, even if people mean to argue for the essentiality of accidents: Their thinking always comes, and is meant to be taken as coming, from beyond those. *That's my maximal respect hypothesis.*

But! Aren't there those intermediate ways of being—human types, racial typing included? In the sixty-some years that I've watched the theories that explode onto and slink off the intellectual scene, human typing has included fat and thin (I forget the fancy somatic designation), inner- and other-directed, civilized and cultured, spiritual and technological, etc., etc., etc. (I've got some doozies of my own, categories much more humanly significant: lovers of Jane Austen versus those of Charlotte Brontë, who despised the former for what she thought was her dispassionate elegance; those who think that the Second Epilogue of *War and Peace*—that short appendix of

Peace to the huge body of War, when the glorious girl-hero-
ine of the great years turns into an obsessively domesticated,
dumpy mother and all the grown-ups assume their final, fixed
shapes—is the acme of the novel and those for whom it's a let-
down. And so on.)

We *think* humanity, *discern* types, *see* faces. The humanity
self-differentiates into types within it and faces upon it. This
is—blow the trumpets—the intrinsic otherness I'm looking
for: self-otherness. To be ourselves we must fall off from our
essence first in schematic and then in more and more detailed
particularization. It's the exact road by which we get to know
each other in the most ardent way: We make our acquaintance as speaking members of our species, we are attracted to
a type of it, but the lime-twig of love is ultimate peculiarity—
that "infinite variety" which was Cleopatra's magic that "Age
cannot wither nor custom stale"—at least that's how it seems
when under the influence of.

What appears to us, the surface looks of people and things
in their bodily impenetrability, these are in principle and hopelessly impenetrable, since however we poke or pierce we are
always on the outside, on the sur-face, always looking *at*.
These superficies have all the features of that "other list,"
the opposing, negative, bad one: nonbeing, multiplicity, variety, hence constitutional non-genuineness and thence inadequacy to thought, *falsity*. This piece of the tradition appeals
to me; it seems right. The world's many-sidedness, oscillation,
mutability, transformations, transgressions, all this too-hot
spice of life, is hard to live with, and what's more confounding, impossible to conceive living without. For one thing, this
surface is the "window of appearance" (Egyptian: the opening where the Pharaoh—rarely—showed himself to his world)
of beauty. I know only one definition of beauty that helps with
this sudden seizure of the senses by unpossessive love. In it
beauty is not a collection of articulable formalisms like proportion and symmetry. Instead Socrates intimates in passing

in the dialogue *Phaedrus* (250) that beauty is brilliance, "sightliness"; beauty is *visibility itself*. It happens when the appearances, the *phainomena*, do their business properly and shine out, when they both display themselves and intimate beyond themselves. Beauty is Being coruscating to the senses. But this vision of beauty presupposes—so I think—that it is effective just because our world is "mired in murk," from dull up to ugly, so that spots of glow can stand out.[6]

That's for one thing; for another, the surface does the opposite: It is, once more, whence passionate love arises; appearances, the skin of things, is where desire begins. What is "falling" in love after all but a growing fixation on one human appearance as being at once inimitably unique and expansively canonical: individual particularity promising generic excellence? Socrates again, in the same dialogue, introduces to the world the powerfully unbeautiful metaphor of the erectile soul, the arousable organ that can rise from the terrestrial surfaces to the celestial heights, from earth's pleasures to heaven's knowledge. As Robert Frost says somewhere, we begin with delight and end in wisdom (though perhaps *he* means disenchantment).

So falsity is folded into us, as multiformity is inherent in our objects. Hence those who enunciate the false require our reserved respect, that is to say our critical hearing—for as hypocrisy is said to be the respect that vice pays to virtue, so critique is the respect truth should pay to falsity.

What's the practical lesson? First, go easy on types: Don't force human beings (especially your students) into re-presenting their putative kind, rather than presenting themselves as their nature and their choice direct. Of course, as we become more mixed, choice—each one's choice—will happily become a necessity. Truth to tell, I abhor these assignments to one's supposed own. When I was an undergraduate at Brooklyn College, which was then largely Jewish, I discovered in myself a propensity for pagan Hellenism. I kept being told that I couldn't escape my history. I hadn't even meant to until then.[7]

When you look at a fellow human being, look through with the intellectual eye to the universal first, but never neglect the fact that you must do that by way of the particulars seen through the imaginative and the sensory eye in conjunction. The foreknown *gestalt* of a type (including race, ethnicity, class, you name the quasi-universal schema) appears in, through, by way of, the unforeseen shapeliness of infinite, unschematizable particularity.

In fact, come to think of it, don't human looks invite that aspect-seeing, the "seeing-as" that so fascinated the last century's philosophers—though not as rabbits slip into ducks and goblet-stems into faces, oscillating in time, but *both at once*, as transparencies of the imagination, now to the fore, now behind? What makes us from time to time wonderful to each other is that the level of our looks fluctuates: sometimes incomparably, uniquely this *one*, sometimes representatively, generally that *group*, sometimes merely, universally essential *humanity*. (I avoid "general," because it is to "universal" as a fudgy collection is to a defined entity.) Respectful looking means seizing the occasion for seeing all in turn, and sometimes—at high moments—all together. Thence comes friendship. For as Plotinus says, "The common and the unique together—that's excellence" (*Ennead* VI 7, 17).

There's, it occurs to me, "a philosophy" in this, a "both-and" philosophy. Is it naïve Hegelianism? (I use Hegel's name because in him is the culmination of all dialectical thinking, though minus my dithering conjecturing.) Maybe, so what? My belief here hangs between the extremes of nominalism, a hard-edged reduction of universals to mere words, and the world-denying flinching from appearances as mere illusion, as Maya, as veils of being. But while the aim is inclusion, it's not to be mush but inclusiveness plus discrimination (a good word fallen on hard times): *Truth* is to be admitted and prized over falsity, as is *good* over bad. When well mastered, they are the in-folded spice and the external shapeliness of beings.

One more case, the last—because, as so often, I've come to the end of my thought-tether long before the topic has reached the end of its thought-compass. It's a matter whose urgency will be current when race is an ancient problem: faith. The standard problem is the opposition "faith vs. reason." But here the problem is the problem: It's a "when did you stop beating your wife" formulation, a type which involves a, usually mildly, vicious "question-presupposition" (a term I recall from my days reading up on "erotetics," the study of questions). The presupposition here, not so mildly injurious, is that the faithful are irrational and the reasoners faithless. The first presupposition is just ridiculous: Saint Thomas has one of the most potent intellects I've come up against, and my fundamentalist friends are—that's my experience—a smidgen more intelligent than the intellectuals who scorn them. What's really worth thinking about is that the reasoners—I'm supposing here that the problem becomes really acute when the abstractions are embodied in human parties—are, by implication, faithless: pure, voided of, faith. There are indeed rationalists who try to reason that reason is ultimate. I suspect that this doctrine doesn't work for human beings in ways I'll try to get hold of. It certainly won't do for approaching in thought a supra-human being, a divinity. There is, to be sure, a kind of self-gaming of the intellect: the ways of analogy, negation, mysticism. These are wonderful ways of thought, not to be missed; moreover, they are *not* "rational" in one legitimate use of the word—in the sense that thought is far more than formal rationality. (This is just old tradition, which goes: "sensing, thinking, thought" or "sensation, reason, intellect" or "sense, understanding, intuition," where thoughtfulness engages each trio.) All this is simply in aid of thinking out why reason can't be pitted against faith just like that.

Let trust mean "dependence on the being-what-they-seem-to-be" of someone or something. Trust would then be surrender to a truth (the related word) in the objective sense I noticed before, when it's not in the telling but in the being. Let faith be truth made potent by ardor always and by doctrine often—love plus *logos*. Have you ever heard an offended scientific type, who is, however, without a clue to its complexities, defend evolution? (I pass over the religious opponents of evolution, whom much should be forgiven if they are indeed as mentally limited as their cleverer critics claim they are.) It's sheer, ardent trust, faith—no willing recognition of the rousing situation that *the* theory of life's diversity, which seems to be an evidential fact, is a conceptual puzzlement.

But that's only an emotional aberration of our most common mental mode: trust on every level. It's the working coordinate of "opinion," the unthought-out thought that must perforce govern the endless utterances of our finite life. (All that comes to me from Plato's *Republic* V–VI.) Trust makes me suspicion-free when I step on the ground, sit down on the chair, engage in innumerable mundane acts. When trust is misplaced, when a chair collapses or a chasm opens, the human consequences can be comical or dreadful. But by and large given nature and made gear are trustworthy. As in life, so in learning: Scientists trust the laws of nature once discovered, mathematicians accept propositions proved long ago. And now my point: Thinking, reasoning itself, is shot through with trust, and even, or especially, when grounded in exigent principles; the logician's explicit conviction is finally a *faith*.

Thinking is an enigma to the thinker—at least, if that's what I'm doing—in two directions. First it *always* begins *in medias res*, it always finds whatever first principles it uncovers from the middle out and then levers them to the top, or more often, digs them into the bottom. Thus its ground is always hypo-thetical, "put-under." Even questions are thus rooted in affairs. I don't mean the formal structure that sets the terms of the answer but its passion-base, what it wants to save, to pull close, to tether.

That's why I trust conjecture; it is devotion to opinion chased down as far as possible; my ultimate opinion *is* the hypothesis. I say "my" with misgivings. It's mine all right, afflicted with my limitations of comprehension and energy. But I don't mean it as mine; I'm after *the* truth, so there's an insuperable tension, now tight-strapped, now nicely twanging. Anyhow, beginnings and ends can't be made, lacking faith. But that's not news.

Here is the other aspect of the enigma of what I will now call, outright, logical thought, *reasoning*. It begins and ends in the middle, but it's also full of middles along the way—interstices. Take the first, the oldest, the simplest formal schema, which is the syllogism, the collection of articulate thoughts into a closing settlement of thinking (which last line alone the Greeks called "the syllogism," the argument-collection). Here is the textbook model of the most straightforward, the "categorical," syllogism:

All men are mortal
Socrates is a man
Socrates is a mortal.

To begin with, where did all that come from? What question were we answering? Was it "Is Socrates mortal?" Could we ever have come to the first, the major, premise or the middle, the minor, premise if we hadn't already supposed that Socrates was mortal? How would we have known what would serve our reasoning? No, finding the conclusion can't be the point, though once the whole syllogism is put down in writing it does look as if we inferred, "brought in," something new. We didn't.

So where's the interest? It is, people agree, in the middle line, and in it the *singular* "man" is crucial. In saying that he's human, it makes a bridge to the individual from the universal, to Socrates from human mortality (or better, from mortals; these terms betoken extensions, that is, collections rather than abstractions). It implicates, involves, entangles Socrates in his mortality and it gives a reason: being human. That's more than mildly interesting, if it's true. But whence comes the truth? A great and current religion claims that there was indeed a person, a mediator between god and man, who was really a man without being, strictly speaking, mortal, and there are several people, living over two millennia apart (Plato, Nietzsche), who think that Socrates was not quite a man but more like a demon of some sort, mediating between heaven and earth. So apart from not quite knowing how a premise comes to us, we're also not likely to find propositions that are completely defensible. And if they are not, the syllogistic sequence can't work.

That's because it isn't a sequence; it's an integral whole, and its linear looks are not the warrant for its connections. Those connections are provided by rules of inference not further justified ("self-evidence" being the cop-out of cop-outs): I may say *"Modus ponens"*—that's one of the rules—and mean that I conclude "by way of putting it down"; it closes no gap, does it? And if the rules *were* grounded, you'd need further rules for applying the rules, *ad infinitum*. Inherent verbal discontinuity seems to be at odds with the desired connectedness of reasoning. That continuity *is* in fact found in space, for example in the schematic pictures called Euler circles. The largest such circle fences off all mortal beings from the indefinite non-class of non-mortals, then corrals all humans into a smaller circle within, and finally herds a single head, Socrates, into a human stall for one. And there is no way to overcome figures, because if you want to avoid spatial logic you have to use figurative phrases like "is included in" as in "enclosed within," or "falls under" as in "drops into a labeled slot"—at least if you are relying on natural-language reasoning as distinct from purely symbolic manipulation. Thus you're caught between visual continuity, which is inarticulate, and verbal discontinuity, which leaves such interstices as to make of each next step of thought a small miracle. So is reasoning without faith? No, the alpha and the omega of thinking calls on faith.

That consideration should leave those who want to go to the edge in thinking at least more tolerant of the faithful who believe a mite sooner in the process. But *tolerance* isn't the point—the *truth* of beliefs that are not mine is the point, both "belief that . . ." and "belief in . . . ." The former seems to me to refer to acceptance of a doctrine as true, the latter to a being as Truth itself. Yet I've set it down for myself: I don't have these beliefs; I have no trust in the doctrine and no faith in the being. No faith?

That's truly bad-faith agnosticism, whose honest form requires keeping possibilities open and collecting more evidence (though being over eighty years old, I'll find out soon enough, anyhow).

I remind myself of what it is I'm after: What is to be respected in the faithful, beyond their mere humanity? Well, first, as I recalled to myself a while ago, there's something more arresting here than the common effect of will stopping reason ("I'll think about that tomorrow"), especially since, it seems, just when intellect has been authoritatively put to rest, spirit begins its struggle. There is the positive capability, or as the side of belief calls it, the gift of faith. This ability to believe, especially as doctrinal ardor, is an even more patent mystery in the overtly faithful than in those of us who live with inadvertent credence, simply because unbelievers aren't so keenly alert to their own faith-permeated moods as are believers, who put credence in propositions that have powerful spiritual resonances.

All this talk of spirit, not a word I use much in talking to myself! What do I mean? I think: that part of my consciousness (oh, why not?—my soul) that breathes more deeply at the thought of Being beyond thinking. Spirit is, in a somatic figure (how else can we even speak of our inwardness?), the respiration of the mind, its drawing in of breezes from beyond.

Spirituality (and I don't mean the flaccid sentimentality and self-manipulating maneuvers that go with it, though that too tells a tale of human need), meaning the spirit at work in others, seems to me a limit case I must try to get hold of.

Human ratiocination appears to have two limits: giving up and giving in. The first, terminal skepticism, that oddly passionate philosophical shoulder-shrugging, seems to me the less illuminating because it's a least-action propensity. The question of thinking *par excellence* is, to my well-influenced mind, the famous "What is . . . ?" question. It is, well and truly, one of those "presupposition-questions," for it supposes that most thoughts are of something that has a "what," called by Aristotle "*the*-what-it-ever-meant-to-be" that thing (*to ti en einai*) and later, its "essence." In brief, that question presupposes that it is an askable question—and that is what skeptics deny. I'm usually all for the cognitive virtue of negativity, but not so much for what I suspect is temperamental negativity—that of a human type or, as it seems to me, a "case."

So when I pass in thought from the light that the "faith-reason" difference casts on certain limit possibilities of the human soul to the matter itself, the positive side—belief—seems to me the more to be regarded. I remind myself that the well-founded opposition seems to be "belief-unbelief" rather than "faith-reason," because, as I've just considered it, I just can't see reason as antithetical to faith simply, so implicated are they with each other. What distinguishes human souls seems rather to be the setting of the flashpoint: where it is that ardor lights up doctrine so that assenting thought leaps over reason's intermediacies. Tertullian's notorious saying should not be read "I believe because it is *absurd*" but "I *believe* because it is absurd," because it is, literally, "discordant" with sequential reasoning.

So asking "How is divinity, as the matter of a believer's belief, worthy of respect?" is almost laughable as a serious question. How could I possibly *not* feel awe before a notion (1) whose very intension, that is, the sum of its properties, whose maximal comprehensiveness, can arguably be said to necessitate the inclusion of being among them (that's Anselm's existence proof) and (2) which is felt as real by so many fellow humans?

As a direct question about God, I've managed to postpone such inquiries, thinking that sometime (now sometime soon) I'll either find out or be past caring. On the other hand, there would be a certain shame in coming to in the Beyond and finding myself a clueless stranger in that afterlife, having pretended (to myself) that I'm living the present one somewhat examinedly. Moreover, sudden flare-ups of dislike for the whole worldly caboodle and normal attacks of *taedium vitae* aside, I have both a temperamental inclination for finding objects of reverence in this world and a ready imagination for figuring the life of paradise in the beyond: a place where the soul's spirit-level is always high and where music manifests to us not only *that* it signifies, but also *what* it signifies—where meaning is ubiquitous and imputations of significance are absolutely warranted. So I'm not so unready.

I'm wandering, though that's maybe not so bad. In meditation, divagation is the direct way; thought that cuts to the chase too soon rides heedlessly by all the contributing scenery and arrives nowhere. To pile it on: If you are purposefully hell-bent you'll get there; in Thurberian rhyme: "Where most of us end up there's no knowing, but the hell-bent get where they are going." Or, yet more vividly:

> They fondly thinking to allay
> Their appetite with gust, instead of fruit
> Chewed bitter ashes, which th'offended taste
> With spattering noise rejected . . .
>
> (Milton, *Paradise Lost* X, 565 ff.),

which could be said of too-earnest philosophical scholarship.

Theology, the—affirming—account of God, is concerned primarily with the high limits of thought-matter, so perhaps my next notion is indeed borderline theology. The world seems to me *infused* with negation, but it is also, as I've thought to myself, *edged* with absolute Otherness. At the edge of all there is, there could be (1) Nothing simply, the abyss, the void of being incomprehensible to thought, infinite as being devoid of definiteness. (Its graphic representation is what is outside of the Euler circles, the region of what used to be called the "infinite judgment," the mere "non-" to what is positively posited: unclaimed void, way beyond "Here be dragons.") Or there could be (2) that goal of the asymptotic direction, the unreachable terminus, which, like the infinite points of space, turns at the edges into an embracing alpha and omega, a divinity, in our days at least, unseen and unheard within physical reality.

The first case, the pure Nothing, there is no coming to terms with that I can think of, except its—this is true irony—determined absorption into self-reliant this-worldliness, into sensualized nihilism:

> What is divinity if it can come
> Only in silent shadows and in dreams?
> Shall she not find in comforts of the sun,
> In pungent fruit and bright green wings, or else
> In any balm or beauty of the earth
> Things to be cherished like the thought of heaven?
> Divinity must live within herself. . . .
>   (Wallace Stevens, "Sunday Morning")

The second possibility, which feels to me like a *deus absconditus*, a "god in hiding," develops scores of temperamental and intellectual snags. My Christian friends, whose intelligent simplicity I love and respect, believe in the divinity as a personal God, who is both in and beyond this world, who both walks *with* and watches *over* them as a divine Father. (I'm not even going to begin to grapple with the mediating notion of the human Son.) Am I watched, regarded, and thus held in respect just by reason of being held to account both in this world and again *sub specie aeternitatis*? It would be a comfort, yes, but also a cloying comfort (or a scary strain); perhaps it erects our being more to live dangerously unsupervised but self-determined: "unsponsored, free." I think my secular friends sometimes turn unbelievers just *because* God is too personal. It is hard to keep one's mind from running to worldly models, and we know that to come under the "personal attention" of a large concern is a chilling experience. Yet the more candid divinity of the philosophers is both too abstracted from its world and too productive of rational puzzles to go to in one's perplexity.

Nonetheless, the God set out by believers, even unbelieved in, has the force of a notionally necessary being: Once thought accepts it, belief is around the corner. As such, as an object of conviction, it acts as a foil, a backstop, for conjecturally attainable truth—I mean as a notion, notionally held, that *all but* morphs into a truth-in-being.

For in the course of thinking out, no, just maundering around, the complex of questions—whether my world is a true neighborhood or just a housing development in the cosmic sprawl; whether it is created and governed by laws approved by, even binding on, the Maker or whether it is without beginning or end and directed according to rational categories that cannot be intelligibly otherwise; whether it has been crafted as a cosmos or is self-generated and conforming to formulas that are inherent in and developed from its own first constituents; whether I am mostly what my genesis determined me to be or largely self-made ("Divinity must live within herself"); and always and above all, who my ultimate watcher is: no one, my fellow humans, myself, or a divinity, with or without the capacity for personal regard—in the course of such meditating I am bound to come on God as a version of the aforethought notion, now in the shape of an Alpha and Omega, an origin and a finality. Once again, it seems to matter here that some fellow humans should actually believe in such a transcendent Beyond-being—not "believe *that* . . ." but "believe *in* . . . ," not as scrunched-up, self-beleaguered bigots, but with sweet simplicity. Why does it matter?

The gods of the thinkers are accessible through studious effort. The Aristotelian divinities are beings

Who, moving others are themselves as stone,
Unmoved . . .

Well, maybe they are not "as stone," because they are stars and made of starry matter, and the chief of them, a matterless unmoved mover, is pure vibrant stasis. He moves other beings by attracting the—unreciprocated—love of the mortal and immortal dwellers in a cosmos he did not make but directs as the intelligible terminus of thought. If such an unmoved mover is a paradox it is not the paradoxicality of a mystery but of thought thinking itself through to finality.

Then there is the Newtonian God who has the whole material world in mind as in a "sensorium," which we experience as absolute space and time.[8]

Though these philosophical theologies would never come to me on my own, I can study them in books and get the idea; that is to say, I can take in the fact *that* there are world-schemes over which these gods preside and *how* these systems are informed by and inform Nature. And I can see that each writer is truly "nature's secretary" and has reason for believing that his account is true. Moreover, there is intellectual satisfaction in beginning to comprehend these theories, for they are not just in themselves magnificent—there are moment-occasions in life on which, and situation-perspectives in thought from which, I too believe that they have truth.

But cosmo-theology is not enough. Serious conjecturing, not just for intellectual fulfillment but for the settling of the soul, longs for trustworthy examples of faith, of belief *in*. Why? Am I not enlightened as Kant defines enlightenment: "the exit of human beings from their self-incurred minority"? I don't feel like a child; what child reads Kant? Or am I subject to a sort of philosophical populism, a trust in the people? Would

I feel this way if I'd never met even one living believer; and if, what's more, I didn't live in a country of believers? (Well, at least the continent *between* the edges from sea to shining sea belongs to the faithful.) Probably not, but let that be: What temperamental conservative, meaning someone (comfortably) imbued with the sense of human limitation, isn't a populist, meaning someone (cautiously) persuaded that plain folks are more safely wise than intellectuals?

What do I learn from people who have faith in what I cannot believe? I learn, to begin with, of a possible necessity— that it is possible that a human being may be turned around, perhaps by scriptural authority or by deep need or by ardent desire, to be sure, but in the first and last instance by a compellingly evident presence. I learn not just to think but to try to feel my way past the edges of my secular world, and then to think from that threshold in—not that I really spend much of my life actively doing it. More often I live passively in? with? by? Bach cantatas, where, in the face of all that undeserved delight, all that elevation of the soul unearned by any serious scaling of heaven, respect turns into reverence.

VIII. Exit: Winter

It is wonderful how the level of the soul rises and falls. Sometimes the investigatory little busybody within dives fairly deep without finding bottom and comes up and makes for a solid shore and sometimes it comfortably splashes about in the muddy shallows. Now I find myself thinking whether liars deserve respect.

Well, in one crude and obvious way, of course. The fact of lying affirms truth; moreover, a really effective liar must actually know it. (There's a Socratic dialogue, the *Hippias Minor*, about that irony—that the true teller of lies must be the actual knower of truth.) But the practiced and practical liar is also *doing* something, something probably low in itself and harmful to others; I've excepted actual bad deeds from the principle of respect. I recall now that Christians (and progressive kindergartners) say that God (or the Caregiver) condemns the sin but doesn't withdraw regard from the sinner. For little kids, it's right, certainly, perhaps also for all human beings in their ultimate humanity. But that's more a matter of solicitous than respectful regard, what the disaffected call "paternalism."

Gulliver's noble horses, once again, who have no word for lying (because they do it too ingenuously ever to notice themselves at it), call it "saying the thing which is not." Surely that's insufficient. "Saying the thing which is not" is our most remarkable ability. I've thought about that before: the ability to say what is not so, to articulate non-being in turn as nothing simply, as negation, as otherness, as fiction, or as falsehood, deliberate or inadvertent, in good faith or with deceitful intent. What are the combinations we can produce? Evidently we are able to think and speak:

> Deceitfully and inadvertently: That's what Socrates calls "the true lie," the one in the soul (*Republic* 382 b)— the mystery of self-deception which attests to the duality of con-sciousness (me with myself), just as lying attests to truth.
> Deceitfully and deliberately: That's the plain old cunning black lie, told deleteriously for profit; it is, however, also the "white" lie, intentional deceit, a social smoothing function.
> In good faith and inadvertently: That's making a mistake, unwitting untruth.
> In good faith and deliberately: That's our most wonderful ability, making fictions, plausibly feigned beings.

Those are distinctive ways I can summon up of saying the thing that is not.

But come to think of it, isn't there a fact of speech that makes liars of us all, always: what we don't say? When we swear "to tell the truth, the whole truth and nothing but the truth" we are perforce forsworn. Who knows the truth, could tell it all in a finite time, and deliver it bare without drawing circumstance into it? That's why cross-examiners curtail the possibilities: "Yes or no. Did you or did you not . . . ?"— to prevent people from actually trying to keep their oath. As anyone knows who has ever been deposed, though innocent as an angel, one begins to feel guilty as hell. Our finitude combined with life's infinity makes us constitutional fibbers; deprived of circumstantiality we of necessity become as barefaced liars.

Kant, the extremist in the cause of virtue, would think that what I've just written, my inventory above, was frivolous. For him intentionality is everything, and a lie can never be well-intentioned. It is unqualifiedly wrong, since by it "is a wrong inflicted on mankind in general," for it makes language lose its trustworthiness; statements will meet no credence. Hence follows Kant's notorious claim that it is a duty to tell a would-be murderer that his victim is in your house. (Think of this "duty" in the time of the Nazis, when a few righteous ones were hiding Jews!)

It is an odd situation: A lie is a wrong done to all mankind and deserves severe civic punishment, says Kant. But this version of "Let justice be done though the heavens fall" forgets that when these heavens fall they do collateral damage to some instance of mankind. Maybe there are sometimes speech occasions when it is right to let go of pure duty, of the universalizing self-consistency of one's maxims, and of regard for the collection called mankind, in order to go for *this* instance of humanity. So I discover in myself misgivings about general principles in morality and a preference for the personal practice of virtue: Summon such occasional courage and such prudential judgment as you have, case by case. Reserve principled duty for up-against-the-wall occasions, perplexed moments when inclinations threaten to skew judgment; use practical judgment in daily life.

Then what about respect for liars? None to be sure, for speech-harm, though maybe some sympathy for the liar who's been driven to the wall—especially children.

An excursus of thought: Imaginative sympathy is the enabling condition of respect as a feeling, a something beyond sober approval. What about pitying sympathy? Is pity compatible with respect? Is it even compatible with sympathy? Isn't it a distancing and denigrating affect: "Thank heavens, not me"? Isn't it first an aversive motion of the soul, even up to horror, away from the object, though immediately checked by a humanity somewhat more pallid as a passion than fellow-feeling, though more persistent as a moral appeal? Clearly there are at least two sorts of pity: the one that cannot help but be disparaging to its object, even against all rhyme and reason, and the other that elevates it, be it God or man, by making love poignant even up to adoration. Such pity is welcome. Othello says, unashamedly touched:

> She loved me for the dangers I had pass'd,
> And I loved her that she did pity them. (I.iii.167)

So I indeed find respectfully pitying sympathy within the inventory of human affectivity. And some of that sympathy goes to liars. Why?

Because the least lovable ones are often daunted souls, and even the exuberantly irrepressible ones are somehow untethered wraiths, and so they display in a whole human character what we all are in part: vulnerable and driven to seize on any available shoddy shield for self-protection. And whoever has become in his whole being a figure for our imperfect parts is worthy of what I'll call respectful contempt. It's a way of saying they're interesting, "egregious" in both its senses: bad and distinguished.

As for all the other, more or less innocent varieties of lying I've listed, their practice by us is ineradicable, so long as we have speech that can reach things (where truth and falsity first reside in complementary togetherness) and minds that contain things that are not, nonbeings (the beings of the imagination that are at once in and before the mind's eye, made and seen by it). The telling of these beings and their doings is called "fiction," which is Latin for both forming and feigning. Imaginative fiction meets all the usual criteria for lying: It says the thing which is not, and the tellers generate cunning unrealities. To me this has long been a fleshed-out fact representing the intimate relation that imaginative productions have to that paradoxically vivid nonbeing called badness: that it is practically the criterion of a great work that its villains have their moments when they glow with the dark glory of hell. That's what Blake means by assigning poets to the devil's party: Milton. Imaginative fiction intends to deceive and the feigners hope to profit; it makes counter-worlds and its creators expect us trustingly to live in them—while themselves remaining its cool manipulators, purveyors of non-being. (Here is what I've just read in the Indo-Persian epic *The Adventures of Amir Hamza*; it's far afield and florid and very apropos: "The pen draws new fictions out of the pit of nothingness, and the fingers exert themselves to unfold this wondrous tale on the paper's bright expanse.")

Volumes are devoted to qualifying this all-too-candid description into—sometimes worshipable—respectability. To me, Socrates does it more honor. He respects it for being equally wonderful and ineradicably disreputable (*Republic* III–IV, X). So lying deserves our disgusted, awed, loving respect for this summary reason: It is a means for making the most, by way of utility or delight, of the way things are not.

I want to say it to myself once more: The Romantic play with evil, its frivolous demotion to the merely esthetic and its dangerous elevation to the acutely fascinating, darkens judgments of action (what, for example, was the attraction offered by the Nazis to the young but Romanticism writ large and made official?), and it is really repulsive. Here is a way to think it out: The world's deeds are usually incomposable disjunctions; their circles don't overlap; to do this means to forgo that; and to set off in one direction leaves the road not taken to nonbeing, for we, the poet says, "could not travel both / And be one traveler." In reasoning, though, it's otherwise; we can entertain both alternatives at once. In fact, logicians prefer what they call the non-exclusive, possibly conjoining "or": "P or Q" can mean p or q *or both*. That's not dithering ambiguity, "negative capability," but an incitement to finding common ground. It is the mode on which I've been meditating. What's a virtue in thinking is, however, often a vice in doing, because in time and space realizing one way consigns the other—Frost is so right—to its opposite, the Unrealized, that is to say, Nonbeing in the realm of the possible. So doing right matters.

Suddenly I've got enough; the soul's level is way down. Let it peter out. The springs will leap up again. Or, to switch figures, there's a lot of what the Greek-talking scholars of old called *paralipomena*, the "leftovers," and that were filed away for *post-mortem* publication. But that's asking for it; better pour it into that mental ramekin where the starter culture for next time sits germinating. Meanwhile, I'll repose in authority:

> For it is necessary to learn both at once: the false *and* the true of being as a whole. (Plato, *Seventh Letter*, 344 b)

· PART TWO ·

CLOSE
READINGS

MADISON'S "MEMORIAL AND REMONSTRANCE"

A Model of American Eloquence

The document entitled "To the Honorable the General Assembly of the Commonwealth of Virginia, A Memorial and Remonstrance" is a jewel of republican rhetoric.[1] Nor has this choice example of American eloquence gone without notice. And yet, compared to the Declaration of Independence and the Gettysburg Address, it has remained obscure—more often admired at a distance than studied in detail. This lack of popularity can in part be accounted for by the circumstances of the document. Addressed to the legislature of a state rather than to the people of a nation, it is concerned with an issue that is critical only sporadically, though then critical indeed. The Supreme Court has, to be sure, searched the document on several occasions for help in interpreting the "establishment" clause of the First Amendment. (See the Appendix.) But this naturally narrow judicial mining of the text has itself served to draw attention away from the depth of its political precepts and the fitness of its rhetorical form, discerningly lauded, for example, by Rives, Madison's nineteenth-century biographer.[2] In part, again, Madison's work has been kept off the roster of canonized public prose because it lacks Jefferson's heady generalities and Lincoln's humane grandeur. But I know this: To study it is to come away with a sense of having discovered, under the veil of Madison's modesty, the great rhetorician of the Founding, whom John Marshall called "the most eloquent man I ever heard." The immediate and the historical efficacy of Madison's appeal shows that despite the deprecating modern estimate that he "could not mesmerize a mass audience" but "only those who sought . . . illumination,"[3] Madison was master of that true eloquence that sometimes turns the former kind of audience into the latter. It is an eloquence of measured passion and sober ardor, which knows what to say when and to whom without bending the truth.

I. The Circumstances Surrounding the Memorial

On December 3, 1784, a bill "establishing a provision for Teachers of Religion" was reported to the General Assembly of Virginia.[4] Its preamble said:

> Whereas the general diffusion of Christian knowledge hath a natural tendency to correct the morals of men, restrain their vices, and preserve the peace of society, which cannot be effected without a competent provision for learned teachers, who may be thereby enabled to devote their time and attention to the duty of instructing such citizens as from their circumstances and want of education cannot otherwise attain such knowledge; and it is judged such provision may be made by the Legislature, without counteracting the liberal principle heretofore adopted and intended to be preserved, by abolishing all distinctions of pre-eminence amongst the different societies or communities of Christians. . . .[5]

The author of the bill, Patrick Henry, had introduced it with a fervent speech tracing the downfall of ancient and modern polities to the decay of religion; the repeal in 1776 of the tithe law, which meant the end of a state-salaried clergy and amounted to the disestablishment of the Anglican Church, was a source of such decay in Virginia. Other eminent Virginians, even more anxious about an increase in laxness of morals and lawlessness than about the precipitous decline of church attendance during and after the Revolution, saw nothing wrong with the bill. Among them were George Washington and John Marshall.

Madison, absolutely opposed, debated Henry on the floor of the Assembly late in November. These speeches contain revealing anticipations of—and contrasts to—the Memorial.[6]

Even with the bill still in committee, Madison's arguments had told. There had been a short-lived attempt to de-christianize it, extending it to all "who profess the public worship of the Deity," be they Mohammedans or Jews. The bill reported out was, furthermore, no longer the General Assessment bill, which had sought in effect to reestablish Christianity (though, of course, not Anglicanism) by a general levy on taxpayers in support of a Christian church. It had been transformed into a Christian education bill, designed partly, as evidenced by the reference in the preamble to those who cannot afford private education, to be a defense against Jefferson's long-tabled secular public education bill of 1779, and partly, as is apparent from its more restricted aims, to be a response to Madison's pressure.

Meanwhile Madison also engaged in some practical politics. In order to remove the oratorical Henry from the scene, Madison had hit on a device both kinder and more efficacious than Jefferson's suggestion "devotedly to pray for his death": he had conspired to elevate him to the governorship. The proud governor-elect had retired to his estates, "a circumstance very inauspicious to his offspring," as Madison wrote with satisfaction to James Monroe.

Also, in exchange for the withdrawal of his opposition to a companion bill for the incorporation of the Episcopal Church, Madison had won postponement of final action on the bill to 1785, so that there might be time to publish its text for consideration by the people. This move was crucial, since in 1784 the bill would probably have passed the legislature with an overwhelming majority.[7] Here as ever, the two facets of Madison's statesmanship—practical maneuvering and principled rhetoric—complemented each other. He had gained a year.

Throughout the spring of 1785, Madison's own inclination was to wait quietly for the popular opposition to manifest itself. The Episcopalians, as old beneficiaries of establishment quite naturally, and the Presbyterian clergy to their shame, supported the bill; the laity and the clergy of the dissenting sects were solidly opposed. By May several supporters but no opponents of the bill had lost their seats. As late as June 21 Madison was assured enough of its unpopularity merely to echo the rebellious common feeling, that although the legislature "should give it the *form*, they will not give it the *validity* of a law . . . —I own the bill appears to me to warrant this language of the people."[8]

Some of his associates in the battle, however, George Mason and the brothers Nicholas, were anxious for more pointed action. They had reason to fear civil disturbances if the legislature, in which the favoring Tidewater counties were overrepresented, should attempt to force the law on the people. They hoped to deter its passage with a large number of well-subscribed identical petitions from all parts of the state, the best device then available for conveying the power of a public sentiment to the legislature. They asked Madison to compose the text.

He wrote the "Memorial and Remonstrance" sometime soon after June 20, 1785, intending it to circulate anonymously. The few friends who knew of his authorship respected his wish, which arose, presumably, from his desire to maintain good working relations with all parties in the legislature. At the time some attributed the work to George Mason, who had drafted the religious liberty clause of the Virginia Declaration of Rights. Though a printer had put Madison's name on a reprint as early as 1786, Madison acknowledged only late in life, in a letter of 1826 to Mason's grandson, that the task of composing such a paper had been imposed upon him.

Mason had the petition printed as a broadside in Alexandria, having seen no reason for changing even one word of the text. The Nicholases saw to its distribution throughout the state. It met, Madison noted in retrospect, "with the approbation of the Baptists, the Presbyterians [who had recanted], the Quakers, and the few Roman Catholics, universally; of the Methodists in part; and even not a few of the Sect formerly established by law [the Episcopalians]."[9]

The Memorial was solidly successful in drawing subscribers. The thirteen circulated copies collected 1552 signatures; 150 freeholders signed one petition in a day. Yet, successful though it was, another, still anonymous, petition, based on the fervently Christian argument that the bill contravened the spirit of the Gospel, ran up more than three times as many signatures on twenty-nine copies. All in all, about eighty opposing petitions with 10,929 signatures came in to Richmond, and only a few in support.

After a brief consideration the bill died in committee in the fall of 1785, having lost, however, by a mere three votes. Madison's petition may well have been crucial.

On January 22, 1786, Madison reported the results of that session to Jefferson in Paris in a modestly jubilant vein:

The steps taken throughout the Country to defeat the Gnl. Assessment, had produced all the effect that could have been wished. The table was loaded with petitions and remonstrances from all parts against the interposition of the Legislature in matters of Religion.

In the same letter he had already told Jefferson even greater news. One element alone of Jefferson's six-year-old revisal of the laws of Virginia had that year been passed into an act, his bill for establishing religious freedom,[10] the most celebrated of all documents concerned with religious liberty.

Advantage had been taken of the crisis produced by the crushing of the religious assessment bill to carry through the Jefferson bill, as Madison put it. The two events were closely connected. The impetus of the collapse of a regressive measure carried over—as sometimes happens—into a sudden advance. The religious clause of the Virginia Declaration of Rights had guaranteed the free exercise of religion to all Christians, but it had not unequivocally banned—witness the assessment bill— the establishment of a non-sectarian state church. During the next nine years the legislature had passed a patchwork of special exemptions, tolerances, and particular measures favoring dissenting sects. Jefferson's bill, which happened to attack compulsory support of religious teachers in its preamble, rode in, as Madison recollected in 1826, under the "influence of public sentiment" manifested in the death of the assessment bill, as a "permanent Barrier agst. future attempts on the Rights of Conscience as declared in the Great Charter affixed to the Constitution of the State."[11] Madison interpreted the petitions against the assessment bill as demands for the enactment of Jefferson's law concerning religious freedom; he thought it an advantage that it had been sanctioned by what was in effect a plebiscite. The Memorial had advanced it as a principle that there should be such invitations to the people to express their sentiments in the course of lawmaking.

II. The Arguments of the Memorial

The Memorial is a petition addressed to the General Assembly of Virginia that remonstrates on fifteen counts (listed in a summary in note 12) against a bill before it establishing a provision for teachers of the Christian religion.[12] Each of these points is set forth in one paragraph in the form of a reflection on one aspect of the right relation between religion and politics. Madison clearly intended to make the argumentation as complete, as principled, as fundamental, and yet as concise, as possible.

The fifteen counts are, furthermore, composed into a symmetrical structure. The eighth, that is, the middle point, addresses the concern immediately central to the occasion—the fear of the decline of social stability—by arguing that state support of religion is not necessary to the civil authority. Clustered about that central claim are the other prudential and cautionary points to be addressed to the Christian communities that hoped to profit from the law. Points 6–7 and again 9–11 display the bill as internally and externally deleterious to Christianity in particular.

By contrast, Points 1–4 and again Points 13–15 have a wider, more encompassing matter: humanity in general. The introductory points proceed on the grandest scale. The first asserts a positive theological principle—the absolute priority of man's relation to God over his social bonds—as the ground for the inalienable character of the right to religious freedom; the second deduces from the first the prohibition of legislative interference in religion. The third point draws the political principle of prompt resistance to civil interference out of the uncompromisably absolute separation of the realms; the fourth draws from the philosophical principle of human equality the political injunction against state support of religion.

The closing numbers cite the forms and practices of popular government that proceed from the foundations established in Points 1–4 as they bear on the bill. Thirteen warns against unenforceable laws, fourteen states the majoritarian principle, and the last point recalls the principle of limited government to the offending legislature. The rhetorical force of this structure will, I think, tell even on a reader who does not apprehend it explicitly.

III. *Rhetorical Analysis of the Text*

PREAMBLE

To The Honorable the General Assembly of the
Commonwealth of Virginia
A Memorial and Remonstrance

We the subscribers, citizens of the said Commonwealth, having taken into serious consideration, a Bill printed by order of the last Session of General Assembly, entitled "A Bill establishing provisions for Teachers of the Christian Religion," and conceiving that the same if finally armed with the sanctions of a law, will be a dangerous abuse of power, are bound as faithful members of a free State to remonstrate against it, and to declare the reasons by which we are determined. We remonstrate against the said Bill. . . .

The preamble[13] alludes to the postponement resolution, which had requested the people of the counties "to signify their opinion respecting the adoption of such a Bill"—the resolution is quoted in the next to last paragraph. The petition, then a common political instrument, is intended to elicit popular opinion in the course of lawmaking. Such moments of communication between the people and their representatives are an important part of Madison's theory of self-government, set out in the penultimate paragraph of the petition.

Not Madison speaks, but "We . . . the citizens." His style could well accommodate itself to a canonical anonymity. He had been trained in a school of rhetoric that eschewed idiosyncrasies, and he never engaged in the luxuriously indignant periodicity peculiar to Jefferson.

This petition is presented in the form of a *remonstrance*, that is, a protest—a protest, suggestively, of the "faithful"—but it is not a mere protest, as are most present-day petitions. It is also a *memorial*, a declaration of reasons—every paragraph begins with a "because"—in the tradition of the Declaration of Independence.

FIRST PARAGRAPH

1. Because we hold it for a fundamental and undeniable truth, "that Religion or the duty which we owe to our Creator and the manner of discharging it, can be directed only by reason and conviction, not by force or violence." The religion then of every man must be left to the conviction and conscience of every man; and it is the right of every man to exercise it as these may dictate. This right is in its nature an unalienable right. It is unalienable, because the opinions of men, depending only on the evidence contemplated by their own minds cannot follow the dictates of other men: It is unalienable also, because what is here a right towards men, is a duty towards the Creator. It is the duty of every man to render to the Creator such homage and such only as he believes to be acceptable to him. This duty is precedent, both in order of time and in degree of obligation to the claims of Civil Society. Before any man can be considered as a member of Civil Society, he must be considered as a subject of the Governor of the Universe: And if a member of Civil Society, who enters into any subordinate Association must always do it with a reservation of his duty to the General Authority; much more must every man who becomes a member of any particular Civil Society, do it with a saving of his allegiance to the Universal Sovereign. We maintain therefore that in matters of Religion, no man's right is abridged by the institution of Civil Society and that Religion is wholly exempt from its cognizance. True it is, that no other rule exists, by which any question which may divide a Society can be ultimately determined, but the will of the majority; but it is also true that the majority may trespass on the rights of the minority.

The first is the most philosophical and the most rhetorically artful paragraph.

Madison begins by reminding the legislature of its own fundamental law; he quotes, as he notes in the margin of his copy, from Article XVI of the "Declaration of Rights and Frame of Government of Virginia," adopted in 1776. Madison himself intervened crucially in George Mason's draft of that article, though not in the clause here cited. (The sentence he affected is given in the fourth and fifteenth paragraphs.) In accordance with the symmetrical structure of the petition, the Virginia Declaration is cited in the first, the fourth, the eleventh, and the fifteenth paragraphs.

The quotation from Article XVI is here introduced in the spirit of the Declaration of Independence—the Virginia Declaration has no such language—as an axiom, an undeniable truth. The consequences of that axiom are then developed in an enchained sequence of sentences which has something of the quality of a liturgical responsory, a kind of rondel of reason. The enchaining brings with it a non-periodic style. (A period, speaking technically, is a circuit-like sentence, whose meaning is not delivered until the whole is complete.) Several sentences are grammatically simple; conjunctions and relatives, regarded in school rhetoric as weakening the vivacity of writing since their function should be carried by the diction,[14] are avoided; the continuity indeed comes from the incantation-like diction.

"The religion of every man must be left to the conviction and conscience of every man": He restates the phrase "reason and conviction" of Article XVI alliteratively and tactfully, avoiding that everlasting dwelling on Reason by which some of the defenders of religious liberty had made themselves suspect.

The recurrent phrase "every man," rather than "all men" as in the Declaration of Independence, carries a subtle emphasis: as Madison's logic notes from college point out, when one turns "all" into "every," the predicate is logically distributed so that it "belongs to every individual."[15] Since religion consists of "voluntary acts of individuals singly and voluntarily associated," Madison's use of "every" rather than "all" conveys the *individual* nature of religion implied by the fundamental axiom: No religious dogma is to be imposed and no religious exercise interfered with—the First Amendment in germ.

Each key word is picked up and elaborated as the argument continues: ". . . it is the *right* of every man to exercise" religion freely. "This *right* is . . . an *unalienable right*. It is *unalienable*, because the opinions of men" are free. "It is *unalienable* also, because what is here a *right* toward men, is a *duty* towards the *Creator*. It is the *duty* of every man to render the *Creator* such homage" as seems right to him. "This *duty* is precedent . . . to the claims of *Civil Society*." "Before a man can be considered a member of *Civil Society* . . . ," etc.

The rhetorical form emphasizes the mutual involvement of the terms. Free exercise of religion is a right and moreover an unalienable right because of an ineradicable feature of human nature—its freedom. This human freedom, the ground of civil liberty, is understood as a bondage of the mind to the dictates of reason and evidence—a dependency clearly expressed in the original opening paragraph of Jefferson's bill on religious freedom, which was deleted by the General Assembly with Madison's reluctant acquiescence.

> Well aware that the opinions and belief of men depend not on their own will, but follow involuntarily the evidence proposed to their minds. . . .[16]

Madison, who had earlier displayed a lively interest in the philosophical question of mental liberty and misgivings about its possibility,[17] must indeed have been sorry to see this pertinent passage disappear from the bill, bartered away for its passage.

The right to religious liberty is inalienable because of man's nature, but also because of man's relation to God, which is that of a subject bound by a duty to his Creator. Religion as defined in the passage from the Declaration of Rights which Madison quotes is a conflation of the Roman notion of obligatory performance and the biblical idea of obedience to the Creator, while the Christian salvational sense, to be introduced in the middle paragraphs, is here missing.

The inalienability of the right is, then, rooted in man's nature as free and as created; it is therefore inalienable by the very reason that makes it a right, namely that it is a *divine* duty that must be *individually* discharged. Succinctly put: "What is here a right towards men, is a duty towards the Creator."

Now comes the crux of the paragraph and indeed of the work. Man's relation as a creature is prior both in time and in degree to his membership in a polity. Before he can be thought of as a citizen of civil society, he must be considered as a subject under the Governor of the Universe; as the former he has rights, as the latter, duties. This priority in time may mean that these duties were his before this or any polity was instituted, even in the Garden of Eden, or that they precede adult citizenship and obligate even children. Precedent in "degree of obligation" must mean that moral duties supersede political obedience and that religion governs citizenship—indeed a creed for citizen-resisters to the usurpations of the civil powers.

Although Madison later himself cites Jesus' "own declaration that his Kingdom was not of this world" in behalf of the separation of worlds,[18] his own remarkable theory is quite distinct from the scriptural doctrine of the two realms, the secular and the spiritual. That doctrine holds this world inferior—Roger Williams, for example, demands a hedge between the garden of the Church and the *wilderness* of the World.[19]

In contrast, the precedence of the religious realm set out in the Memorial is not seen from the perspective of the world beyond, but from the position of a practicing citizen of *this* world, albeit with prior obligations. That is precisely why the functionaries of civil society may not invade the realm of religion—because that realm is here conceived as belonging to the active life of the world, not to civil society but certainly to society. The suspicion and contempt of the world, on the other hand, against whose intrusions the soul and the church must be guarded, belongs to *Christian* liberty—a *theological condition* and not a *civil right*. (The defense of religious liberty from the scriptural point of view is rousingly made in Milton's

Treatise of Civil Power in Ecclesiastical Causes; Madison may have known it.)

Madison is proposing a civil theology[20] in which the political arena is circumscribed by religion. From the point of view of political theory, men come out of (though in a sense they never leave) the Lockean state of nature and its right to self-preservation; from the point of view of the civil theology, man first and last remains "a free-born subject under the crown of heaven owing homage to none but God himself."[21]

Madison, however, does not advocate the cause of a deistic supersect with its positive rationalist doctrines, so confidently set out in Jefferson's bill concerning religious freedom, which knows and approves "the plan of the holy author of our religion . . . to extend it by its influence on reason alone." Encompassing all religions, whether propagated by reason, revelation, or force of tradition, Madison's civil theology is a far more genuine grounding for religious pluralism.

The conclusion is that rights of conscience are reserved from the authority of the political power. As Jefferson puts in it Query XVII of the *Notes on the State of Virginia* (1781):

> Our rulers can have authority over such natural rights only as we have submitted them. The rights of conscience we never submitted, we could not submit. We are answerable for them to our God.

There follows in the Memorial an intricately wrought analogy containing more subtleties than bear articulating:

> As 1. a member of Civil Society 2. who enters into any subordinate Association 3. must always do it 4. with a reservation of his duty 5. to the General Authority,

> Much more so must 1. every man 2. who becomes a member of any particular Civil Society 3. do it 4. with a saving of his allegiance 5. to the Universal Sovereign.

The climax of the deduction from the axiom of religion as a duty to God is the radical proposition that "no man's right is abridged by the institution of Civil Society and Religion is wholly exempt from its cognizance." That is to say: (1) individual religious rights are not alienated upon entering civil society and (2) the realm of common religious observance is wholly out of its jurisdiction.

This is the seminal secular statement concerning religious liberty as a civil right in the public realm, since Jefferson's law, to which Madison later gave the honor of being the standard of expression on the subject, was, though prior in the drafting (1779), posterior in publication (1785).

The political consequences are reserved for the last paragraph of the petition. Madison, however, here adds an afterthought that brings these fundamental principles into the political arena. It is an antithesis acknowledging in capsule form the paradox of majoritarianism, a clash of truths in the world of action:[22] "True it is" that the will of the majority alone can settle divisive differences, "but it is also true" that the majority may try to infringe the rights of the minority. The penultimate paragraph will counterbalance this reservation by an expression of full faith in the majority as a last court of appeal in cases of infringements on liberty.

SECOND PARAGRAPH

2. Because if Religion be exempt from the authority of the Society at large, still less can it be subject to that of the Legislative Body. The latter are but the creatures and vicegerents of the former. Their jurisdiction is both derivative and limited: it is limited with regard to the co-ordinate departments, more necessarily is it limited with regard to the constituents. The preservation of a free Government requires not merely, that the metes and bounds which separate each department of power be invariably maintained; but more especially that neither of them be suffered to overleap the great Barrier which defends the rights of the people. The Rulers who are guilty of such an encroachment, exceed

the commission from which they derive their authority, and are Tyrants. The People who submit to it are governed by laws made neither by themselves nor by an authority derived from them, and are slaves.

Now the doctrines of the first paragraph are applied, a fortiori, to government: If religion is beyond the political community, so much the more is it beyond the legislature. For as human beings are God's creatures, so the legislature is civil society's creature. (The manner of this legislative subordination is again taken up in the corresponding next-to-last paragraph.) The double limitation on its jurisdiction is stated in a succinct presentation of the theories of checks and balances and of limited government. It displays Madison's genius for articulating a full complement of fine but fundamental distinctions in the smallest compass: He speaks of the "metes and bounds" (a phrase possibly adapted from Locke's *Letter Concerning Toleration*[23]) that contain the departments of government, and of the "great Barrier" that circumscribes government itself.

That barrier, the limitation of legislative jurisdiction, is the political palisade before the "wall of separation," in Jefferson's famous metaphor for the First Amendment, which is to be erected between church and state.[24]

The language of the following sentences grows terse and absolute (although Madison manages to tuck in definitions of both tyranny and slavery): The rulers who encroach are tyrants, the people who submit, slaves. The theory of prompt resistance to be set out in the next paragraph is prepared.

THIRD PARAGRAPH

3. Because it is proper to take alarm at the first experiment on our liberties. We hold this prudent jealousy to be the first duty of Citizens, and one of the noblest characteristics of the late Revolution. The free men of America did not wait till usurped power had strengthened itself by exercise, and entangled the ques-

tion in precedents. They saw all the consequences in the principle, and they avoided the consequences by denying the principle. We revere this lesson too much soon to forget it. Who does not see that the same authority which can establish Christianity, in exclusion of all other Religions, may establish with the same ease any particular sect of Christians, in exclusion of all other Sects? that the same authority which can force a citizen to contribute three pence only of his property for the support of any one establishment, may force him to conform to any other establishment in all cases whatsoever?

The first sentence is often quoted, and "viewing with alarm" has, of course, become a cant phrase of American rhetoric. Here the key word "liberties" first appears; the phrase "religious liberty" is missing from the work.

The Revolution is invoked in favor of a "noble" mode of political response. In the remarkable phrase "prudent jealousy" Madison conflates republican duty with the principle of honor, the citizen's calculation of consequences with the nobleman's propensity for quick offense.

The necessity for a ready response lies, of course, in the fact that absolute principles, not compromisable interests, are involved; "the least interference with religion would be a flagrant usurpation." The Revolution, being the complex event of both principle and interest, was in fact slow in coming:

> mankind are more disposed to suffer, while evils are sufferable, than to right themselves by abolishing the forms to which they are accustomed. (*Declaration of Independence*)

Nevertheless, Madison here propagates the view, for the sake of the "revered lesson" it contains, that the three-penny tax on tea moved the "free men of America" to revolt because it was a first signal of oppression, not the last straw.[25] This view was evidently dear to him, for later he wrote:

The people of the U.S. owe their Independence and their liberty, to the wisdom of descrying in the minute tax of 3 pence on tea, the magnitude of the evil comprized in the precedent.[26]

The lesson he urges is immediate recognition of and resistance to breaches of principle, and especially of the principle of religious liberty, because it stands and falls as a whole. As Locke says: "The civil power can either change everything in religion . . . or it can change nothing."[27]

Two balanced rhetorical questions next address first the churches and then the individual citizens: As the authority to establish Christianity implies the power to establish one sect, so the authority to touch a citizen's property implies the power to force him into religious conformity. This passage reveals Madison's universal view of religious liberty. He writes here, in hopeful suppression of the fact admitted in the eleventh paragraph, that Virginia still had a Christian establishment, as if the establishment were an incipient event to be feared by the sects. His vigorous promotion of Jefferson's bill concerning religious liberty shows that he knew otherwise. An episode that occurred during its consideration in the Assembly shows where his sentiments lay.

For the sake of passage, Madison acquiesced in several deletions urged by men who objected to the aggressively deistic tone of the bill, although he thought these defaced the text somewhat—to him its expressions were ever the "true standard of religious liberty," even if his own inclination was to phrase that liberty as a right to the "full and free exercise" of religion rather than to its nonexercise. What he refused to agree to was an insertion that was attempted; as Madison much later recalled it:

An experiment was made on the reverence entertained for the name and sanctity of the Saviour, by proposing to insert the words "Jesus Christ" after the words "our lord" in the preamble.[28]

Madison, ever vigilant of words, fought the insertion and it was dropped. On January 22, 1786, he reported to Jefferson in Paris in a spirit of modest triumph that the enacting clauses had passed without alteration and, "I flatter myself, have in this country extinguished forever the ambitious hope of making laws for the human mind." The rejection of the insertion proved, Jefferson later said, that "the Jew and the Gentile, the Christian and Mohametan, the Hindoo and Infidel of every denomination" were within the mantle of its protection. Those were exactly Madison's intentions, and indeed he was to receive expressions of gratitude from American Jews and to give encouragement to them.[29]

So, although in the Memorial he writes to and for and—unemphatically but unquestionably—as a Christian, there can be no question about the universal application of his principle of religious liberty. No more can there be doubt about his uncompromising steadfastness in its application. Of many proofs let me choose only three.

His early draft of those amendments to the Constitution which were to become the Bill of Rights specifically prohibits the establishment of a "national religion."

Even in later life he retained his rhetorical vigor in fighting Christian establishments. He apostrophizes his country:

> Ye states of America, which retain . . . any aberration from the sacred principle of religious liberty, by giving to Caesar what belongs to God, or joining together what God has put asunder, hasten to revise and purify your systems.[30]

As ever, he attacks the perverse wedlock of church and state on the ground of Christianity itself.

The most striking, almost comical, examples of his scrupulous avoidance of even the slightest trespass are his presidential Thanksgiving Messages during the War of 1812. Forced from him by a Congressional resolution, he phrased them as exhortations to free choice of worship rather than to public piety.[31]

The strong Madisonian meaning of the word "liberty" as applied to religion, to be adumbrated throughout the petition, begins to emerge.

Religious liberty is a civil right that is grounded in relations of duty to God antecedent to political society and therefore incapable of being abrogated. These relations are determined by the nature of the human conscience, which is free in a philosophical sense, that is, determined not by external force but only by the internal compulsion of evidence, be it reason or revelation; they are also determined by the original nature of the human being, which is dependent in a theological sense, that is, created by God (Para. 1). Delicate because it must be maintained absolutely (Para. 3), this liberty requires the government to abstain completely from interference, for the purpose either of supporting or of obstructing the exercise of religious obligations (Para. 2). The government must protect religion, but only by abstaining evenhandedly from interference and by safeguarding each sect from the intrusions of the other sects (Para. 8). As a right held on the same political terms as the other natural rights that are reserved to the individual, religious liberty stands or falls with them (Para. 15).

FOURTH PARAGRAPH

4. Because the Bill violates that equality which ought to be the basis of every law, and which is more indispensable, in proportion as the validity or expediency of any law is more liable to be impeached. If "all men are by nature equally free and independent," all men are to be considered as entering into Society on equal conditions; as relinquishing no more, and therefore retaining no less, one than another, of their natural rights. Above all are they to be considered as retaining an "*equal* title to the free exercise of Religion according to the dictates of Conscience." Whilst we assert for ourselves a freedom to embrace, to profess,

and to observe the Religion which we believe to be of divine origin, we cannot deny an equal freedom to those whose minds have not yet yielded to the evidence which has convinced us. If this freedom be abused, it is an offence against God, not against man: To God, therefore, not to man, must an account of it be rendered. As the Bill violates equality by subjecting some to peculiar burdens, so it violates the same principle, by granting to others peculiar exemptions. Are the Quakers and Menonists the only sects who think a compulsive support of their Religions unnecessary and unwarrantable? Can their piety alone be entrusted with the care of public worship? Ought their Religions to be endowed above all others with extraordinary privileges by which proselytes may be enticed from all others? We think too favorably of the justice and good sense of these denominations to believe that they either covet pre-eminences over their fellow citizens or that they will be seduced by them from the common opposition to the measure.

The proposed bill violates the natural equality of men affirmed in Article I of the Virginia Declaration of Rights, now quoted by Madison. Such equality is presented here as an *internal* condition of all law. The more liable a law is to the charge of invalidity or inexpediency, the more important such equality becomes. The dictum that equality "ought to be the basis of every law" refers to the inner equity of the law, which ought to affect everyone equally, not to the familiar demand for equality of treatment under the law; the law must be such as to be *capable* of equal application.

A succinct statement of the contract theory of rights that underlies this demand is given: All men being by nature equally free, they must enter civil society on equal conditions; they must give up and retain exactly equal rights. "To embrace, to profess, and to observe the Religion which we believe to be of divine origin," to join, to declare, and to exercise whatever religion seems to us to be truly a religion, is the essence of these rights with respect to religion.

In the conclusion of his *Letter Concerning Toleration* Locke says that "the sum of all we drive at is that every man may enjoy the same rights that are guaranteed to others." Madison italicizes this one word in the petition—*equal*—when he quotes for the first time that clause of Article XVI of the Virginia Declaration of Rights for whose form he himself was responsible. Equality of applicability *and* application was for Madison, as for Locke, important above all else. Although it intends to preserve the "liberal principle" of Article XVI, by "abolishing all distinctions of pre-eminence" among the different sects, the Assessment bill is inequitable because it burdens all in support of a religious service that will peculiarly burden non-Christians and peculiarly exempt those Christians who do not wish to take advantage of its benefits. The rhetorical question, what sects besides those mentioned would fall under the latter category, would have the obvious answer: above all the Baptists, whose opposition to any kind of state intervention was a matter of theological principle.

There can never be a moral or theological pretext for interference, because the abuse of the right of religion is not subject to human punishment. Madison had restricted Mason's broad reservation in the original draft of Article XVI, that the magistrate might restrain free exercise if, "under colour of religion, any man disturb the peace, the happiness, or the safety of society," to the condition that "the preservation of liberty and the existence of the State are manifestly endangered." His record shows that as a magistrate he would have found no occasion to apply it; presumably he was glad finally to see the whole clause drop out.[32]

A bilaterally symmetrical sentence, the only one in the petition to contain the word "God," presents this central point: God alone punishes offenses of faith.

Early American documents mention the names of God profusely enough to intrigue a medieval theologian.[33] In this petition he is the Creator to whom man owes the duties of a dependent creature; the Governor of the Universe to whom man is a subject rather than a citizen (Para. 1); the God before whom alone man can sin (Para. 4); the Author of our Religion who hands down its teachings in scripture (Para. 6); the Supreme Lawgiver of the Universe from whom illumination of the legislature is requested (Para. 15). Not mere unreflective Enlightenment epithets, these names must be genuine expressions of Madison's understanding of the facets of humanity's relations to God, for they delineate just such a God as would be the ground of religious liberty.

In his work on Article XVI of the Declaration of Rights,[34] the young delegate to the Revolutionary Convention of May 1776 had offered but one draft article, on religion. Patrick Henry, who had himself sponsored it, had quickly disclaimed it when challenged on the floor to explain whether he actually intended to disestablish the Church. Madison had, of course, intended just such disestablishment:

> That Religion or the duty we owe to our Creator, and the manner of discharging it, being under the direction of reason and conviction only, not of violence or compulsion [a stylistic emendation of Mason's "force or violence"], all men are equally entitled to the full and free exercise of it according to the dictates of Conscience.

No man or class of men, the article continues, should receive special privileges or be subjected to special penalties for religious reasons, a prefiguration of the two prongs of the First Amendment, the establishment and free exercise clauses.

Madison, having been forced to withdraw his own draft, scrutinized Mason's version, which promised "the fullest *toleration* in the Exercise of religion." Perhaps he alone in that assembly took one word of it seriously enough to forestall a danger.[35]

That word was "toleration," which implies not a right to religious liberty but a privilege granted. That was absolutely insufferable for Madison, for toleration accorded with, and so confirmed, ecclesiastical establishment (as in modern times it can accompany an anticlerical policy).[36]

Although he wrote respectfully of the Dutch "experiment of combining liberal toleration with the establishment of a particular creed,"[37] Madison would certainly have rejected Spinoza's views in the *Theologico-Political Treatise* (Ch. XIX), that the possessor of sovereign power has rights over spiritual matters but should *grant* religious liberty on matters of outward observancy, only inward piety being private and inalienable. In any case, it is unlikely that he knew Spinoza's writings, especially since Locke, whose *Letter* he had probably read (as external likelihood and internal evidence in the Memorial indicate), admitted to little acquaintance with Spinoza's work.[38] Although called a "Letter Concerning *Toleration*," Locke's work, by a typical cunning twist, shifts the meaning of the term: not *granted* to dissenting Christians by the ecclesiastical establishment and its state sponsors, toleration is *required* of the magistrate toward all churches—Mohammedans, Pagan, idolaters (though *not*—and here Madison differed—to atheists); the magistrate has no right to interfere with either the internal or the external aspects of religion. This "tolerance" was not the notion Tom Paine excoriated in the *Age of Reason* as "not the *opposite* of Intolerance, but . . . the *counterfeit* of it," but a demand for a right under cover of a less aggressive term. Madison might well have taken his lead from the thought of the *Letter Concerning Toleration* at the same time that he balked at the use of the term "toleration" in fundamental law.

FIFTH PARAGRAPH

5. Because the Bill implies either that the Civil Magistrate is a competent Judge of Religious Truth; or that he may employ Religion as an engine of Civil policy. The first is an arrogant pretension falsified by the contradictory opinions of Rulers in all ages,

and throughout the world: the second an unhallowed perversion of the means of salvation.

The brief but resounding paragraph ("arrogant pretension"—"unhallowed perversion") appears to have been retained from the debate on the floor of the Assembly. Madison's notes show that he employed his large theological erudition[39] to bring home to the Assembly, with that muted irony of which he was capable, the politico-theological consequences of the bill. It would require a legislative definition of Christianity: It would require that the lawmakers choose an official Bible—Hebrew, Septuagint, or Vulgate—decide the method of its interpretation, confirm a doctrine—Trinitarian, Arian, Socinian—as orthodox, and so forth. The sentiment of the paragraph is Lockean: "neither the right nor the art of ruling does necessarily carry along with it the certain knowledge of other things and least of all of the true religion."

In this paragraph alone Madison speaks of religion as a "means of salvation," in contrast to its employment as an "engine of civil policy." In the argument for religious liberty the obligations of religion, not its blessings, count most.

SIXTH PARAGRAPH

6. Because the establishment proposed by the Bill is not requisite for the support of the Christian Religion. To say that it is, is a contradiction to the Christian Religion itself, for every page of it disavows a dependence on the powers of this world: it is a contradiction to fact; for it is known that this Religion both existed and flourished, not only without the support of human laws, but in spite of every opposition from them, and not only during the period of miraculous aid, but long after it had been left to its own evidence and the ordinary care of Providence. Nay, it is a contradiction in terms; for a Religion not invented by human policy, must have pre-existed and been supported before it was established by human policy. It is moreover to weaken in those who profess this Religion a pious confidence in its innate excellence

and the patronage of its Author; and to foster in those who still reject it, a suspicion that its friends are too conscious of its fallacies to trust it to its own merits.

Madison leaves the universal considerations of religious liberty to attend to the particularly Christian interest in it. The seven core paragraphs of the petition are devoted to that Christian point of view, an arrangement that tellingly mirrors both the encompassing necessity for a philosophical foundation and the immediate fact that a Christian constituency is speaking. Establishment, prohibited in a purely political context for the sake of the free exercise of religion, is to be yet more eschewed for the sake of Christianity itself.

His notes for the floor debate show that he intended to divert the argument from the preoccupation with the social need for religion to the "true question": Are religious establishments necessary for religion? The proponents' concern with "the peace of society" was, so he implies later, in part a cover for concern with the declining importance of the churches. The end of war, laws that cherish virtue, religious associations that would provide personal examples of morality, the education of youth, and precisely the end of governmental intrusion, not state intervention, were the "true remedies" for the decline of religion which he recommended to the legislature. Note the neoclassical notion that the laws should promote virtue.[40]

Madison's Christian defense of liberty is in the great tradition of Protestant dissenting writings, especially Milton's *Treatise of Civil Power in Ecclesiastical Causes* (1659), in which he shows "the wrong the civil power doth; by violating the fundamental privilege of the Gospel, . . . Christian libertie,"[41] that is, freedom from forcible impositions in matters of worship. Indeed, Milton's whole argument is drawn from scripture, especially from the Pauline letters.

Madison, too, alludes to scripture: "every page" of religion "disavows a dependence on the power of this world." The Baptists, whose whole petition was based on the grounds that the bill was "repugnant to the Spirit of the Gospel," however, outdid him in this line of argument. For them, as for other opposing Christians, disestablishment dated from Jesus himself. "Render to Caesar the things that are Caesar's and to God the things that are God's" (Mark 13:17).

The paragraph next exposes the contradictions of the bill's premise that Christianity cannot be diffused "without a competent provision" for its teachers. The contradiction *of fact* is that Christianity has indeed flourished at all times without aid—and Madison gives a believer's capsule history of its two epochs, the era of miracles and the era of ordinary providence. The more serious contradiction *in terms* is twofold: the dependence of religion, which is preexistent, on human policy and the failure of the faithful to trust in God for its support. The argument is rendered in a beautifully branching and balanced coda.

Fifty years later, Madison would feel entitled to answer the "true question" definitively from the accumulated evidence of the American experience, which had "brought the subject to a fair and finally decisive test." Left to itself, religion would flourish; indeed the danger lay rather in its extravagances.[42] Madison insisted that "every successful example of a perfect separation . . . is of importance," and that he regarded such success as an indispensable empirical test of the principle of religious liberty. At the same time, he was certain that the test would never fail since "there appears to be in the nature of man what insures his belief in an invisible cause. . . ." But what would Madison have said in the face of an observable decline of "religious commitment" and the increasing legal expulsion of religion from communal life?[43]

SEVENTH PARAGRAPH

7. Because experience witnesseth that ecclesiastical establishments, instead of maintaining the purity and efficacy of Religion, have had a contrary operation. During almost fifteen centuries

has the legal establishment of Christianity been on trial. What have been its fruits? More or less in all places, pride and indolence in the Clergy, ignorance and servility in the laity, in both, superstition, bigotry and persecution. Enquire of the Teachers of Christianity for the ages in which it appeared in its greatest lustre; those of every sect, point to the ages prior to its incorporation with Civil policy. Propose a restoration of this primitive State in which its Teachers depended on the voluntary rewards of their flocks, many of them predict its downfall. On which Side ought their testimony to have greatest weight, when for or when against their interest?

Proof positive that religion could flourish on its own was a half-century in the future, but the evidence of fifteen centuries, that is, dating back roughly to the Conversion of Constantine, showed that legal establishments corrupted Christianity, because they hampered freedom of conscience, "the truly Christian principle."[44]

Here, as elsewhere, Madison allows himself the most spirited language for clerical degeneracy, without, however, giving way to that automatic anticlericalism that possessed Jefferson. Even in his youth, in an early letter to his friend William Bradford (January, 1774), echoing the spirit of the fourth part of Hobbes's *Leviathan*, "Of the Kingdom of Darkness," he had given a similar catalogue of clerical and lay vice, of the "Pride ignorance and Knavery among the Priesthood and Vice and Wickedness among the Laity," which he thought was evident in his home country; worst of all:

> That diabolical Hell conceived principle of persecution rages among some and to their eternal Infamy the Clergy can furnish their Quota of Imps for such business.

The Protestant supporters of the bill would preach the life of early Christianity, but they do not want to live like the first disciples, much less like the first Teacher himself. This passage deals with church business without resorting to the word "church," which never occurs in this petition. Madison opposed not only the "incorporation with Civil policy" effected by a bill proposing state-salaried religious teachers, but the "encroachments and accumulations" encouraged by the legal incorporation of churches.[45] He desired neither state-supported nor richly endowed churches, but small congregations that would directly support their ministers.

EIGHTH PARAGRAPH

8. Because the establishment in question is not necessary for the support of Civil Government. If it be urged as necessary for the support of Civil Government only as it is a means of supporting Religion, and it be not necessary for the latter purpose, it cannot be necessary for the former. If Religion be not within the cognizance of Civil Government how can its legal establishment be necessary to Civil Government? What influence in fact have ecclesiastical establishments had on Civil Society? In some instances they have been seen to erect a spiritual tyranny on the ruins of the Civil authority; in many instances they have been seen upholding the thrones of political tyranny; in no instance have they been seen the guardians of the liberties of the people. Rulers who wished to subvert the public liberty, may have found an established Clergy convenient auxiliaries. A just Government instituted to secure & perpetuate it needs them not. Such a Government will be best supported by protecting every Citizen in the enjoyment of his Religion with the same equal hand which protects his person and his property; by neither invading the equal rights of any Sect, nor suffering any Sect to invade those of another.

At the middle count, Madison takes up the main point supposedly agitating the proponents of the bill: the dangerous decline of morality that the bill was supposed to halt.

In his first extant expression concerning religious liberty, a youthful letter to Bradford (December, 1778), Madison had asked this politico-theological question: "Is an Ecclesiastical

Establishment absolutely necessary to support civil society in a supream Government?"

In this petition Madison has prepared the ground for answering the question in such a way that he can dispose of it by a mere syllogism (*modus tollens*): Only if religion is within the cognizance of government can the question of necessary legal establishment arise. But it is not, by the first paragraph. Therefore establishment is not necessary. With equal logic, he disposes of the circular arguments of the supporters, who say that establishment is necessary to government only insofar as government is a necessary means of supporting religion; since the latter contention has been shown false by the preceding paragraph, the former falls also.

So logical a resolution of the great question was not universally appealing. After he heard these arguments, Henry Lee wrote to Madison: "Refiners may weave as fine a web of reason as they please, but the experience of all times shows Religion to be the guardian of morals." Not really in disagreement with Lee's premise, Madison only disclaimed the inference that government ought to support the churches; he certainly never went as far as Jefferson, who claimed that "the interests of society require observation of those moral precepts only on which all religions agree,"[46] which amounts to saying that sectarian churches arc unnecessary to society.

There are some instances of establishments supplanting governments, many instances of their upholding tyrannies, none of their supporting liberty. "A just government, instituted to secure and perpetuate it, needs them not," concludes Madison, in the language reminiscent of the Declaration of Independence: "That to secure these Rights, Governments are instituted among Men, deriving their just Powers from the Consent of the Governed."

How does a just government protect religious rights? It protects them precisely as it protects property and other rights. In a short essay "On Property,"[47] written in 1792, Madison elaborates a remarkable theory of religious rights which goes further—Rights *are* property: "In a word, as a man is said to have a right to his property, he may equally be said to have a property in his rights. . . ." And earlier in the same essay: "He has a property of peculiar value in his religious opinions, and in the profession and practice dictated by them. . . ." Just government is instituted to secure property, in the large sense in which the term includes anything that a person values as his *own* (leaving to everyone else a like advantage), of which dominion over external things is only a part. Religious rights so conceived establish a kind of internal personal and external sectarian territoriality that government is to protect by "neither invading the equal rights of any Sect, nor suffering any Sect to invade those of another." Those worried about inhibitions put on the free exercise of religion by the Supreme Court's enforcement of the establishment clause of the First Amendment might well look to Madison's theory of religious rights as property rights.

NINTH AND TENTH PARAGRAPHS

9. Because the proposed establishment is a departure from that generous policy, which, offering an Asylum to the persecuted and oppressed of every Nation and Religion, promised a lustre to our country, and an accession to the number of its citizens. What a melancholy mark is the Bill of sudden degeneracy? Instead of holding forth an Asylum to the persecuted, it is itself a signal of persecution. It degrades from the equal rank of Citizens all those whose opinions in Religion do not bend to those of the Legislative authority. Distant as it may be in its present form from the Inquisition, it differs from it only in degree. The one is the first step, the other the last in the career of intolerance. The magnanimous sufferer under this cruel scourge in foreign Regions, must view the Bill as a Beacon on our Coast, warning him to seek some other haven, where liberty and philanthropy in their due extent, may offer a more certain repose from his Troubles.

10. Because it will have a like tendency to banish our Citizens. The allurements presented by other situations are every day

thinning their number. To superadd a fresh motive to emigration by revoking the liberty which they now enjoy, would be the same species of folly which has dishonoured and depopulated flourishing kingdoms.

Now Madison inserts two complementary considerations, humanitarian and practical, which had figured in the floor debates under the heading of "Policy." The bill might close Virginia as a religious asylum and also drive out dissenters, and might thus at once prevent much-needed immigration and further thin a population already moving westward at an alarming rate. Madison did not have to spell out to his fellow farmers the bad economic results of this policy: a yet greater shortage of labor power and further declining land prices.

The politically regressive consequences, however, needed telling. Citing again his maxim of the contiguity of the least and greatest breach of liberty, he does not hesitate to compare, though with reasonable qualifications, a Protestant Estabishment with the Catholic Inquisition.

The springiness of style that derives from the adroit juxtaposition of two kinds of English diction, short and polysyllabic words, is noteworthy; for example: "What a *melancholy mark* is the Bill of *sudden degeneracy?*"

ELEVENTH PARAGRAPH

11. Because it will destroy that moderation and harmony which the forbearance of our laws to intermeddle with Religion has produced among its several sects. Torrents of blood have been spilt in the old world, by vain attempts of the secular arm, to extinguish Religious discord, by proscribing all difference in Religious opinion. Time has at length revealed the true remedy. Every relaxation of narrow and rigorous policy, wherever it has been tried, has been found to assuage the disease. The American Theatre has exhibited proofs that equal and compleat liberty, if it does not wholly eradicate it, sufficiently destroys its malignant influence on the health and prosperity of the State. If with

the salutary effects of this system under our own eyes, we begin to contract the bounds of Religious freedom, we know no name that will too severely reproach our folly. At least let warning be taken at the first fruits of the threatened innovation. The very appearance of the Bill has transformed "that Christian forbearance, love and charity," which of late mutually prevailed, into animosities and jealousies, which may not soon be appeased. What mischiefs may not be dreaded, should this enemy to the public quiet be armed with the force of a law?

A crowd of notions familiar in early American rhetoric is now brought to bear on the threat of sectarian strife raised by the bill: Time has revealed, and America is the stage to test and prove, the remedies to old problems; liberty once instituted, innovations may be dangerously regressive.

The paragraph permits itself some hyperbole, in the claim of complete religious freedom in Virginia, which flies in the face of the fact that the same Article XVI that Madison cites establishes Christianity, if not as a state church, at least as *the* public morality; moreover, in 1781 Jefferson had indignantly noted that although "statutory oppression" had ceased, common law permitting all sorts of persecution was still on the books.[48]

In this section Madison prudently suppresses his opinion that a vigorous variety of sects is an even more practically efficacious guarantee of liberty than a bill of rights,[49] and that disestablishment promotes church prosperity very much as factions well-managed produce political stability. The unstated premise is, of course, that doctrinal enthusiasms are as much an irrepressible force of human nature as special secular interests.

I can detect no strain in this opinion of Madison which might equate it with the insouciant dogma that truth is a private predilection and that everything is "true for" them that believe it. His preference for sectarian variety rests on limits and necessities of observed human nature, not on a doctrinal disavowal of the search for truth.

TWELFTH PARAGRAPH

12. Because the policy of the Bill is adverse to the diffusion of the light of Christianity. The first wish of those who enjoy this precious gift ought to be that it may be imparted to the whole race of mankind. Compare the number of those who have as yet received it with the number still remaining under the dominion of false Religions; and how small is the former! Does the policy of the Bill tend to lessen the disproportion? No; it at once discourages those who are strangers to the light of revelation from coming into the Region of it; and countenances by example the nations who continue in darkness, in shutting out those who might convey it to them. Instead of Levelling as far as possible, every obstacle to the victorious progress of Truth, the Bill with an ignoble and unchristian timidity would circumscribe it with a wall of defence against the encroachments of error.

In his notes for the floor debate Madison had proposed to himself at about this place in the argument a vindication of disestablished Christianity, a "panegyric of it on our side." He omits it in the Memorial in favor of an appeal to the missionary urge. The offending Bill is altogether too parochially conceived. Not only in Virginia but throughout mankind should Christianity be propagated. Instead the bill will act to prevent conversions by discouraging "strangers to the light of revelation," that is, infidels (Madison had first written "light of truth" and then christianized the term), from "coming into the Region of it," which implies that a free America ought to be the natural ground on which revealed religion may be experienced.

The final sentence of the Christian section is reminiscent of the great peroration of the preamble to Jefferson's bill establishing religious freedom, that truth is great and will prevail if left to herself: that she is the proper and sufficient antagonist to error and has nothing to fear from the conflict unless by human interposition disarmed of her natural weapons, free argument and debate,

except that the truth of this paragraph is the truth of revelation, and the freedom here called for Christian liberty, a very Madisonian harmonizing of the spirit of enlightenment and the claims of Christianity.

THIRTEENTH PARAGRAPH

13. Because attempts to enforce by legal sanctions, acts obnoxious to so great a proportion of Citizens, tend to enervate the laws in general, and to slacken the bands of Society. If it be difficult to execute any law which is not generally deemed necessary or salutary, what must be the case, where it is deemed invalid and dangerous? And what may be the effect of so striking an example of impotency in the Government, on its general authority?

Again balanced phrases: "enervate the laws . . . slacken the bands," "necessary or salutary . . . invalid and dangerous." The rhetorical questions are intended to give pause to legislators who are ignoring the dangerous political effects of an unenforceable law: Madison's associates anticipated rebellion in some counties.

FOURTEENTH PARAGRAPH

14. Because a measure of such singular magnitude and delicacy ought not to be imposed, without the clearest evidence that it is called for by a majority of citizens, and no satisfactory method is yet proposed by which the voice of the majority in this case may be determined, or its influence secured. "The people of the respective counties are indeed requested to signify their opinion respecting the adoption of the Bill to the next Session of Assembly." But the representation must be made equal, before the voice either of the Representatives or of the Counties will be that of the people. Our hope is that neither of the former will, after

due consideration, espouse the dangerous principle of the Bill. Should the event disappoint us, it will still leave us in full confidence, that a fair appeal to the latter will reverse the sentence against our liberties.

In accordance with the symmetry of the composition, the penultimate paragraph returns to the beginning. The resolution that occasioned the petition is cited, though with a little rhetorical interjection ("indeed") reflecting on its insufficiency.

Self-government, Madison argues, demands both that the voice of the majority be determined and that its influence be secured. That is to say, the legislature's occasional solicitation of petitions is not a methodical enough polling of opinion, and electoral qualification as well as legislative apportionment are not fair enough for either the Delegates or the Senators to be truly representative.[50] Truly representative representatives, namely, those elected from districts fairly apportioned and responsive to their constituents, would have been less likely to support the dangerous abuse of power perpetrated by the bill. The petitioners hope, however, that even the legislature as presently constituted can be brought to reconsider its dangerous course. The paragraph concludes with a veiled threat of an organized grassroots campaign for repeal should the bill nonetheless be passed.

Here is set out an important aspect of Madison's theory of self-government. It is the idea that when major and controversial legislation is in progress, the people should be given some systematic opportunity to express themselves, because such a plebiscitic element is a trustworthy preventive of legislative usurpation and an added sanction for laws. (There is, however, no evidence that Madison was proposing that this "method" for determining the voice of the majority be incorporated in the Constitution.)

Accordingly, the fact that Jefferson's law on religious liberty had been overwhelmingly passed in the wake of this and other petitions was regarded by Madison as a consummating factor: it had the "advantage of having been the result of a formal appeal to the sense of the Community and a deliberate sanction of a vast Majority. . . ."[51] The majoritarian faith Madison expresses here is, of course, qualified in other contexts, where he designs devices, "moderations of sovereignty," for protecting liberties from the people as well as from the legislature.

FIFTEENTH PARAGRAPH

15. Because finally, "the equal right of every citizen to the free exercise of his Religion according to the dictates of conscience" is held by the same tenure with all our other rights. If we recur to its origin, it is equally the gift of nature; if we weigh its importance, it cannot be less dear to us; if we consult the "Declaration of those rights which pertain to the good people of Virginia, as the basis and foundation of Government," it is enumerated with equal solemnity, or rather studied emphasis. Either then, we must say, that the Will of the Legislature is the only measure of their authority; and that in the plenitude of this authority, they may sweep away all our fundamental rights; or, that they are bound to leave this particular right untouched and sacred: Either we must say, that they may control the freedom of the press, may abolish the Trial by Jury, may swallow up the Executive and Judiciary Powers of the State; nay that they may despoil us of our very right of suffrage, and erect themselves into an independent and hereditary Assembly, or, we must say, that they have no authority to enact into law the Bill under consideration. We the Subscribers say, that the General Assembly of the Commonwealth have no such authority: And that no effort may be omitted on our part against so dangerous an usurpation, we oppose to it, this remonstrance; earnestly praying, as we are in duty bound, that the Supreme Lawgiver of the Universe, by illuminating those to whom it is addressed, may on the one hand, turn their Councils from every act which would affront his holy prerogative, or violate the trust committed to them: and on the other, guide them into every measure which may be worthy of his [blessing, may re]dound to

their own praise, and may establish more firmly the liberties, the prosperity and the happiness of the Commonwealth.

The right of religious liberty is now examined not insofar as it is grounded in transpolitical conditions, as in the opening paragraph, but with respect to its situation in the political realm. Madison again quotes his free exercise clause of Article XVI of the Virginia Declaration of Rights (as he evidently had in the floor debates) together with a sonorous adaptation of its full title:

> A declaration of rights made by the representatives of the good people of Virginia, assembled in full and free convention; which rights do pertain to them and their posterity, as the basis and foundation of government.

The purpose of the citation in the fourth paragraph was to emphasize the equal *application* of the right; the point now is the equal, or even superior, *standing* that it has compared with the other fundamental rights. The religious right is equal with them in its natural origin, in its importance, and in its place of promulgation in fundamental law. (In the Declaration it had in fact been given the ultimate, most emphatic position, even beyond the article of exhortation to virtue and "frequent recurrency to fundamental principles.")

Since it is coequal with the other fundamental rights, religious liberty stands or falls with them. The argument, presented in two parallel sets of alternatives, recurs to the all-or-nothing reasoning of the third paragraph, which is now extended. The least breach of the religious right endangers all the rights at once: Either the will of the legislature is unlimited or this particular right is untouchable; either they may sweep away all rights or they cannot enact the present bill. All the phrases are precise and suggestive: "Will of the legislature" is opposed to "voice of the people" of the previous paragraph; the "plenitude of their authority" conveys legislative high-handedness; "sacred" is used in the double sense of holy and inviolable. The rights of which the legislature "may despoil us"—Madison had first written "may abolish" but then remembered that natural rights cannot be abolished—are then enumerated from the Declaration, but their order is almost exactly reversed, ending with the most specifically political right, a "fundamental article in Republican Constitutions," the right of suffrage.[52] The whole appeal is couched in terms of the constraints of reasonable speech: "Either we must say . . . or we must say. . . ." It concludes determinedly: "We the Subscribers say, that the General Assembly of this Commonwealth have no such authority."

The final pronouncement of the citizens, then, supersedes all the previous considerations. It is the principled denial of legislative authority to enact the bill at all: The legislators may not arm it "with the sanctions of a law," in the words of the preamble. Into the last paragraph of his law concerning religious freedom Jefferson had written just such a denial: No assembly can constrain a future one equally elected by the people, but it is free to shame it by declaring that if it should repeal or narrow the law, "such an act will be an infringement of natural right."

The subscribers' pronouncement introduces the submission of the Memorial in a peroration that counters the simplicity of the opening with a grand, intricately branching rhetorical period, praying, as religious duty demands, that two coordinate illuminations might descend on the lawmakers, that they may both refrain from violating their trust and pass measures that will make them worthy of God's blessing, will procure for them the praise of men, and will establish for the citizens liberty, prosperity, and happiness.

Observe the careful enumeration of goods in triads and subtriads; such triples belong to the familiar rhythms of American rhetoric: "Life, liberty, and the pursuit of Happiness" rise most immediately to the ear. The prayer for the establishment of these goods echoes the title of Jefferson's famous Bill: "A Bill for *Establishing* Religious Freedom," which proclaims the republican appropriation of the offending term. The petition ends as it began, with a reference to the Commonwealth.

IV. Madison's Rhetoric

How is the rhetoric of the Memorial to be characterized and how is it to be accounted for, reticent and rousing, calculated to persuade and designed for truth-telling, concisely compendious and artfully structured, as it is?

In his essay "Of Eloquence," Hume complains of the deficiency of modern eloquence. It is "calm, elegant, and subtile," but also lacking in passion and sublimity as well as order and method: It is mere "good sense delivered in proper expressions." The Memorial has the precise virtues and precisely lacks the shortcomings Hume names. It is at once "argumentative and rational," grandly passionate and carefully constructed. It is almost as if Madison had composed to Hume's standards, standards probably more appropriate to written than to spoken eloquence. Unlike Jefferson, whose style failed him on the floor, Madison, incidentally, was a persuasive though undeclamatory speaker. He seems to have addressed assemblies with just the same educated elegance with which he wrote, suiting his matter rather than his form to the occasion.

The terms and criteria for judging style used to be fairly fixed; they were to be found in textbooks of rhetoric, or—the preferred word in the eighteenth century—of eloquence, and they were universally employed in characterizing and judging productions. The loss of such a set of critical vocabulary is not much mourned by modern writers on rhetoric, who regard it as meaningless and unprofitable, and demand more fluid, sophisticated criteria. But its disappearance is a loss. To be sure, a writer was unlikely to improve his style merely through learning Quintilian's maxim that the first virtue of eloquence is perspicuity or clarity, that vivacity or liveliness of imagery is next in order of importance, that elegance or dignity of manner is also required, and that the intellect has the prerogative of being always the faculty ultimately addressed in speech. (My source here is Campbell's *Philosophy of Rhetoric*, 1776, a work based mainly on Humean principles of human nature and a popular textbook in the colleges of the early Republic.[53]) Yet it seems to me a suggestive fact that in the era when these criteria were considered significant, prose was produced that indeed satisfied them. Certainly they describe Madison's style with accuracy.

They were, I suppose, not so much the instigators as the precipitates of a well-defined and uncompromising taste—well-defined insofar as a deviation truly offended, and uncompromising because no one, certainly not Madison, lowered his language for any audience or occasion. All the manifestos, pamphlets, correspondences, petitions, memoranda, and memorials of the time that come in one's way show the same educated correctness of style.

Such correctness, then called "purity," that is, speech true to its rules, is said by Campbell to be the lowest—and indispensable—rhetorical virtue: "Where grammar ends, eloquence begins." It was in such basic studies that Madison, and everyone of his class, was amply trained, and that early, in boyhood.

At twelve, Madison recalls in his autobiography, he was learning Greek and Latin, studies that, if not absolutely indispensable to good style, at least ensure that knowledge of syntax and vocabulary that prevents illogical constructions and faulty diction, while shaping the Latinate English appropriate to political writing. "Miscellaneous literature" was also embraced by the plan of the school he attended. Madison devotes a special paragraph to one such work of literature that he read early to great advantage, namely, the *Spectator*, especially Addison's numbers, and in recommending it late in life to his nephew, he writes:

> Addison was of the first rank among the fine writers of the age, and has given a definition of what he showed himself to be an example. 'Fine writing,' he says, 'consists of sentiments that are natural, without being obvious'; to which adding the remark of Swift, another celebrated author of the same period, making a good style to consist 'of proper words in their proper places,' a definition is formed, which will merit your recollection.[54]

Madison has here conjoined precepts from one writer of satiny sweetness and another of mordant savor. Both together evidently guided his taste.

The young student apparently had an interest in rhetorical lore; at one point he copied out and annotated a long poem on the tropes of rhetoric:

> A metaphor compares with out the Sign
> [Madison's marginalia: "as, like, etc."]
> Virtue's A star and shall for ever shine.[55]

Studies conducive to good style and rational discourse continued in Princeton. There he filled a copybook with notes on a course of logic, probably given by the president, Dr. Witherspoon, much of which naturally bore on argumentation.[56] There, too, he is very likely to have heard Dr. Witherspoon's lectures on eloquence, of which extensive notes taken, among others, by Madison's college friend William Bradford in 1772, are still extant.[57] Witherspoon was fully conscious that he was speaking to young men destined for political responsibilities, who might one day have to address "promiscuous assemblies." He tried to convey to them the dignity and efficacy of rhetorical studies. He deals with the usual topics: types of language, such as the sublime and the simple; the use of tropes or figures of speech; his own set of characteristics for eloquent writing—for example, it is just if it pays "particular attention to the truth and meaning of every sentence" and elegant if it employs "the best expression the language will afford." Furthermore, he treats of invention, organization, and style, always giving examples, and among them Addison and Swift.

But what seems to me most likely to have penetrated to his young auditors was his introductory list of five rules for good writing: (1) "Study to imitate the greatest examples." (2) "Accustom yourselves to early and much composition and exercise in speaking." (3) Acquaint yourselves with the "branches subordinate" to eloquence, namely, grammar, orthography, punctuation. (4) Notice and guard against "peculiar phrases," namely, idiosyncrasies of speech. (5) "Follow nature," meaning, gain clear conceptions and follow the truth. Who now is bold enough to give such good advice so authoritatively?

Rives thought that Witherspoon had had a major part in forming Madison's style. Both show

the same lucid order, the same precision and comprehensiveness combined, the same persuasive majesty of truth and conviction clothed in a terse and felicitous diction,

words that surely describe Madison's style faithfully. Evidently, good style, if not great eloquence, *can* be taught.

One far from negligible feature of this early training was the prodigious amount of studying Madison—and Jefferson as well—did in their youth. Madison reports that he lost his health and nearly his life at Princeton through all too successfully cramming two year's work into one. But as a result both men were masters of their style early: Jefferson was thirty-three when he wrote the Declaration and Madison composed the Memorial at thirty-four. Yet these efforts, being completely self-imposed, never spoiled the savor of study for either man.

Madison went to his books throughout his life; for example, no sooner had he been appointed deputy of the Constitutional Convention than "he turned his attention and researches to the sources ancient and modern of information and guidance as to its object. Of the result of these he had the use both in the Convention and afterwards in the 'Federalist'." And later, at the close of his public life, he devoted himself to his farm and his books.[58] Such continuous, ready recourse to reading both for private pleasure and political practice is surely a chief contributor to fluent expression.

But of course, the most minute history of his studies is as insufficient to account for Madison's eloquence as the most time-honored rubrics of eloquence are to describe it. Finally, it seems to me, his rhetoric is shaped by that rare aptitude for conjoining speech and action which caused Jefferson in his own autobiography to couple in his noble description of Madison "the powers and polish of his pen, and the wisdom of his administration." That capacity was part of a

> habit of self-possession which placed at his ready command the rich resources of his luminous and discriminating mind. . . . Never wandering from his subject in vain declamation, but pursuing it closely in language pure, classical, copious, soothing always the feeling of his adversaries by civilities and softness of expression. . . . With these consummate powers were united a pure and spotless virtue which no calumny has ever attempted to sully.

In the traditional understanding, the rhetorical art has three parts: first, and least, elements of style, such as copious diction and felicitous syntax; next, devices of persuasion, such as "civilities," prudent omissions and emphases together with well-placed passion; and finally, the very conditions of good speech, the veracity of the speaker and the verity of his thought. By these criteria, Madison was a consummate rhetorician.

Madison's "Memorial and Remonstrance" seems to me in truth among the finest of those works of republican rhetoric in which adroit enunciation of the principles of liberty elicits their practice. In particular, that strict separation of church and state which implies the total secularization of public life and which, when promoted with heedless or rabid rationalism, causes me, at least, some unease, is set forth in the Memorial with such respectful, even reverent reasonableness that my scruples are dissolved in a certain enthusiasm for Madison's principles and in the gratitude that a Jew and a refugee must feel for the safe haven he made.

And yet the question obtrudes itself whether such texts, for all their fineness, are not relics of an irrecoverable art. A document to whose phrases the highest court of the land has recourse in formulating decisions affecting every school in every district of the country can, of course, hardly be relegated to history. Nonetheless, it is perhaps no longer a possible model of public discourse. I ask myself why that might be.

I can imagine four reasons that would be readily forthcoming. It will be said that the public will no longer listen to educated speech, and it will be said that politicians can no longer be expected to have the requisite training. And again, it will be claimed that the level of language itself has fallen, and also that the complexity of our condition precludes any grandly perspicuous statement of principles.

These may be true reasons, but they are also bad excuses. They merit indignant refutation as miserable collusions with mere or imaginary circumstance. How we will be spoken to, how we and our representatives will be educated, to what level the language will rise, how our thought will dispose the world—these matters are not yet in the hands of Society or the Historical Situation, but in ours. And in the exercise of liberties in which that truth is realized, Madison is not only a possible, but the best possible, model.

Appendix: The Memorial in Supreme Court Decisions (up to 1981)

The after-history of the petition is chiefly that of its citation by the Supreme Court.[59] The Court has recurred to the Memorial for elucidation of the "establishment" clause of the First Amendment, both because the latter was also drafted by Madison and because the Memorial is concerned with religion in education, as are so many cases involving that clause.

The relevant part of the First Amendment runs:

> Congress shall make no laws respecting an establishment of religion, or prohibiting the free exercise thereof.

It includes two clauses, one prohibiting aid, and the other, obstruction to religion. That is to say, the "establishment" clause prohibits official support of religious institutions, while the "free exercise" clause guarantees absence of coercive invasions of any individual's religious practice (Justice Clark, 1963). In this country, happily, the court has to deal far more often with putative attempts at establishment than with more direct interference with the free exercise of religion. Therefore the question of the precise meaning of the term "establishment" remains continually acute.

Madison's wording of the establishment clause is not vague but extremely careful—careful, that is, to use the most encompassing language. Thus the phrase "a law respecting" an establishment conveys a wider notion than would have been contained in the briefer phrase "a law establishing" religion, and, as Justice Rutledge points out, an "establishment of religion" is a wider notion than would have been an "establishment of a church." Such observations, however, are only the beginning of an interpretation; the central matter is the recovery of Madison's meaning of the word "establishment" itself, and here the Memorial, which was composed to combat an establishment of religion, is naturally the most pertinent document.

The Memorial played its chief role in the *Everson* decision of 1947. Everson, as a district taxpayer in New Jersey, filed a suit challenging a statute authorizing local Boards of Education to reimburse parents of parochial-school students equally with parents of public-school students for money expended on bus transportation. The argument was that such state aid to religious education constituted an establishment of religion under the First Amendment as made applicable to the states by the Fourteenth. Although the Court held that this particular statute did not constitute such an establishment, Justice Black in the course of his opinion paraphrased the Memorial at the climax of his argument for a very strong interpretation of the First Amendment:

> The "establishment of religion" clause of the First Amendment means at least this: Neither a state nor the Federal Government can set up a church. Neither can pass laws which aid one religion, aid all religions, or prefer one religion over another.

Justice Rutledge canvassed the Memorial at yet greater length for his dissent, to find in it that broad meaning of the word "establishment" which would be consonant with the evident breadth of language of the First Amendment just pointed out. He found the word to have a wider scope of application than that current in England, where it usually meant a state church established by law.[60] Establishment, he showed, could encompass measures of all sorts and degrees, including, above all, state aid to any activity associated with religion, especially when coming out of tax money. He argued that all such government support whatsoever was vigorously proscribed under the name of establishment by the Memorial and hence by the First Amendment. Therefore the New Jersey statute supporting the children's way to parochial schools was unconstitutional. Rutledge thought the Memorial so fundamental a document that he appended it to his dissent. It might be argued that so broad an interpretation of the Establishment clause was bound to bring it into conflict with the Freedom of Exercise clause.

Be that as it may, the justices who have cited the Memorial have almost all understood it as enjoining an absolute separation of church and state, and have construed the First Amendment accordingly—a construction named by a Jeffersonian phrase the "wall of separation" doctrine. Justice Frankfurter cites the Memorial once again in 1948, in the *McCollum* opinion, finding unconstitutional the device of so-called "released time," which permitted religious groups to come into public schools to instruct children who were released from the classroom for that purpose. He alone, incidentally, had an ear for that note of the document which could hardly get full hearing in a judicial context: its "deep religious feeling." Again, in 1963 Justice Clark quotes from the third paragraph, that "it is proper to take alarm at the first experiment on our liberties," to support prohibition of even minor incursions of the state into religion, such as the reading of a supersectarian prayer in school.

But this agreement on intent has not been sufficient to decide cases. The Memorial has several times been used on both sides, as in the *Everson* case and, much earlier, in the Mormon marriage case of 1879. There Judge Waite endorsed its doctrine that religion was not within the cognizance of the government, but found nevertheless that it did not protect religious practices made criminal under the law of the land, such as polygamy. Madison himself had confessed "that it may not be easy, in every possible case, to trace the line of separation between the rights of religion and the Civil authority,"[61] though he thought that the doubts would arise on inessential points. In other words, like all fundamental documents, the Memorial is necessary but not sufficient for determining cases.

It should be noted that the one judge who wished to give the Memorial and Madison's views a narrowly historical interpretation, Justice Reed in his *McCollum* dissent, cites as traditionally permissible involvement of the government in religious affairs, the existence of chaplains of Congress and of the armed forces—evidently unaware that Madison had most emphatically opposed the first and only tolerated the latter.[62] (Such toleration is rationalized by present-day courts under the category of "neutralizing" aids, breaches of the wall of separation permitted to counterbalance restrictions on the free exercise of religion incidental to meeting governmental demands, such as service in the armed forces.) Madison, however, excused such practices only reluctantly by the aphorism "the law ignores trifles."[63]

Furthermore, the judge who rejected most forcefully "a too literal quest for the advice of the Founding Fathers" (Brennan, 1963), largely on the grounds that conditions of education have changed, failed to recall that the two new issues he mentions, universal public schooling and religious diversity, were precisely among the chief preoccupations of both Jefferson and Madison.

It is as hard to find fault with the strong interpretation of the First Amendment in the light of the Memorial as it is to deny the principles themselves of the Memorial. Yet one must wonder whether, were Madison alive now, he would not recognize certain complicating circumstances, especially where education is concerned.

Within the context of the Constitution the Establishment clause is essentially ancillary to the Free Exercise clause. It is because state aid to religion inevitably in some way restricts someone's free exercise that it is prohibited. Furthermore, the Court has repeatedly held that irreligion, secularism, and humanism are all entitled to protection under the First Amendment, that is to say, they are in some manner of speaking religions, "belief systems": "the day that the country ceases to be free for irreligion it will cease to be free for religion . . ." (Justice Jackson, *Zorach v. Clauson*, 1952). Consequently there is, by the Court's own admission, a sense in which secular schools are not neutral in respect to religious doctrine.

Might not Madison, the fairest of men in such arguments,[64] have honored the point, if moderately made, that the enormous preemption of a child's time for secular purposes implied by modern school-attendance requirements, considered together with the financial hardship that Justice Rutledge admits the policy of total separation imposes on parents wishing to give their children religious schooling, amounts to a state invasion of religious rights? Would he not have lent an attentive ear to the admission made by Justice Black (*Epperson v. Arkansas*, 1968) that non-religious schooling cannot help but be, as, for example, in the teaching of evolution, in some sense anti-religious, and that the mandated secularism[65] of the public schools is indeed, in the sense before explained, a kind of religious establishment, possibly in need of counterbalancing by fairly vigorous "neutralizing aids?" To study Madison's writings on religious liberty is to conceive an ardent wish that he might be here to consider these dilemmas.

More by E.B. on Political Texts and Subjects

"Concerning the Declaration of Independence." *The College* 28, 2 (1976): 1–16. Also: Chicago: Nightingale–Conant Corporation, audiocassette, record, pamphlet.

"Politics and the Imagination." *The St. John's Review* 36 (1985): 10–18.

"Literacy, Culture, and the Shaping of Democracy." *Nebraska English Journal* 33 (1988): 2–7.

"Learning to Deliberate." In *Deliberation in Education and Society*, edited by J. T. Dillon. Norwood, NJ: Ablex, 1992.

"Was Jefferson a Philosopher?" In *Law and Philosophy: The Practice of Theory: Essays in Honor of George Anastaplo*, edited by John A. Murley, Robert L. Stone, and William T. Braithwaite. Athens, OH: Ohio University Press, 1992.

"Education and the Constitution." In *Is the Supreme Court the Guardian of the Constitution?* edited by Robert A. Licht. Washington, DC: AEI Press, 1993.

"Democratic Distinction." *Key Reporter* 58, 4 (1993).

"The Founding and Higher Education." Paper delivered at the New American College Institute on Education for Democracy, St. Mary's College, Moraga, CA, June 19, 1997.

"Jeffersonian Ambivalences." In *Philosophers on Education*, edited by Amelie Rorty. New York: Routledge, 1999.

A READING OF LINCOLN'S "GETTYSBURG ADDRESS"

I. The Speech as a Whole

The most obvious feature of this "Address Delivered at the Dedication of the Cemetery at Gettysburg" (VII, 23) is its brevity. It consists of ten sentences which can be spoken in a little over two minutes. It is so short that on the occasion of its delivery in the open air, before a crowd of more than 15,000 people, although the speaker delivered his words "in a clear, full voice," he seemed to have finished before the sound had really begun to carry.[1]

This fugitive character of the live speech is the obverse of its endurance as a piece of prose. We know that Lincoln meant the speech to survive as a written text, since he himself prepared several copies for publication, the last one over three months after its delivery.[2] And although Lincoln punctuated this speech, as he did all his speeches, in the manner of a speaker,[3] using the commas of grammar to mark the commas or pauses of the rhetoric, yet there is something deliberately set and permanent about it as well.

Furthermore, Lincoln had chosen his format quite deliberately. For he answered Everett, who had generously written to

FINAL TEXT OF THE ADDRESS DELIVERED
AT THE DEDICATION
OF THE CEMETERY AT GETTYSBURG

Four score and seven years ago our fathers brought forth on this continent, a new nation, conceived in Liberty, and dedicated to the proposition that all men are created equal.

Now we are engaged in a great civil war, testing whether that nation, or any nation so conceived and so dedicated, can long endure. We are met on a great battle-field of that war. We have come to dedicate a portion of that field, as a final resting place for those who here gave their lives that that nation might live. It is altogether fitting and proper that we should do this.

But, in a larger sense, we can not dedicate—we can not consecrate—we can not hallow—this ground. The brave men, living and dead, who struggled here, have consecrated it, far above our poor power to add or detract. The world will little note, nor long remember what we say here, but it can never forget what they did here. It is for us the living, rather, to be dedicated here to the unfinished work which they who fought here have thus far so nobly advanced. It is rather for us to be here dedicated to the great task remaining before us—that from these honored dead we take increased devotion to that cause for which they gave the last full measure of devotion—that we here highly resolve that these dead shall not have died in vain—that this nation, under God, shall have a new birth of freedom—and that government of the people, by the people, for the people, shall not perish from the earth.

Abraham Lincoln
November 19, 1863

him that "I should be glad if I could flatter myself that I came as near to the central idea of the occasion in two hours as you did in two minutes" that

> In our respective parts yesterday, you could not have been excused to make a short address, nor I a long one. . . . (VII, 24)

Edward Everett, who had been both a professor of Greek at Harvard and a distinguished statesman, had been chosen to be the main speaker at the dedication as a national cemetery of the piece of ground bought by the eighteen Northern states who had lost men at the battles of Gettysburg. Lincoln, as chief of state, had been invited, but only two weeks before the ceremony. Everett had courteously sent him his own two-hour speech,[4] composed in the classicizing style for which he was famous, so that Lincoln might consider it in writing his own (VII, 24). We might therefore expect Lincoln's speech to be composed as a counterpoise to Everett's; in fact, in spite of Lincoln's expressed admiration (VII, 24), it seems to be a tacit and tactful repudiation of Everett's learned rhetoric.

Everett begins his speech with a reference to the funeral ceremonies for the soldiers of ancient Athens, reported by Thucydides in the second book of the *Peloponnesian War* (paras. 35 ff.), and ends it by quoting from Pericles's oration, as Thucydides gives it. Everett's speech was thus intended to be "classical" in tone. In a malicious but not totally inept editorial, the *Richmond Examiner* had said of Everett's performance: "So far the play was strictly classic"; and then of Lincoln's speech "To suit the general public, however, a little admixture of the more irregular romantic drama was allowed"; the latter term *might* conceivably be applied to a speech which, in its revealing and moving brevity, was like the serious complement of a folksy Lincolnian anecdote.

There are certain other points in which the two speeches differed. Everett's was heavily dactylic; a stress version of the

Greek epic foot of one long and two short syllables appeared often, beginning with the first words:

Stánding beneáth this seréne sky,

through phrases like:

the gráves of our bréthren beneáth our feet
the éloquent sílence of Gód and Náture
It was appoínted by láw in Áthens,

to the final words:

thát which relátes to the Báttles of Géttysburg.

Lincoln's composition, on the other hand, shows the prevailing disyllabic, mostly iambic, pattern natural to sober English speech—and of Shakespearean tragedy. So after the two long beats of a grave and mournful spondee the pattern sets in:

Foúr scóre and séven yéars agó,

and in the last paragraph particularly, sequences of iambic pentameter are discernible.

In respect to diction, Everett's prose was classical and Latinate, while, it has been reckoned, Lincoln used only 32 words of Latin origin on this occasion, in contrast to his practice when addressing a select body like Congress, as in the peroration of his Annual Message of 1861:

With a reliance on Providence, all the more firm and earnest, let us proceed in the great task which events have devolved upon us. (V, 53)

As far as the antecedents are concerned, Everett conceived his effort as part of a monumental tradition of military funeral oratory. He ends by embellishing upon Pericles's magniloquent saying that "the whole earth is the sepulchre of illustrious men." Lincoln, in contrast, assigns to the dead neither the earth with which he ends his speech, nor the continent with which he begins, nor even the battlefield upon which he dwells in the middle, but soberly, a mere modest "portion of that field." So also Everett, beginning as Pericles had begun, with a reference to the law in Athens, makes much of the antique sanction for such funeral ceremonies, which included an obligatory oration delivered by an orator chosen for the purpose. Lincoln, on the other hand, in his first written draft, says brusquely, "This we may in all propriety do" (VII, 17–18), intimating that such dedications are an indulgence of the living, and moderates this in delivery to a brief statement of common propriety:

> It is altogether fitting and proper that we should do this. (VII, 23, cf. VI, 497)

And then he immediately goes on to call the whole ceremony in question:

> But, in a larger sense, we can not dedicate—we can not consecrate—we can not hallow—this ground. The brave men, living and dead, who struggled here, have consecrated it, far above our poor power to add or detract. . . .

Lincoln is implicitly making the significant point that it is *not* the law in America to have such obsequies and such speakers, that honor, particularly for the dead, is not an established public concern in America.

With respect to content, what is most striking is that Everett touches on a number of matters about which Lincoln has not one explicit word to say. Everett refers to the Confederate "invasion" of Maryland and Pennsylvania and compares it to the Persian invasion of Greece. Lincoln, on the other hand, had, in a letter to General Halleck, specifically objected to the phrase "drive the invader from our soil" used by General Meade in his order thanking the army for the victory at Gettysburg. For, Lincoln said, "the whole country is our soil," mindful of the fact that the opponent was not a foreigner. Hence he says nothing of the strategic circumstances of the battle credited with ending the danger of a Confederate occupation of the North, circumstances which make up the bulk of Everett's text, nor does he, as did Everett, assign responsibility for the war, take up specific constitutional questions or mention explicitly the fundamental issues of slavery and Union. It is worth mentioning these omissions, because, as will be shown, they shape the speech.

Thus Lincoln presents an alternative to the classicizing style, which is an undemocratic style designed, at bottom, for the secret and separate satisfaction of the speaker and some connoisseurs. This appears most clearly at a point in which Lincoln can be contrasted with the classical models, with Thucydides and his Pericles themselves, not through Everett and as a student of the *Peloponnesian War* (there is no evidence that he was), but as an American with an Athenian statesman. Everett's choice of model had, after all, been an academic, a politically blind choice. For in the American tradition Pericles is, of necessity, a dubious figure, the leader who, as Alexander Hamilton says in *The Federalist* No. 6, was for personal motives

> the primitive author of that famous and fatal war . . . which . . . terminated in the ruin of the Athenian commonwealth.

It is only necessary to remember that that war was a civil war to see that Pericles is Lincoln's natural antique antagonist. How then do they contrast with respect to political rhetoric?

The single sentence of Lincoln's speech which had the greatest effect at the time and was most singled out for anecdote and quotation (for instance, by the *Philadelphia Press* and *Harper's Weekly*) was the following generous pretense:

> The world will little note, nor long remember what we say here, but it can never forget what they did here.

The word *did* was the only word underscored (First Draft, VII, 17).

In this emphasis on the soldiers' *deed*, Lincoln expresses his sense of urgency in that late fall of 1863, when, after the summer battles of Gettysburg, he had been disappointed, as the pressing letters to his generals show (cf. VI pp. 327–328, 466–467), by the indecisive maneuvering in the east. Lincoln felt oppressed by a sense of unfinished business, and had for that reason said that his speech would be "short, short, short." The "unfinished work," "The great task remaining before us" are what curtail the format of the speech, and in the precipitous ellipses of the last sentence, even affect its grammar, for the sentence lacks all the connectives here conjecturally supplied:

> It is rather for us to be here dedicated to the great task remaining before us—[which means] that from these honored dead we take increased devotion to that cause for which they gave the last full measure of devotion—[and] that we here highly resolve that these dead shall not have died in vain—[so] that this nation, under God, shall have a new birth of freedom—and that government of the people, by the people, for the people, shall not perish from the earth.

Thus the sentence gives a headlong, fiercely condensed, overview of the remaining task's two spiritual requirements: increased *devotion* and its consequent *resolve*, and of its two political purposes: a new *conception* of the nation in the principle of liberty (revivification of the Declaration) and the *preservation* of the government already established to realize that principle (enforcement of the Constitution).

But the more significant aspect of Lincoln's depreciation of "what we say here" can be best seen by contrast with a corresponding sentence from Pericles's opening. He says:

Most of my predecessors in this place have commended him who made this speech part of the law, telling us that it is well that it should be delivered at the burial of those who fall in battle. For myself, I should have thought that the worth which had displayed itself in deeds, would be sufficiently rewarded by honours also shown by deeds; such as you now see in this funeral prepared at the people's cost. And I could have wished that the reputations of many brave men were not to be imperilled in the mouth of a single individual, to stand or fall according as he spoke well or ill. *(Peloponnesian War* 11.35)

The deprecating phrases barely hide Pericles's persuasion that the dead must rely on him for their life in the city's memory and for honor, that his speech is worth a battle, just as Thucydides thought his history worth a war. Contrast Lincoln's assertion that the dead are best honored by their own deeds and do themselves honor, that the task at hand overshadows all ceremony, and his avoidance of the pronoun "I."

The rhetorical character of Pericles's speech is writ large in Plato's dialogue *Menexenus*, in which Socrates recites to Menexenus an excruciatingly blown-up caricature of Pericles's funeral oratory, as he claims to have learned it from Pericles's mistress Aspasia. It is essentially a democratic adaptation of the "noble lie" of the *Republic* (414 f.). For in it the Athenians are told that they are all autochthonous, all equally descended from those who sprang from the earth, their mother, and so share equally in a high and heroic lineage *(Menexenus,* 237 ff.). By the prolonged repetition of this and other falsities, orators, as Socrates describes it,

bewitch our souls . . . so that even I, Menexenus, when so lauded by them feel thoroughly noble, and each time I stand and listen enthralled and think that I have become suddenly bigger and nobler and more handsome. . . . And this exaltation remains with me for more than three days. (235)

Now compare a speech in which Lincoln deals with the matter of traditional celebrations, his Chicago speech of 1858 (II, 484). He calls attention to the nation's non-aboriginal nature, to its beginning 82 years ago; he calls the founders the "men we claim as our fathers and grandfathers," not heroes, but "iron men"; he approves of the annual celebration of the ancestral founders of our present prosperity and says drily that "we go from these meetings in better humour with ourselves." But then he stops and remembers that half the present citizens of the country are not blood descendants of the founding fathers, and he finds that the true common "father" of all Americans is in fact a declaration of "moral principle," and through it all Americans are "blood of the blood, and flesh of the flesh, of the men who wrote that Declaration" (II, 499–500).

In Lincoln's rhetoric, then, general prosperity takes the place of proud deeds; a significant founding act replaces continuity of habitation; and a permanent mood of sober self-approbation substitutes for the exaltation of the day; a tradition of principle supersedes a lineage of blood. And for all these reasons together, the American speaker is not a master manipulator, but a *political teacher*, the only vocation open to a man who believed, in distinct opposition to the thesis that "some men are too *ignorant*, and too *vicious* to share in government" (II, 222),

> that no man is good enough to govern another man, *without that other's consent*. . . . (II, 266)

The Gettysburg Address will, accordingly, turn out to be a distillation of Lincoln's political philosophy, which he, on this occasion as on many others, attempted to infuse into the nation at large, a nation distinguished by the fact that its prosperity "has a philosophical cause" (IV, 168). It is for this reason that the written versions of the speech have no formal salutation—it is addressed to all citizens. And the very brevity that made its ten sentences at the time so fugitive in the hearing make them a "permanent possession" for later absorption. For because of its shortness the speech is readily learned by heart, and is, or used to be, in fact learned by heart by many schoolchildren. So that Lincoln has succeeded in lodging in the *heart* those very propositions, essential to the national life, which are too difficult—and perhaps too dubious—to be continually kept in *mind*. Lincoln recognized that

> In this age, in this country, public sentiment is everything,

since in America significant political action depends entirely on such sentiment. Consequently, as a republican statesman, he made it his continual rhetorical task to guide public feeling, that is, to convert the sound principles of the founding documents into the sober passion of the citizens, in unconscious accordance with Montesquieu's advice in the *Spirit of the Laws*. For he says in the chapter "Of Education in a Republican Government" that the peculiar republican virtue, "love of the laws and of our country," requires a kind of self-renunciation, a "constant preference of public to private interest," and that "to inspire it ought to be the principal business of education" *(Spirit of the Laws* 11.5). But such love of things public is precisely the product of propositions transformed into sentiments: Lincoln's rhetoric is based on the conversion of political principle into "moral sentiment" (II, 499).

Thus Lincoln, who deprecates what *he* says, must make every word poignant with a world of meaning, and his contemporaries recognized that he did just that. The *Springfield Republican* commented:

> His little speech is a perfect gem; deep in feeling, compact in thought and expression, and tasteful and elegant in every word and comma. . . . Turn back and read it over, it will repay study as a model speech. Strong feelings and a large brain were its parents—a little painstaking its *accoucheur*.

In undertaking such a study of this model speech I will begin with a brief scanning of the whole, which will bring out its grand framework: In time it spans the past ("Four score and seven years ago"), the present ("Now we are engaged in a great civil war") and the future ("this nation . . . shall have a new birth of freedom"), while in space it comprises the battle ground on which it is delivered (middle sentences), the continent on which the nation was born (first sentence) and the earth which it is to save (last sentence).[5]

II. The First Paragraph

Lincoln begins:

Four score and seven years ago . . .

"Four score," with its long oh's, repeated in several assonances, and the first of many alliterations, sounds a more mournful and solemn note than the words "eighty-seven years," but the choice of the phrase is not only a matter of sound; it also carries a special meaning. It is the language of the Bible, as in Psalm 90: 10:

The days of our years are threescore years and ten; and if by reason of strength they be fourscore years, yet is their strength labour and sorrow; for it is soon cut off, and we fly away.

With the psalm in mind the phrase means: just beyond the memory of anyone now alive, too long ago for living memory. Now we know that from his youth on Lincoln was concerned with a peculiarly American danger: the death of sound political passion. In his youthful speech on "The Perpetuation of our Political Institutions" (1838),[6] Lincoln drew a clear parallel with the early community of Christians, the danger to whose continuity lay in the fact that the first generation of disciples and eye-witnesses was followed by a second which had only heard by word of mouth, by a third which had in part only read of Christ, and a fourth which had begun to forget. So in the American community; the scenes of the revolution

> *cannot be* so universally known, nor so vividly felt, as they were by the generation just gone to rest. . . . (I, 115)

The men who had seen the Revolution, who were its "living history" are now gone:

> They *were* the pillars of the temple of liberty; and now, that they have crumbled away, that temple must fall, unless we, their descendants, supply their places with other pillars, hewn from the solid quarry of sober reason. . . . (I, 115)

The danger that the living enthusiasms of the Revolution might become mere myths has advanced to a fact in 1863, the time of the fourth generation from that event; the national edifice has to be rebuilt "from the solid quarry of sober reason." This is the age for a deliberate mining of the first accounts, for rereading the founding documents.

"Four score and seven years ago," then, points to that quarry, that mine, of reason. Subtract 87 from 1863 and the result is 1776. Lincoln considers that this nation was both conceived in and born with the *Declaration of Independence*.[7] On July 7, 1863, in response to a serenade on the occasion of the victory of Gettysburg, under the influence of the providential coincidence that both the victory of that battle and of Vicksburg had been announced on the Fourth of July, and that Jefferson and John Adams had both died on that day, he had said:

> How long ago is it—eighty odd years—since on the Fourth of July for the first time in the history of the world a nation by its representatives, assembled and declared as a self-evident truth that "all men are created equal." That was the birthday of the United States of America. . . . (VI, 319)

And in earlier speeches he had often counted back the eighty or eighty-two years to 1776 (II, 491–492). In repeatedly fixing on the signing of the Declaration as a crucial date, Lincoln is making a deliberate political judgment concerning the hierarchy of founding events, different for instance from that of Toombs of Georgia who had begun a speech in 1850 in this way:

> Sixty years ago our fathers joined together to form a more perfect Union and to establish justice . . . [8]

referring the *founding of the republic* to 1790 (the date when the last original stare ratified the Constitution), and quoting from its Preamble. Lincoln refers rather to the *birth of the nation*.

He goes on:

> . . . our fathers brought forth on this continent, a new nation, conceived in Liberty, and dedicated to the proposition that all men are created equal.

The "fathers"—he calls them fathers, although they are only forefathers, in order to bring the Revolution close—are a definite group of men. In another context he had said:

> I suppose the "thirty-nine" who signed the original instrument [here the Constitution] may be fairly called our fathers who framed that part of the present government. . . . (III, 523)

In this speech, then, "our fathers" must be those men, in part identical with the signers of the Constitution (II, 267), who devised and signed the Declaration, especially Jefferson—the Founding Fathers.

These men "brought forth": this is again Biblical diction; the phrase is used, for instance, in *Luke* 1:31 in the annunciation of the Messiah's birth. They "brought forth on this continent" (all versions but the last two had "upon"): there are undertones here of 'begot upon the body of this land," "fathered on this fallow continent as mother;" the child nation is safe in the lap of the whole continent, capable of protecting it from foreign interference and of providing those apparently unlimited riches which are its material condition.

The new nation was "conceived in Liberty" ("liberty" being the only noun capitalized besides "God"): not conceived in love as are blessed children, but conceived in the love of liberty as are blessed nations (cf. II, 276). We might balk at a male bringing forth, a male giving birth. But the begetting of this nation was a begetting of reason; "bringing forth" can mean "uttering reasons" (cf. *Isaiah* 41:21), once primarily a male act; as in Aeschylus's *Eumenides* the begetting of the wisdom of Athens, the conception of Athena, is exclusively male (line 736); America is a fatherland, not a Menexenean motherland, and this lends Lincoln's "patriotism" a special cast. Upon this conception, the nation-child was dedicated to a proposition, as in a baptism. The proposition, "that all men are created equal," was in quotation marks in the first draft (VII, 17) since it is directly quoted from the second paragraph of the Declaration of Independence.

If these are the associations of the first, and shortest, of the three paragraphs of increasing length, what is its significance?

Consider first the continent, the first of the nation's three parts, which are "its territory, its people, and its laws" (V, 527). *The Federalist* No. 2 says

> This country and this people seem to have been made for each other. . . .

Tocqueville makes the same point of the United States:

> . . . God himself gave them the means of remaining equal and free, by placing them upon a boundless continent. . . . (*Democracy in America*, I. xvii)

Lincoln too, especially in his Annual Messages to Congress, spoke almost with awe of the continent, "the ever-enduring part" of the nation, whose riches gives liberty its material, whose impregnability fosters an uninvidious patriotism, and whose integrity makes secession a chimaera:

> Physically speaking, we cannot separate [1861, IV, 269] . . . the land we inhabit . . . would, ere long, force reunion, however much blood and treasure the separation might have cost. [1862, V, 529]

Such a continent makes the fittest ground for a seed of principle, for a continental space is needed to safeguard the first embodiment of the democratic idea.

Next, what of the birthdate of 1776? Consonant with *Federalist* No. 2, Lincoln held that the Declaration of Independence was *preceded* by the Union, formally established by the Articles of Association of 1774, and was *succeeded* by the establishment of the Constitution in 1787 (IV, 265). This sequence was of the greatest significance, for it meant that the nation's birth was also the birth of principle, a birth made possible by the antecedent union of the people, and made secure by allowing the practical instrument of its life, the Constitution, to follow its conception. Thus, using phrases borrowed from *Proverbs* 25:11, Lincoln wrote of the principle "Liberty to all" as expressed in the Declaration:

> The assertion of that *principle*, at *that time*, was *the* word, *"fitly spoken"* which has proved an "apple of gold" to us. The *Union* and the *Constitution* are the *picture of silver*, subsequently framed around it. . . . (IV, 169)

Here "subsequently" must, in the case of the Union at least, mean not later in time, but in political priority.

Lincoln, then, held the Declaration to be far more than a declaration of *independence* (cf. IV, 236, 240), and indeed, it would then have been a peculiar document to cite in a war to fight secession. And it *is* much more; for its writer, Jefferson,

> had the coolness, forecast and capacity to introduce into a merely revolutionary document an abstract truth, . . . (III, 376);

and it is precisely by the omission of this truth that the various "merely revolutionary" Declarations of Independence adopted by the Union's adversaries are characterized (IV, 438). For this reason Lincoln can say:

> I have never had a feeling politically that did not spring from the sentiments embodied in the Declaration of Independence. . . . It was not the mere matter of the separation of the Colonies from the motherland; but that sentiment in the Declaration of Independence which gave liberty, not alone to the people of this country, but, I hope, to the world, for all future time. ("Speech in Independence Hall, Philadelphia [Feb. 22, 1861]," IV, 240; cf, II, 407, IV, 169)

Now what is of prime importance in the speech is *how* these principles, which mark the true beginning of the nation, are held. Lincoln denominates them *"conceptions"* and *"propositions."* In the Declaration the fathers had held that they were *"self-evident Truths."* Something has happened between the founding and the present which forces Lincoln to call the axioms of the Declaration mere propositions. This is what had happened: the Declaration had been called in public "a self-evident lie," a phrase Lincoln often cited with repugnance (II, 275, 318; 111, 375; cf. II, 130–131), for it creates a fatal situation:

> One would start with great confidence that he could convince any sane child that the simpler propositions of Euclid are true; but, nevertheless, he would fail, utterly, with one who should deny the definitions and axioms. The principles of Jefferson are the definitions and axioms of free society. . . . (III, 375)

Lincoln had made a special effort to study texts concerned with, and to ponder the nature of, axiomatic self-evidence and logical consequence. In his short autobiography he particularly mentions that he had "studied and nearly mastered the six books of Euclid since he was a member of Congress" (IV, 62). He understood that self-evidence is a peculiarly delicate affair, since when once impugned, when once only denied in public, a self-evident truth turns into a debatable proposition. Yet, as the axiom, precisely by reason of its self-evidence, was unprovable, so the proposition has no rational proof from higher principles, but can be verified only from its consequences or—dreadful prospect—from the fatal consequences of its contrary. This, then, is the peculiar danger of a nation which lives on a tradition of explicit principle rather than of ingrained myth, a principle affirmed at its very beginning in one event whose impact no later events, with the unhappy exception of some catastrophe, can match—that it grows blind to the self-evidence of its conceptions until a catastrophe opens its eyes.

And now, what, more precisely, are these principles whose standing has changed? In the words of the Declaration they are:

> that all Men are created equal, that they are endowed by their Creator with certain unalienable Rights, that among these are Life, Liberty and the Pursuit of Happiness.

Here equality of creation, equality before God, precedes, and is the condition of, the other rights, of which only some are named. One striking omission is of positive importance, since except for this omission Lincoln could scarcely have cited this document in that year which had begun, in the Emancipation Proclamation of January 1, 1863, with what was admittedly a destruction of the property of many Americans (V, 531). In Locke's recurrent formula "life, liberty and property" (or some equivalent for the last, *The Second Treatise of Civil Government*, e.g. paras. 123, 135, 137), Jefferson had substituted for property "the Pursuit of Happiness," leaving the original phrase to be picked up in the Constitution (III, 533). Except for this substitution the Declaration could hardly have been so close to the heart of Lincoln, who remembered with approval

> that the Jefferson party were formed upon its supposed superior devotion to the *personal* rights of men, holding the rights of *property* to be secondary only, and greatly inferior, . . . (III, 375)

But a moment of national crisis and the occasion of commemorating the war dead is scarcely an opportune time to dwell on the specifically personal rights to life and the pursuit of happiness. There remain, out of the Declaration, first equality and then, liberty.

Now Lincoln seems in his speech to reverse this order in setting liberty as the original conception, as he had before termed "Liberty to all" *the* principle of the Declaration (IV, 169). But elsewhere he says:

> I believe the declara[tion] that "all men are created equal" is the great fundamental principle upon which our free institutions rest; (III, 327)

it is the founding principle to be kept in view, for instance, when the territories pass out of a state of nature and the foundations of political society are laid. What does Lincoln consider to be the real relation of these two principles?

Tocqueville in the chapter inquiring "Why Democratic Nations Show a More Ardent and Enduring Love of Equality than of Liberty" (*Democracy in America*, II. ii. 1) considers liberty and equality two diverse and independent notions, of which equality pertains primarily to the social, liberty to the political sphere. Yet he admits that ultimately, radically, considered the two are what would be called in logical terms "commensurately universal," that is, they imply each other:

It is possible to imagine an extreme point at which freedom and equality would meet and blend.

Lincoln takes exactly this "extreme" view. He habitually sets out his understanding of the principle of equality with respect to the slavery question, which would appear to be primarily a question of liberty. On the other hand, he interprets equality of creation to mean precisely the possession of "unalienable rights," chief among which is political liberty. The Declaration, although by no means declaring men equal in *all respects*,

> does mean to declare that all men are equal in some respects; they are equal in their right to "life, liberty and the pursuit of happiness". . . . (II, 520, cf. III, 16)

As Rousseau (*The Social Contract*, II. xi) had already claimed, equality is the *condition* of all rights, and liberty its necessary *consequence*, while, conversely, the rights define equality. Thus the order of the speech simply signifies that a community conceived in the spirit of liberty is congenitally devoted to the enunciated condition of its conception, the axiom of equality. Lincoln is able to interchange the two conceptions in this way precisely because he does not make Tocqueville's division between the social nature of equality and the political nature of liberty. For equality, the ruling article of Lincoln's political thought, is not fundamentally a social, or even a political matter; it is prior to human affairs. Lincoln asserts the converse of Tocqueville's statement that

> Men who are similar and equal in the world readily conceive the idea of the one God, governing every man by the same laws and granting to every man future happiness on the same conditions. The idea of the unity of mankind constantly leads them back to the idea of the unity of the Creator; . . . (*op. cit.*, II. I. 5)

The converse of this passage is that the idea of one God implies the essential similarity and equality of men. Its effect is a deep doctrine regarding man's original nature as a creature and his consequent standing in what Lincoln calls "the economy of the Universe," namely his common submission to "the justice of the Creator to his creatures . . . to the whole great family of man";[9] it is a deep-felt revival of Jefferson's discarded version of the Declaration, which had asserted that

> all men are created equal and independent; that from that equal creation they derive rights inherent and inalienable. . . .[10]

This creaturely equality implies no social homogeneity—the authors of the Declaration

> did not mean to say all were equal in color, size, intellect, moral developments, or social capacity. . . . (II, 405)

It is, in fact, compatible with the practical superiority of one race (III, 16). But it does mean that men have each a will of their own and a sufficient amount of good common sense for the earthly realization of their equality in civil liberty, which, in effect, means self-government; it is on this view of human nature that Lincoln's trust in the wisdom of the people concerning the basic matters of ordinary life depends. The American social situation is, then, the *consequence* of political principles; for example, where a state of nature exists, Congress with the aid of that "standard maxim for free society" (II, 406), the principle of equality, "lays the foundations of society" (III, 327)—politics precedes society, not the reverse (II, 222). Thus, since society is *originally* based on political principles, which themselves have a moral and, finally, a *religious* basis, American life depends ultimately on a higher source. And so, by his reference to the principle of equality, Lincoln reminds the nation which lacks the earth-born equality of a common birth-place, touted for Athens in the *Mene-*

xenus, of a common high paternal origin; it is a nation equal "under God."

III. *The Second Paragraph*

Now we are engaged in a great civil war, testing whether that nation, or any nation so conceived and so dedicated, can long endure.

In his middle paragraph Lincoln passes from "four score and seven years ago" and "our fathers" to "now" and "we," and from the generation of the Revolution to the generation of the Rebellion, of the "great civil war." He had in the days of the victory of Gettysburg termed this war, in its enormity, a "gigantic Rebellion" (VI, 320, also VI, 264), using Miltonic language. Indeed there was to him something of the Fall in the wanton

> destruction of our national fabric, with all its benefits, its memories and its hopes. . . . Will you hazard so desperate a step, . . . while the certain ills you fly to, are greater than all the real ones you fly from? . . . ("First Inaugural Address," IV, 266–267)

Yet in that very speech Lincoln maintained the right of revolution (IV, 269), which he had already asserted in the House as a "sacred right" during the war with Mexico, in a speech attacking the President for waging, without consulting Congress, a long, aggressive and immoral war (I, 438). But, he maintained, the action of the southern states was not revolution, or secession, but "rebellion" (IV, 432).

Why was it not secession? The word, he declared to Congress, implies the legality of states leaving the Union. But, he had said,

> I hold, that in contemplation of universal law, and of the Constitution, the Union of these States is perpetual. . . . (IV, 264)

He held this because the Union represents the fundamental social compact; as Locke says in *The Second Treatise of Civil Government*:

> That which makes the community and brings man out of the loose state of nature into one politic society is the agreement which everybody has with the rest to incorporate and act as one body, and so to be one distinct commonwealth. The usual and almost only way whereby this union is dissolved is the inroad of foreign force making a conquest upon them. . . . (para. 211, cf. 243)

Secession of any sort therefore does violence to political society itself and is on the simplest practical grounds insupportable. However, formally it was a theory of statehood which allowed Lincoln to maintain the absolute perpetuity of the Union, a theory which again turned about the date and wording of the Declaration of Independence. He observed that that document first declared the "United Colonies" "Free and Independent States" (IV, 433), so that the Union, which had preceded independence, had certainly preceded statehood. Accordingly he denied that the new Confederacy was right in claiming that the Articles of Confederation adopted by Congress in the year after the Declaration, according to which "Each State retains its sovereignty, freedom, and independence" (Art. II), represented a kind of prototype period, a state of nature, so to speak, for the States, in which their original sovereignty displayed itself. For the Union, having preceded the Declaration, *a fortiori* preceded any organic law, as shown by the Preamble of the Constitution, which speaks merely of establishing "*a more perfect union*" (IV, 263). The States had never existed "out of" the Union, but had entered it, insofar as they were entities at all, only as colonies, or, if territories, from the state of nature (III, 328):

> Our States have neither more nor less power than that reserved to them . . . , in the Union, by the Constitution—no one of them ever having been a State *out* of the Union. The original ones

passed into the Union even *before* they cast off their British colonial dependence; . . . The new ones only took the designation of States, on coming into the Union, while that name was first adopted for the old ones, in and by, the Declaration of Independence. . . . Having never been States, either in substance, or in name, *outside of* the Union, whence this magical omnipotence of "State rights," asserting a claim of power to lawfully destroy the Union itself? . . . (IV, 433–434, cf. IV, 194)

Hence the assumption of the States' power of lawful withdrawal was a "sophism" (IV, 433). Lincoln's term "civil war" implies precisely the denial of the Confederate view, that the war was a "war between the States."

This argument is only apparently an appeal to mere dates. Here history, in the providential course it seems to run on this continent, displays the nature of the case, for the Union comes naturally before the States, being the ground and guarantor of that popular government which is the incarnation of the founding principles. This is expressed in the instrument of popular government, the Constitution, in two places. First in its Preamble: The very phrase, "We, the People," is meant to indicate that only a united people, speaking in its own voice, can sanction republican fundamental law—as Lincoln had pointed out, it had been precisely this phrase which was altered in the new southern document to "We, the deputies of the sovereign and independent States," in accordance with the fact that the new southern Declarations had omitted the words "all men are created equal." "Why this deliberate pressing out of view the rights of men and the authority of the people?" he asks (IV, 438). Secondly in its body: the Constitution provides that "The United States shall guarantee to every State in this Union a republican form of government" (Art. IV, Sect. 4), so that

if a State may lawfully go out of the Union, having done so, it may also discard the republican form of government, . . . (IV, 440, cf. VII, 55)

Hence the Union is responsible not only for the establishment but also for the pervasiveness of republican institutions. Yet Tocqueville says:

> The sovereignty of the Union is an abstract being . . . ; the sovereignty of the states is perceptible by the senses, easily understood, and constantly active. . . . (*Democracy in America*, I. VIII)

Lincoln's effort is, therefore, without detriment to the distinctiveness of the States (III, 17), to turn this abstraction into a palpable feeling, in the Gettysburg Address as much as anywhere, although out of tactful respect for the fact that it is a national but not a federal cemetery which is being dedicated, the word "Union" never appears.

Now the right of secession having been rejected, what happens to the right of revolution? Lincoln thinks on this crucial matter as a radical conservative. That is, when charged with revolutionary views he protests his conservatism:

> . . . What is conservatism? Is it not adherence to the old and tried, against the new and untried? We stick to, contend for, the identical old policy on the point in controversy which was adopted by "our fathers who framed the government under which we live;" . . . (III, 537)

But since the controversy referred to is the extension of slavery, which Lincoln opposed with all his might, his very opposition to change is made in the spirit of the Revolution. In other words, in this country, whose original government was constituted by revolution, the most progressive side, he claims, tries most faithfully to return to the beginnings, so that even innovations are made in a context of rational argument with the Fathers (III, 534–535). This side has once and for all preempted the Revolution, embodied in the process of change by majority decision, so that henceforth all rebellion is counterrevolution. In a well-founded polity, justice is almost coincident with organic law, and a sense of justice with the intention to preserve the law.

In practice this view implies, on the one hand, that, though bad laws

> should be repealed as soon as possible, still while they continue in force, for the sake of example, they should be religiously observed (1, 112),

even if it is expected that they will be held unconstitutional (V, 531). On the other hand it means that no law or decision need become "a rule of political action" (II, 516; cf. II, 494) until it is judged to harmonize with the intention of the Founders. The right to revolution does remain; however it is clearly circumscribed, and in such terms as to reveal the chief function of the Constitution in a working democracy:

> If, by the mere force of numbers, a majority should deprive a minority of any clearly written constitutional right, it might, in a moral point of view, justify revolution—certainly would, if such right were a vital one. . . . (IV, 267)

The issue must, then, be one of constitutional rights denied, or extra-legal action upon it constitutes an uprising against the people. So Lincoln says of the secessionists:

> These politicians are subtle and profound on the rights of minorities. They are not partial to that power which made the Constitution, and speaks from the preamble, calling itself "We, the People." (IV, 436–437)

Thus any sectional or factional uprising, no matter how worthy of sympathy its cause, being directed against that government which is itself the first living and prospering incarnation of the revolutionary principle,

conducing more essentially to the ends of civil and religious liberty (1, 108)

than any previously known, a government without viable
alternative, and moreover as Lincoln emphasized, containing
the means of its own amendment within itself (IV, 267–270),
is a catastrophe of a peculiarly awful sort. Lincoln declined to
participate in such a deed even where his sense of justice was
completely outraged (II, 323). For the man who

> proposes to abandon such a Government, would do well to con-
> sider in deference to what principle it is that he does it; what
> better he is likely to get in its stead; whether the substitute will
> give, or be intended to give, so much of good to the people. . . .
> (IV, 438)

The question is thus always, in Lincoln's adaptation of Ham-
let's weighing of suicide (III. i. 8.2):

> Will you hazard so desperate a step, . . . while the certain ills
> you fly to, are greater than all the real ones you fly from? . . . (IV,
> 266–267)

This war, Lincoln goes on to say, is a *test*. The crisis has the
nature of a test, because as he had said in his message to the
Congress which he had called into special session to meet on
that fateful date of July 4, at the beginning of the war in 1861,
this government is an experiment:

> Our popular government has often been called an experiment.
> Two points in it our people have already settled—the *success-
> ful establishing*, and the successful *administering* of it. One still
> remains—its successful *maintenance* against a formidable [inter-
> nal] attempt to overthrow it. . . . (IV, 439)

As the final phase of an experiment the war represents one ultimate test for all cases, for the Union represents the model case

of a nation established on explicit principles, in which two necessary founding conditions, namely the wisdom of the Fathers
and the receptivity of the continent, had been optimal; if this
nation fails then it is demonstrated that "any nation" must
fail. This is how the American enterprise had been understood
from the founding; "it seems to have been reserved," says *Federalist* No. 1,

> to the people of this country, by their conduct and example, to
> decide the important question, whether societies of men are really
> capable or not, of establishing good government from reflection
> and choice, . . .

and this very circumstance had moved Tocqueville to write his
book (I. xvii, end). When the Thucydidean Pericles calls the
whole city "an education to Greece" (II. 41) he means that Athens is the unique and inimitable cynosure of the *Greeks*; when
Lincoln calls the government an experiment and the present
war a test for all nations he offers America as a practical political pattern to the *world*.

The fundamental issue, which in the course of the war had
become "distinct, simple and inflexible," is an issue which can
only be tried by war and decided in victory (VIII, 151). But
how can a war be a test of anything? The war will, Lincoln
says at its beginning, teach that

> when ballots have fairly and constitutionally decided, there can
> be no successful appeal back to bullets. . . . (1861, IV, 439)

Is Lincoln not self-contradictory here? How could the successful use of bullets in this war prove that there can be no
successful appeal to bullets in republics? Or, if the argument
is that strength at war is the converted strength of the ballot
box, will it not be necessary to say that every outcome proves
the principle of popular sovereignty? Certainly, Lincoln found
his old "faith that right makes might" (e.g., III, 550) corrobo-

rated by the popular support the Union commanded (IV, 437–441; VIII, 101; VIII, 149–150); to him the solid conservatism of the majority was a sign of political soundness. But as the war went on he looked more often to a higher judge, to "the God of battles" of the Revolution (II, 121), whom the theoreticians of popular government had not been able to avoid invoking.

In the *Second Treatise of Civil Government*, Locke says, not perhaps with much inner conviction, but rather driven by the argument, that

> where there is no judicature on earth to decide controversies amongst men, God in heaven is Judge. (paras. 241–242, cf. V, 404)

And Lincoln's Second Inaugural Address (1865) is a fervent reference to Psalm 19:9:

> the judgments of the Lord, are true and righteous altogether. (VIII, 333)

(Cf. "Letter to A. G. Hodges [April 4, 1864]," VII, 281–282, which anticipates the Inaugural.) So also in a private meditation on the divine will "not written to be seen of men" in 1862, he ascribes the direction and the outcome of the war entirely to the will of God, who uses the contestants as his "human instrumentalities" (V, 403–404; cf. IV, 482). While there is still peace, God's judgments are given by his "great tribunal, the American people" (First Inaugural, IV, 270), but once at war, the Almighty adjudicates. From the day Lincoln left for Washington, as President-elect, he did what the American people have always expected their fallible fellow citizens who rule them to do—he committed himself to God (IV, 190), as the only power high enough to oversee the tendency of the whole, and in this spirit he continued:

> . . . I claim not to have controlled events, but confess plainly that events have controlled me. Now at the end of three years strug-

gle the nation's condition is not what either party, or any man devised, or expected. God alone can claim it. . . . ("Letter to A. G. Hodges [April 4, 1864]," VII, 282)

Exactly what the test was to prove Lincoln had stated already in his "Perpetuation" speech of 1838. It was to be

> a practical demonstration of the truth of a proposition, which had hitherto been considered, at best no better than problematical; namely, the *capability of a people to govern themselves.* . . . (I, 113; cf. I, 278–279)

"The experiment is successful," he had then added, but as the self-evidence of the axiom of equality had begun to fade, so its practical consequence, the government, was thrown in doubt. The more precise form of the question now is:

> . . . whether discontented individuals, too few in numbers to control administration, according to organic law, in any case, can always, upon the pretenses made in this case, or on any other pretenses, or arbitrarily, without any pretense, break up their Government, and thus practically put an end to free government upon the earth. . . . "Is there, in all republics, this inherent and fatal weakness?" "Must a government, of necessity be too *strong* for the liberties of its own people, or too *weak* to maintain its own existence?" (IV, 426)

That a nation, heir to the "fundamental blessings" of the "fairest portion of the earth" invulnerable to invasion, as well as to a free government, could only "die by suicide" (I, 108) had seemed plain to Lincoln early on, though at the time (1838) he had thought that this internal trial would take the form of a perversion of democracy which he called "mobocracy," in which the people cease to act as persons. Now it turns out that in his century the test of endurance has taken the form of civil war, in which a whole segment of the nation refuses to submit to its own government.

Lincoln goes on:

We are met on a great battle-field of that war.

But he avoids any particularization of the circumstances of the greatest battle of the great war; Everett had treated that at length.

We have come to dedicate a portion of that field, as a final resting place for those who here gave their lives that that nation might live. It is altogether fitting and proper that we should do this.

A part of the field, which had, incidentally, been called Cemetery Hill even before the battle, is being set aside as the earthly domain of those newly dead soldiers who, as the fathers gave the nation birth, insured its continuing life.

IV. The Third Paragraph

But, in a larger sense,
we can not dedicate—
we can not consecrate—
we can not hallow—
            this ground.

The third paragraph has features of an incantation, repetition and rhyme, but of a negative incantation. It begins by warding off an error: Fit and proper though it may be in a narrow sense to conduct dedication ceremonies, there is danger that we, the present generation, substitute the rituals of dedication, consecration and devotion for the dedication of the fathers, that dedication of a piece of ground may take the place of the larger dedication to a proposition called for by the great war. Hence the steady iambs of Lincoln's three-line rhyming refrain is perturbed by the warning emphasis on "we."

The brave men, living and dead, who struggled here, have consecrated it, far above our poor power to add or detract.

In this sentence Lincoln honors at once the Union dead, the Union su:vivors, and, generously but tactfully, the enemy, for the phrase "the brave men, living and dead, who struggled here" applies also to the other side, of whom about an equal number, 23,000 men, had died (VI, 327). Lincoln, unlike Pericles in speaking to the Greek Athenians, always keeps before him the terrible fact of the civil war that Americans were fighting Americans. Lincoln says not one derogatory word of the temporary enemy; three weeks after the Address, he issued a Proclamation of Amnesty and Reconstruction giving full pardon to all ordinary citizens who would resume allegiance to the Union (VII, 54). As always, he avoids making divisions and invidious distinctions for:

> Our strife pertains to ourselves—to the passing generations of men; and it can, without convulsion, be hushed forever with the passing of one generation (V, 529; cf. IV, 270),

and

> What I deal with is too large for malicious dealing. (V, 346)

He goes on:

> The world will little note, nor long remember what we say here, but it can never forget what they did here.

It is known that Lincoln considered the speech a failure as a spoken speech, for he had told a friend right after its delivery: "Lamon, that speech won't *scour*. It is a flat failure and the people are disappointed." The same thing had happened with respect to his second most renowned speech, the Second Inaugural, about which he had written to a friend:

> . . . I expect the latter to wear as well as—perhaps better than—anything I have produced; but I believe it is not immediately popular. . . . (VIII, 356)

Nonetheless, in view of Lincoln's usually correct appraisals of his speeches, the sentence from the Address cannot be regarded as a comment on the Address; rather it serves as the counterpart of one of his previous Annual Message:

> ... We *say* we are for the Union. The world will not forget that we say this. . . . (V, 537)

In Congress words count, but on a battlefield, deeds.

And finally come the last two sentences, half the speech in length. They develop its explicit theme, the second *dedication* of the nation, in this consecrated place, *here* (Lincoln removed a fourth "here" from the final version).

> It is for us the living, rather, to be dedicated here to the unfinished work which they who fought here have thus far so nobly advanced.
>
> It is rather for us to be here dedicated
> to the great task remaining before us— . . .

Practically, the "unfinished work," "the great task remaining before us," is the winning of the war (cf. VIII, 333), but in significance it is something greater, the successful completion of the experiment of popular government.

The next two clauses, again in that spell-like diction in which successive cola have identical or near-identical endings, give the nature of this new dedication; it means

> that from these honored dead we take increased devotion to that cause for which they gave the last full measure of devotion—
> that we here highly resolve
> that these dead
> shall not have died
>   in vain— . . .

In invoking the dead, Lincoln is touching what in his First Inaugural he called

> the mystic chords of memory, stretching from every battle-field and patriot grave, to every living heart and hearth-stone, . . . (IV, 271)

For this purpose he mingles the language of church and legislative assembly. The dedication, the consecration, the hallowing, the devotion Lincoln urges is of a political sort. He had urged it already in 1838, in his speech on "The Perpetuation of our Political Institutions."

> Let reverence for the laws, . . . become *the political religion* of the nation; and let the old and the young, the rich and the poor, the grave and the gay, of all sexes and tongues, and colors and conditions, sacrifice unceasingly upon its altars. (I, 112)

Lincoln is deliberately consecrating politics by calling on the great human agency of reverence, memory, where all things "seem hallowed" (I, 367).

The last two clauses give the effect of the new dedication:

> that this nation, under God, shall have a new birth of freedom— . . .

The words "under God" were not in the first draft; they were reported in the newspaper versions of the speech as delivered and incorporated by Lincoln later (cf. VII, 395). Why did he add them?

Under the heading "Of Civil Religion," the last in *The Social Contract*, Rousseau describes the civil religion of republics which it is the business of the sovereign to set out, not as religious dogma but as "sentiments of sociability." They ought to be

> simple, few in number, precisely fixed, and without explanation or comment. The existence of a powerful, wise, and benevolent

> Divinity, who foresees and provides the life to come, the happiness of the just, the punishment of the wicked, the sanctity of the social contract and the laws. . . . (IV. viii)

This is precisely the nature of Lincoln's public pronouncements (V, 403–404; VI, 496; VII, 535; VIII, 333). The nation is under a "beneficent Father who dwelleth in the Heavens" (VI, 497). It has a double parentage—the forefathers and the Father above. With the words "under God," Lincoln, then, invokes at once faith, the personal trust in a superior being, and religion, the public obligation to reverence.

This nation will have a "new birth of freedom." Those words are not, and were not at the time felt to be, innocuous. For if "of freedom" is read not as an objective genitive (so that the nation is not said to give birth to a new freedom) but as a parallel to "conceived in Liberty," (so that the nation itself is said to be reborn) the sentence becomes very strong. The *Chicago Times*, in commenting on the speech, said that in this phrase "Mr. Lincoln did most foully traduce the motives of the men who were slain at Gettysburg," for they fought only to preserve the old government. Now, as has been shown, Lincoln in fact agreed with this conservative view of the struggle; he had said so explicitly:

> I am exceedingly anxious that this Union, the Constitution, and the liberties of the people shall be perpetuated in accordance with the original idea for which that struggle was made, and I shall be most happy indeed if I shall be an humble instrument in the hands of the Almighty, and this, his almost chosen people, for perpetuating the object of that great struggle. (IV, 236)

And yet the *Chicago Times* was right to suspect an underlying radical intention, a radical opposition to the Democratic party's kind of conservatism expressed in their slogan "The Constitution as it is and the Union as it was." In 1854 Lincoln had said at Peoria:

Let us re-adopt the Declaration of Independence, and with it, the practices and policy, which harmonize with it. Let north and south—let all Americans—let all lovers of liberty everywhere—join in the great and good work. If we do this, we shall not only have saved the Union; but we shall have so saved it, as to make, and keep it, forever worthy of saving. We shall have so saved it, that the succeeding millions of free happy people, the world over, shall rise up, and call us blessed, to the latest generations. (II, 276)

The last phrases are a paraphrase of the Magnificat, the words of the mother-to-be of the Messiah: "For behold, from hence forth all generations shall call me blessed" (*Luke* 1:48). It is Lincoln's awesome idea that the generation of the civil war, under his leadership, is at once the savior and the parent of the savior nation, that America is to politics "almost" as Israel was to the spirit. Hence for the Union side the war is a kind of second coming, a second bringing-forth, after four score and seven years. Lincoln had converted Jefferson's extravagant opinion that "a little rebellion, now and then, is a good thing" ("Letter to Madison," January 30, 1787) into a serious conception concerning the periodic rebirth of the Revolution—to occur, evidently, in fullest force in the fourth generation, once in a century.

In this idea Lincoln recognizes that a country founded by a revolution is bound to have a generational problem. For the document constituting its government is ordained and established, as the principle of popular government demands, in the first person plural; it begins: "We the people." Yet this can mean literally only the ratifying generation, for thereafter the fundamental act of self-government is inherited. But self-determination by tradition is a kind of paradox, and it is this difficulty which lay behind Jefferson's advocacy of a regular revolution:

Can one generation bind another, and all others, in succession forever? I think not. The Creator has made the earth for the living, not the dead. . . . A generation may bind itself as long as its majority continues in life; when that has disappeared, another majority is in place, holds all the rights and powers their predecessors once held, and may change their laws and institutions to suit themselves. Nothing then is unchangeable but the inherent and unalienable rights of man. ("Letter to J. Cartwright," June 5, 1824)

Jefferson's radical solution to the problem of changing generations was opposed by Lincoln on the ground that majority rule itself, as well as minority rights, were guaranteed by nothing but a commitment to the fundamental law of governmental institutions.

The very material success of "the popular principle applied to government" acerbates the problem. On several occasions, for instance to Congress in 1861 and 1862, Lincoln had given exultant accounts of the fantastic increase of population, eight-fold since the founding and continuing even through the war (VI, 496; VIII, 55), adding projections, based on the same rate of growth, of 250 million by 1930 and a proportionately even greater increase of prosperity (V, 529, 533). But when making up such an account a quarter of a century earlier, in the speech "On the Perpetuation of our Political Institutions," he had added:

We, when mounting the stage of existence, found ourselves the legal inheritors of these fundamental blessings. We toiled not in the acquirement or establishment of them—they are a legacy bequeathed us, by a *once* hardy, brave, and patriotic, but *now* lamented and departed race of ancestors. . . . (I, 108)

The generational dilemma raised by success is that the *epigoni*, the successor generations, bred in that most desirable ignorance, the ignorance of anarchy and despotism, and mistaking the routines of their parents for the tradition, will combat apathy by giving current problems a cataclysmic cast, that they will be willing to cure dissatisfaction by catastrophe. A deliberate return to the founding revolution alone can forestall such an event, or if, as in the case of the Civil War, it becomes an accomplished fact, turn it into an act of salvation. Lincoln continually makes the effort to convert the war in this way, even comparing its financial funding to that of the Revolution (IV, 431–432).

There is, of course, an assumption in this course of action which goes beyond Jefferson's reliance on the mere principles of 1776. It is that constitutional government is, in fact, the best means of realizing these principles and that it is, therefore, to be cherished equally with them. Lincoln held this assumption in full awareness of the mixed and mammoth character which the nation was to attain in the next century, and this is why he saw the incidents of the Civil War as "philosophy to learn wisdom from" "for any future great national trial" (VIII, 101).

What then, exactly, does Lincoln mean by "a new birth of freedom"? As the nation was conceived in liberty and dedicated to equality, so it is to be reborn in freedom. That means that in this speech "freedom" covers both equality of creation and "liberty," that is, civil freedom, which Lincoln elsewhere calls the jewel of liberty within the family of freedom; it stands at once for man's nature as a creature under God and for his means of fulfilling that nature in civil society, as part of a nation (cf. II, 501). This means is self-government, which Lincoln respects equally with its object (i.e. freedom), calling it "right—absolutely and eternally right" (II, 265). In fact, he defines it coextensively with liberty, which means for "each man to do as he pleases with himself" (VII, 301):

> I trust I understand, and truly estimate the right of self-government. My faith in the proposition that each man should do precisely as he pleases with all which is exclusively his own, lies at the foundation of the sense of justice there is in me. . . . (II, 265; cf. II, 493)

It is implied in this view first of all, with respect to politics, that submission to a government must be by the consent of the governed, understood as

> A majority, held in constraint by constitutional checks and limitations, and always changing easily with deliberate changes of popular opinions and sentiments . . . (IV, 268),

as discovered in elections, for

> We can not have free government without elections; . . . The strife of the election is but human-nature practically applied to the facts of the case. . . . (VIII, 101)

And secondly, with respect to economics, this view means that people must be able to acquire and hold something of their own, must have, not the assurance, but the possibility of acquisition; Lincoln made this aspect of self-government a subject of his first Annual Message to Congress in 1861 (V, 52; cf. III, 478–479).

Now when Lincoln in the decade before and during the war set out his thoughts on freedom, he did it almost invariably in reference to its antithesis—slavery (cf. II, 265 and 350). By "a new birth of freedom" Lincoln means the readoption of the Declaration in a very specific sense, a sense which the ordinary "conservatives" strongly disapproved.

During the war Lincoln expressed his views on the slavery question succinctly in a private letter. They are characteristic of the double nature of his political opinions, reverence for the laws combined with radicality of principle. He said:

> I am naturally anti-slavery. If slavery is not wrong, nothing is wrong. I can not remember when I did not so think, and feel. And yet I have never understood that the Presidency conferred upon me an unrestricted right to act officially upon this judgment and feeling. (VII, 281; *cf.* II, 493; V, 388–389)

For, as he said in his First Inaugural, not only did he have no lawful right to do so under the Constitution, but he even held himself bound by his oath of office to enforce the constitutional provision for the reclaiming of fugitive slaves (III, 386; IV, 263)—it was more important to preserve the very basis of liberty than to secure immediate justice. At the same time he found himself able to base his uncompromising public opposition to slavery on the opinions of the Founding Fathers (e.g. II, 129) and on the founding documents. Whether or not he knew of Jefferson's "philippic against Negro slavery" which Congress deleted from the final draft, he had no question that the Declaration meant to include negroes, a view he set out in his debate with Douglas:

> I should like to know if taking this old Declaration of Independence, which declares that all men are equal upon principle, and making exception to it where will it stop. If one man says it does not mean a negro, why may not another say it does not mean some other man? . . . (II, 500; cf. II, 405 ff; III, 327–328)

And he had equally no question about the intention of the Constitution. He often repeated the argument from "necessity." It was that to get the Constitution at all the framers had had to compromise, but that they had found a way to save in the long run the principle which they could not assert at the moment (II, 266, 274, 403 ff., 501, 520; III, 327), for

> when the fathers of the government cut off the source of slavery by the abolition of the slave trade, and adopted a system of restricting it from the new territories where it had not existed, I maintain that they placed it where they understood, and all sensible men understood, it was in the course of ultimate extinction. . . . (III, 276; cf. II, 492, 515)

Accordingly Lincoln who, as a responsible participant in actual political life, could not support the extreme of abolition, became the implacable foe of the *extension* of slavery—this single issue dominates his speeches before the war (e.g. I, 347–348; II, 361). In fact it brought him, as it had Jefferson (II, 128), back into politics, which had begun to lose its interest for him (III, 512). It was an issue important to him in part because it was so peculiarly connected with one aspect of the axiomatic character of the founding principles, namely with the question *of their universality* (cf. 11, 270–271; 111,204). Propositions of this sort, precisely because they are principles of human nature, and are pronounced concerning "all men," must eventually either fail altogether or altogether prevail, both in respect to institutions:

> I believe this government cannot endure, permanently half *slave* and half *free* (II, 461),

and to individuals:

> This is a world of compensations; and he who would *be* no slave, must consent to *have* no slave. Those who deny freedom to others, deserve it not for themselves; and under a just God, can not long retain it. (III, 376; cf. II, 323; III, 95)

Lincoln did not regard it as impossible that the nation might fail, which would mean that the false principle might become generally accepted and that the nation would degenerate into despotism (II, 323). It was precisely his political task to prevent this. So, once the war had revealed itself as the final means of resolving the issue, and precisely because his "paramount object" was to

> save the Union, and . . . not either to save or destroy slavery . . . (V, 388–389),

he recognized, in his Second Inaugural Address, that that "eighth of the whole population" who were slaves, were "somehow, the cause of the war" (VIII, 332), and that

In giving freedom to the *slave*, we *assure* freedom to the *free*. . . .
(V, 537)

For slavery was "that only thing which ever could bring this
nation to civil war" (VIII, 41). And he gave this not only
a political, but as fitted the nature of the case, an economic
interpretation, on the principle that bad labor drives out good.
So he told a labor delegation that

> the existing rebellion means more, and tends to more, than the
> perpetuation of African slavery—that it is, in fact, a war upon
> the rights of all working people. (VII, 259; cf. II, 364–365)

This conception of the war caused him, just after the victory at
Gettysburg, to call it

> a gigantic Rebellion, at the bottom of which is an effort to over-
> throw the principle that all men are created equal. . . . (VI, 320)

Lincoln had several times made a point of the fact that the
word "slavery" does not occur in the Constitution:

> Thus, the thing is hid away, in the constitution, just as an afflicted
> man hides away a wen or a cancer, which he dares not cut out at
> once, lest he bleed to death; with the promise, nevertheless, that
> the cutting may begin at the end of a given time. (II, 274)

In accordance with this omission the Address does not contain
the word either, although for a different motive: as the founders
had to violate their feelings about slavery out of political necessity, so the time had come at the beginning of that year, 1863,
when Lincoln could indulge his out of military necessity. He
used what he considered to be the president's war powers to put
the Emancipation Proclamation in force for the states in rebellion (VI, 29–30), a move he defended with the argument that
the black regiments were indispensable to military success (VII,
281–282; 499–501). Since the Union slave states, like Maryland

(VII, 302), were proceeding with voluntary emancipation, it was plain that the thing was on the way out. The Union was to be reconstructed without slavery, and this is what the "Proclamation of Amnesty and Reconstruction" Lincoln issued three weeks after the Gettysburg Address provided (VII, 53 ff., cf. VIII, 399 ff.). The "new birth of freedom" meant for Lincoln the re-adoption of the Declaration (II, 276) and the amendment of the Constitution (V, 530; VIII, 149) in such a way as to make explicit their true intention; it meant "returning slavery to the position our fathers gave it" (II, 276), and restoring the republican example to "its just influence in the world," by securing it from the charge of hypocrisy (II, 255). Lincoln made of the war a purification—the nation was to be purged of inconsistency.

And now the last clause:

> and that government of the people, by the people, for the people, shall not perish from the earth.

How, first of all, should we imagine that Lincoln read this phrase, this memorable definition of "popular government"? Did he stress the prepositions "of," "by," "for" or the noun "people"? The dissyllabic rhythm of the speech is best preserved by reading trochees:

> óf the péople, bý the péople, fór the péople,

a rhythm which gives equal weight to the people and its relation to the government.

As was the beginning, so the end of the speech is directly adapted from the American oratorical tradition, namely from an abolitionist sermon given, appropriately, on July 4 (1858) by the Rev. Theodore Parker, who had said:

> Democracy is direct self-government, over all the people, for all the people, by all the people.

Besides changing the rhythm, Lincoln had, significantly, soft-
ened "over" to "of," avoiding even a hint of despotism and
instead alluding to the people's ultimate authority. Thus the
people govern 1. as the final source of sovereignty, 2. by representatives chosen from among themselves, and 3. ruling in the
popular interest—a description the President himself exemplified (cf. VII, 512).

Lincoln does not say "this" government as he had said
"this" nation, for it is the preservation of popular, that is,
elected, government *anywhere* which is at stake, though the
immediate cause for resorting to force was certainly the preservation of *this* government. But the wider and narrower cause
came to the same thing; thus near the beginning of the war
Lincoln had told Congress, called by him into special session,
again on a July 4 (of 1861), that he regretfully found that

> the duty of employing the war power in defense of the govern-
> ment [had been] forced upon him . . . no popular government can
> long survive a marked precedent, that those who carry an elec-
> tion can only save the government from immediate destruction,
> by giving up the main point upon which the people gave the elec-
> tion. . . . (IV, 440)

Lincoln had begun with the Revolution and its statement
of principle, the Declaration; he ends with government and its
instituting document, the Constitution. This represents the
difference in the commitments of the first and the fourth generations:

> . . . As the patriots of seventy-six did to support the Declaration
> of Independence, so to the support of the Constitution and Laws,
> let every American pledge his life, his property, and his sacred
> honor; . . . (I, 112; cf. *Declaration*, end)

It also represents the relation of the Declaration to the Constitution; the latter is merely the instrument of the former, as

shown in a sentence Lincoln quotes from the second paragraph of the Declaration:

> That to secure these Rights, Governments are instituted among Men, DERIVING THEIR JUST POWERS FROM THE CONSENT OF THE GOVERNED. . . . (II, 266)

The government is a *means*, and thus a compromise of evils. Thus Madison says in *The Federalist* No. 51:

> But what is government itself but the greatest of all reflections on human nature? If men were angels, no government would be necessary.

But the founding principles themselves, which government is supposed to realize and protect, are always present to Lincoln (III, 14), and it is that sense of presence which allows him to appeal, even in political matters, to "the better angels of our nature" (IV, 271). Thus for him the Declaration, based on final principles, stands permanent, while the Constitution, as a means, is amendable; the two together stand for America's double root in what is absolutely best and what is merely most practicable. Yet Lincoln regards this government as being eminently well instituted to maintain the principle. He says of the Constitution that

> It can scarcely be made better than it is,

and he warns:

> Don't interfere with anything in the Constitution.—That must be maintained, for it is the only safeguard of our liberties. (II, 366)

In this way the preservation of popular government is linked to the defense of the American Constitution.

This government "shall not perish from the earth"—that is the "work,' the "task," the "cause." Lincoln has ended, as he began, with language heavy with the Bible:

> The good man is perished out of the earth: and there is none upright among men: they all lie in wait for blood; they hunt every man his brother with a net. (*Micah* 7:2)

If this rebellion prevails, his allusion warns, so that "these institutions shall perish" (IV, 440), men will return to that universal state of war, the war of each against all, which precedes the institution of government; the Rebellion would undo the Founding:

> [F]or when men, by entering into society and civil government, have excluded force and introduced laws for the preservation of property, peace, and unity amongst themselves, those who set up force again in opposition to the laws do *rebellare*—that is, bring back again the state of war—and are properly rebels; . . . (Locke, *Second Treatise of Civil Government*, para. 226)

In Lincoln's words:

> Plainly, the central idea of secession, is the essence of anarchy. A majority, held in restraint by constitutional checks and limitations, and always changing easily with deliberate changes of popular opinions and sentiments is the only true sovereign of a free people. Whoever rejects it, does, of necessity, fly to anarchy or despotism. (1861, IV, 268)

And finally, there is an allusion to *Jeremiah* 10:11:

> The gods that have not made the heavens and the earth, even they shall perish from the earth. . . .

False gods shall perish, but the government of the people shall not perish.

V. The Speaker

After having, at length, considered the speech, it is permissible to consider the speaker.

Lincoln is, at his height, a public man:

> If ever I feel the soul within me elevate and expand to those dimensions not wholly unworthy of its Almighty Architect, it is when I contemplate the cause of my country; . . . (I, 178)

But the American speaker, who, like Lincoln, means to put his whole heart and ambition (III, 334) in the service of the body politic, has a peculiar problem, which is rooted in that quality of American life that Tocqueville describes in the chapter "Of Some Sources of Poetry Among Democratic Nations":

> Nothing conceivable is so petty, so insipid, so crowded with paltry interests—in one word so anti-poetic—as the life of a man in the United States. (*Democracy in America*, II. I. 17)

The cause of this paltriness is that in a democracy men have given up the source of aristocratic poetry, the past, while the very principle of equality deprives them of the present as a source of poetry, by making all contemporaries equally mediocre. There remain, Tocqueville says, only three sources to democratic poets: the nation, the future, and God—precisely the very themes of Lincoln's public poetry. But, as he observes in the chapter on "Why American Writers and Orators Often Use an Inflated Style," it is difficult to present these themes at the middle range:

> In democratic communities, each citizen is habitually engaged in the contemplation of a very puny object: namely, himself. If he ever raises his looks higher, he perceives only the immense form of society at large or the still more imposing aspect of mankind. His ideas are all either extremely minute and clear or extremely general and vague; what lies between is a void. (*Ibid.*, 18)

Clearly, then, the principles of equality and liberty themselves are responsible for this American problem of the void at the middle, not only because they induce mediocrity, but for deeper reasons as well. First, since they are axioms of openness, that is, propositions of reason which are by their very nature incapable of serving as the theoretical bases of a total system, they provide no specific authoritative "public philosophy." Hence each issue must be decided anew on the basis of principles which can give no univocal guidance. Second, since they are intended precisely to insure "the pursuit of happiness," that is, a prosperous privacy, they seem less poignant the more successfully they are at work. For they are principles of pure potentiality, the possibility of goods but not themselves goods, and certainly not public goods; significantly, French "fraternity," a concrete social bond, has never been the complement of liberty and equality in America.

In his speeches, Lincoln wrestles with just these and similar difficulties, which might be characterized with the aid of a classical term: By the very nature of their political foundation Americans tend to act not as a *polis*, a political community held together by friendship (Aristotle, *Nicomachean Ethics*, VIII. i. 4.), but as a modern society, a collection of private persons who jostle each other into some sort of balance; Lincoln's effort in his speeches is precisely to prove this tendency inessential, to persuade the nation that it *is* held together by "bonds of affection" (IV, 271).

Lincoln, then, attempts to fill the agitated national void with sober sentiment "hewn from the solid quarry of sober reason," the founding principles. Once the spontaneous dedication of the Revolution is gone, he says in his speech on "The Perpetuation of Our Political Institutions," a new situation arises:

> Passion has helped us; but can do so no more. It will in future be our enemy. Reason, cold, calculating, unimpassioned rea-

son, must furnish all the materials for our future support and defense.—Let those materials be moulded into *general intelligence; sound morality*, and, in particular, a *reverence for the constitution and laws*; . . . (I, 115)

Lincoln's solution of the "historical" problem, the receding of the moment of greatness for succeeding generations, is bold: He offers a new, sober passion, a passion of reason—reverence, a lawyer-like love for the instruments which have accomplished the miracle of a stable democracy; his rhetoric incorporates and so elicits it.

At the same time, true to the openness demanded by the principles, he usually abstains from rhetorical compulsion in favor of specific pleas; these sentences of his last public address, dealing with the most burning problem of the moment, are typical:

In the Annual Message of Dec. 1863 and accompanying Proclamation, I presented *a* plan of re-construction (as the phrase goes) which, I promised, if adopted by any State, should be acceptable to, and sustained by, the Executive government of the nation. I distinctly stated that this was not the only plan which might possibly be acceptable; . . . (VIII, 401–402)

Instead of attempting to compel the people to a course deduced dogmatically, in the manner of an ideologist, he presented, in the words of the *London Spectator*,

A political transparency, in which the nation could see an individual character of great power working out the problems set before them all. . . .

He manages to make these problems supremely absorbing, and he does it by making almost every speech an interpretation of the founding documents in which he reveals at once their unaging radicality and their enduring applicability. He is, in fact, giving Americans a secular complement to Scripture (I, 115).

It is a significant aspect of Lincoln's effort that he never attempts to raise the question of the truth of the democratic principles, nor even to supply a definition, except in extremely simple and negative terms. So he says,

> The world has never had a good definition of the word liberty, and the American people, just now, are much in want of one.

And he provides it. In simple terms, liberty means

> for each man to do as he pleases with himself, and the product of his labor; . . . (VII, 301)

while he expresses his "idea of democracy" in the form of the familiar religious precept "Do unto others as you would have them do unto you":

> As I would not be *a slave*, so I would not be a *master*. This expresses my idea of democracy. Whatever differs from this, to the extent of the difference, is no democracy. (II, 532)

Thus he treats the principles of American politics as plain precepts for the happiness of humanity, which are at the same time standards of moral perfection, and about which he offers no theoretical reflections:

> The Savior, I suppose, did not expect that any human creature could be perfect as the Father in Heaven; but He said, "As your Father in Heaven is perfect, be ye also perfect." . . . So I say in relation to the principle that all men are created equal, let it be as nearly reached as we can. . . . (II, 501)

Indeed, deep public inquiries would hardly be in accordance with the object of his rhetoric. For the strictly rational basis of democracy is to be found in the theory of "natural rights" set out by Hobbes and Locke, a theory which regards precisely what is common in men and not what is elevated; it is therefore scarcely conducive to a public feeling of piety. What Lincoln does instead is, by invoking Scripture (II, 501), to raise these principles from self-evident propositions to articles of faith, returning to a foundation in fact deeper, as Tocqueville showed (*op. cit.*, I. ii), than the rational beginnings provided by the founding fathers.

To explain why "*the spirit of religion* and the *spirit of liberty*" are anciently incorporated with each other in America, Tocqueville had appealed to the classical tradition concerning the need for public piety to support the body politic:

> Liberty regards religion as its companion in all its battles and its triumphs, as the cradle of its infancy and the divine source of its claims. (*Op. cit.*, I. ii)

And he had found this theory corroborated in America:

> Religion in America takes no direct part in the government of society, but it must be regarded as the first of their political institutions. (*Op. cit.*, I. XVII)

Lincoln came to hold the converse of this expedient view: Religion does not serve politics, but the reverse—republican government is itself a great religious institution; in his own words "the only greater institution" is the church (I, 115). The rock of reason of Washington's foundation has the same basis as Peter's church. That reverence for the laws which Lincoln calls "the political religion" of the nation (I, 112) is based on a trans-political faith. It must be urged that this is not an opinion Lincoln holds routinely or perfunctorily—for him, the Republic, which puts the good of the whole finally into the hands of a numerical majority (VIII, 149), is plausible only as a community of the faithful, protected by a beneficent provision that few shall be totally without grace and that of all those who come into the world, only a small percentage are natural tyrants. . . . (II, 264)

Were it otherwise, democracy would be a continual gamble with the body politic.

Accordingly the Gettysburg Address begins and ends not only with phrases borrowed from American oratory but with the diction of the Bible. To Lincoln the people of the Revolution is also the second people of the Book, the "almost chosen people" (IV, 236). All Americans, he said in his Second Inaugural,

> read the same Bible and pray to the same God; . . . (VIII, 333)

Lincoln himself was not only, as were most backwoodsmen, brought up on the Bible, but he could still write to his friend Speed in the year before his death:

> I am profitably engaged in reading the Bible,

and in the same year he said to a committee which had presented a Bible:

> . . . it is the best gift God has given to men.
> All the good the Savior gave to the world was communicated through this book. But for it we could not know right from wrong. All things most desirable for man's welfare, here and hereafter, are to be found portrayed in it. . . . (VII, 542)

Lincoln's commitment to the Bible was not that of an orthodox Christian, for, as he said,

> I have never united myself to any church, because I have found difficulty in giving my assent, without mental reservation, to the long, complicated statements of Christian doctrine which characterize their Articles of Belief and Confessions of Faith. (Remark to H. C. Demig, c. 1862; cf. I, 382)

For him the Bible was rather a political source book, in two contrasting respects. On the one hand it provides him a language at once solemn and popular, beyond both that of the demagogue and of the intellectual. It is a language of salvation with which he magnifies the American enterprise—with its diction he speaks as "Father Abraham," as the first patriarch of a new generation of Founding Fathers. And on the other hand, it supports him in a view of the nature of things which damps the hysterical activity filling the American void, and reduces it to a sound if somewhat melancholic deliberation. For Lincoln had been from his youth a believer in an inner counterpoise to political liberty, which he understood to be called the "Doctrine of Necessity,"

> that is, that the human mind is impelled to action, or held in rest by some power, over which the mind itself has no control; . . . (I, 382)

That power is God who, though "not a person," can yet directly exercise his will in human affairs:

> By his mere quiet power on the minds of the now contestants, He could have either *saved* or *destroyed* the Union without a human contest. . . . ("Meditation on the Divine Will [Sept. 3, 1862]," V, 404)

This god, in whom Lincoln, by the peculiar power of his faith, recognizes at once "Nature's God" and the God of the Bible, is Lincoln's and the people's political master; he imposes strict limits on the power of human contrivance. The humanity which is the consequence of Lincoln's view is embodied in Lincoln's last speech to the nation before his assassination, the Second Inaugural Address, which is a classical American poem drawing particularly on Tocqueville's third source of democratic poetry, God.

The same speaker who is so eminently democratic in theme is, remarkably, the very reverse in form. Again Tocqueville provides the criteria, namely in his chapter on "Literary Characteristics of Democratic Times":

> Taken as a whole, literature in democratic ages can never present, as it does in periods of aristocracy, an aspect of order, regularity, science and art; its form, on the contrary, will ordinarily be slighted, sometimes despised. Style will frequently be fantastic, incorrect, overburdened, and loose, almost always vehement and bold. Authors will aim at rapidity of execution more than at perfection of detail. Small productions will be more common than bulky books. . . . (*Democracy in America*, II. i. 13)

Now, this so frequently accurate description is conspicuously inapplicable to Lincoln's writing. The Gettysburg Address is small, to be sure, but it was not rapidly executed—Lincoln had brought a worked-over draft from Washington; he re-worked this in Gettysburg on the eve of delivery, and he emended each of the three known copies he made over the next three months. Although, as he said, not a master of language nor in possession of a fine education (II, 491), he *was* careful:

> Gentlemen, Judge Douglas informed you that this speech of mine was probably carefully prepared. I admit that it was. . . . (II, 491)

By means of this care he succeeded in giving his thoughts a most detailed perfection of form. For this purpose he had, at the age of twenty-three, set himself to study English grammar, "imperfectly, of course, but so as to speak and write as well as he does now" (IV, 62), enabling him to write to a man who had submitted to him an edited version of one of his speeches:

> So far as it is intended merely to improve in grammar, and elegance of composition, I am quite agreed; but I do not wish the sense changed, or modified, to a hair's breadth. And you, not

having studied particular points so closely as I have, can not be
quite sure that you do not change the sense when you do not intend it. . . . (IV, 58)[11]

His style, too, is the very opposite of that of the typical democratic writer, as described by Tocqueville in his chapter
"How American Democracy Has Modified the English Language" (*ibid.*, II. i. 16). Such a writer, from lack of care, love
of change, and desire for bigness, uses old words in indeterminate senses, introduces vast numbers of new words, usually
borrowed from technical vocabularies, and loads his speech
with abstract and general expressions. Tocqueville had called
lawyers the aristocrats of America (*ibid.*, I. xvi), and in part
Lincoln's care is that of a lawyer interpreting law. But the lap-
idary precision of form which carries the patriarchal grandeur of Lincoln's oratory—he was unable to deliver a mere
dry lecture (IV, 40)—is something more, namely a sign of a
novel kind of aristocracy—republican aristocracy. Lincoln had
tacitly rejected Everett's cold classicism as inappropriate to a
democratic speaker, whose whole object it ought never be to
demonstrate or exert his own superiority. His ambition was,
rather, as he told his friend Herndon, "to be distinctly understood by the common people,"[12] and to use his power, as had
his model, Clay, in the service of democratic *deeds*:

> All his efforts were made from practical effect. He never spoke
> merely to be heard. He never delivered a Fourth of July oration,
> or an eulogy on an occasion like this. . . . ("Eulogy on Henry
> Clay [July 6, 1852]," II, 126; cf. 125–126)

And yet Lincoln's rhetoric displays precisely the characteristics
of ancient aristocratic writers, of which Tocqueville writes in
the chapter entitled "The Study of Greek and Latin Literature
Is Peculiarly Useful in Democratic Communities":

Nothing in their works seems done hastily or at random; every line is written for the eye of the connoisseur and is shaped after some conception of ideal beauty. No literature places those fine qualities in which the writers of democracies are naturally deficient in bolder relief than that of the ancients; no literature, therefore, ought to be more studied in democratic times. (*Ibid.*, II. i. 15)

Lincoln himself is, therefore, in Tocqueville's sense an aristocratic writer, even to the point of finding his sources in the past. The man who had had from youth the "peculiar ambition"

of being truly esteemed of my fellow men, by rendering myself worthy of their esteem, (I, 8; cf. III, 334)

and who said he hoped he understood "that which constitutes the inside of a gentleman" (II, 513), could have no quarrel with the essence of aristocracy. In fact, in the weeks just before the delivery of the Gettysburg Address he had received visitors who urged him at the earliest occasion to present the Union to the public "as fighting the battle of democracy for all the world" and the war as being one "of the people against the aristocrats"—he had accepted the former and rejected the latter suggestion. For he was himself a living corroboration of Jefferson's contention, set out in his correspondence with Adams (October 28, 1813), that aristocracy and democracy, the rule of the best and the rule of the people, have become compatible in the United States, that the citizens in free election can and will "in general" choose from among themselves the "natural *aristoi*," the best by nature. The Gettysburg Address is the utterance of such an *aristos*, a man at the same time excellent in the antique sense and good in the common understanding.

THE PARADOX
OF OBEDIENCE

By "The Paradox of Obedience" I mean this: You, the men and women of the United States Air Force, are citizens of the world's oldest and largest democratic republic, which, in its best moments, values human freedom as the highest civic good. You are also members of a military order which, by its very nature, makes obedience a central virtue. How can that be? How can you embody your civic right to do as you will, together with its opposite, the renunciation of that right in favor of obedience to orders?

I imagine that you have already run up against this paradox, implicitly and half-consciously. I want to try to think it out with you explicitly.

The writings, philosophical and practical, on military obedience to orders that I have read—not very many but very reputable ones—all focus on the problem of *disobedience*, on your duty to disobey orders that are illegal or (and here's where really hellishly difficult dilemmas arise) just immoral, that is, inhumane. But I want to ask a less acutely practical and

Lecture Given at United States Air Force Academy, November 18, 2004, in the Joseph A. Reich Sr. Distinguished Lecture Series on War, Morality and the Military Profession.

yet, it seems to me, a deeper and more life-disposing question. Put it this way: Why is your obedience not servitude? Why are you even entitled to think of yourselves as free, perhaps even as most nobly free?

When we're trying to puzzle something out, it often happens that we come upon a book serendipitously to our purpose. I was reading Aristotle's *Metaphysics* not long ago—Aristotle is where I go when I want sensible thinking carried to wildly wonderful heights. There I found the following remarkable sentence:

> . . . [I]n a household it is the free persons who may least do what suits them but all or most of what they do is under standing orders [*tetaktai*], while the slaves taken in war [*andrapoda*] and the animals have little common responsibility but mostly do what they do at random. (1075 a 19)

What goes for something as hands-on as household management is well known to hold for something as free of practical purpose as theoretical thinking: The freer it is, the more obedient it is to orders coming from a hidden but potent source, the truth. So here is another version of my question tonight: Is it possible that human freedom *requires* some sort of obedience? Might the ethics of the free and the morality of the military be much more than barely compatible?

You can hear from the tone of my question that I think so, but the thought needs working out. Why might that working out to be of interest to you? Why not just do it—for the moment obey or, if need be, disobey, as intelligently and as conscientiously as you can; later on issue orders in the same spirit, and leave it at that? The answer is: Because human beings who haven't thought out the condition of their life, especially if it is, as is yours, a marked life, marked by the uniform you wear and the mission you accept—which is to do efficiently what others are forbidden to do, to take human life when so ordered—such thoughtless persons are quite seriously not all there. A callow, unthinking warrior is a fearful thing, to my citizen's mind.

I do know how intrusive and unwelcome this demand to be reflective might be. I know that your being here tonight is just one more thing you've been ordered to do. I know from my visits to the Naval Academy, our neighbor across the street in Annapolis, as well as from teaching my share of ensigns, lieutenants, and lieutenant commanders who have come to St. John's College for their graduate work, that it is a deliberate policy of the Naval Academy to hound and hassle the midshipmen so as to train them to perform the tasks of warmaking and peacekeeping under acute pressure. And such pressure is exactly the opposite of the leisure needed to work out our thoughts and to collect and settle in our soul those rules of conduct that we can call on in a pinch. Everyone seems to agree that the time needed to develop character, to transmute moral thinking into personal structure, is in hopelessly short supply in the service academies; I imagine it is no different in Colorado than in Maryland or New York.

It then becomes irresistible, especially when noisy scandals focus public attention on military mores, to try to be efficient about character formation, to appoint an ethicist who lectures on different systems of morality, to invite someone to give a Thursday evening talk on an ethical problem, to hand out manuals with power points on conduct. But these devices are better for showing goodwill than for being morally effective. In matters of the soul an efficient use of time is an impossibility. I'm not, however, criticizing the service academies for trying; I'm rather pointing out a part of the paradox you must live with: that you have to become morally mature in a forbidding environment. By "morally mature" I mean what philosophers call being "autonomous," a Greek word (in our world most terms of reflection are Greek) that means being "a law unto yourself," living by a self-given law. And that, of course, is just what you are also training not to be and do. Learning to be a pilot of a military aircraft and learning to steer your own soul do have certain common features, such as making correct split-second decisions in action, yet the time frame for learning to do the right thing in both senses is very different.

But both tasks must be done, and my guess is that the second, the moral growth, takes place mostly in the interstices of your working time, above all when you're not being talked at, as I'm doing now, but when you talk to each other in the squadrons, decks or barracks. I would say that the human quality of the members of a service academy is truly evaluated by what is not accessible to measurement: the occasional moral seriousness of the conversation among themselves. I know perfectly well that to some remaining degree you are sometimes just kids shooting the breeze and throwing the bull, that some halfmen think it's manly to talk crudely about each other and vulgarly about women (in fact, all the country knows that some of your predecessors disgraced their uniform by their misconduct toward women).[1] So too some not-yet-women think it's their female prerogative to be bitchy about each other and gross about men.

Yet these facts of life don't eclipse another important fact: that you are owed a special—even awed—respect from the civilian world, not only because in this time of long-term asymmetric war you represent the straight and lawful side of the deadly equation, but just because and insofar as you have deliberately chosen a life of service that involves you in moral demands and complexities beyond those facing civilians.

I'll tell you how that comes home to me personally. In my town of Annapolis I see a lot of people, especially young ones, in dark blue uniform. They wear a characteristic look, a look of innocence and naiveté—I would almost say purity. I know full well that they are just as accomplished at being hell-raisers as are our scruffy and knowing kids at my college and that mandatory grooming has a lot to do with their clean young look, but that's only its lesser cause. The greater is that they have committed themselves to a mission, submitted themselves to an order that can ask everything of them, even their life, and that choice confers on them a certain fine straightness. But if any of this straight simplicity comes from the comfort of just following orders, it is an ignorant rather than a noble simplicity, which needs to be shaken.

I might say, incidentally, that we visitors from across the wall discovered, when invited to observe, that midshipmen who transgressed did it at least partly from a kind of virtue, namely loyalty. In this ardent pressure cooker they lived in, it was not the institution that had succeeded in winning their most passionate loyalty. That was reserved for their peers, for whose protection they were, in certain cases, willing to put themselves in danger of ignominious dismissal. So a certain virtue, absolutely crucial in battle, put them in direct opposition to the Naval Academy's honor code. I doubt that they had thought deeply, more universally, more largely, about the hierarchy, the scale, of their loyalties: how to put their heart into obeying non-human, impersonal imperatives without losing the intensity of comradeship that is the cement of the services. For my part, I have a certain faith that, subjected to thoughtful recognition, these paradoxes, so logically obvious and so urgently felt by any human being who is all there, are resolvable, or if not resolvable, at least absorbable into a certain steadiness of judgment that reconciles prompt obedience with ultimate autonomy.

While I learned about these perplexities and dilemmas of military education as a sympathetic civilian in Annapolis, both the sympathy and the perplexities have earlier roots in my life. I think it's worth saying a brief word about myself because in my effort to present you with food for thought, I'm also, against my better judgment, preaching at you, and so you have a right to my *bona fides*.

My father was a field doctor in a German cavalry regiment in the First World War and a holder of the Iron Cross (second class). I remember when I was a twelve-year-old discovering his regimental history in our home library and reading and rereading the paragraphs where his colonel told of mentioning him in dispatches for his bravery under fire. My mother was a front-line nurse; in fact both my parents, a decade before meeting each other, were present at the bloody battle of Verdun in 1916. When I found the regimental history it was 1941, and we were packing up to emigrate. Why did we leave Germany so late? Partly, I am sure, because my parents, loyal Germans first and Jews second, simply could not imagine that the country they had served was about to visit such evil on us. I remember vividly how, as the sealed train destined for the boat to America was passing the Maginot Line (with all the guns visibly trained in the wrong direction), my mother opened the window to the crack that it was allowed to open, and tossed both her own and my father's decoration into the French countryside. Thus unburdened we came to America, and my younger brother eventually became an American soldier, who enlisted to fight in Korea. So much for the sources of my sympathy for people in uniform, which are also the causes of the perplexities I am considering with you tonight. It might be pertinent to add that my whole extended family lives in Israel, and every last one of them was once or is now or will be serving in the Israel Defense Forces, since, as you probably know, military service is a universal obligation in that endangered country.

Why did the German Officer Corps permit itself to serve a criminal regime? It is a historical problem more vivid to me by reason of my own origins. One partial answer has to do with a flawed conception of obedience.—I am not thinking so much of the army's willingness to condone and even help to carry out great war crimes, but of a prior condition of submission. In its corporate thinking the traditionally Prussian Officer Corps was Lutheran and Kantian. I quote and report a relevant thought from each of these, first from Luther and then from Kant. In his tract of 1526, "Whether a Soldier Too Can Be Saved," Luther asks rhetorically:

> Well then, if the king keeps neither God's law nor the law of the land, ought you to attack him, judge him, and take vengeance on him? Who commanded you to do that?

Such rhetoric, clearly implying that judging the morality of the authorities is not a soldier's affair, does not encourage military resistance to evil.

On the other hand, Kant carries his respect for personal integrity to such extremes that he considers lying—under any circumstances whatever, and oathbreaking in particular—so great an offense against the duty owed to moral law that it must destroy all self-respect. It is a severe teaching which can have, in some human contingencies, dangerous unintended consequences. In 1934, for example, Hitler had cunningly played on the Kantian convictions of the officers by extracting from them this oath:

> I swear by God this sacred oath, that I will render unconditional obedience to Adolf Hitler, the Fuehrer of the German Reich and People. (William Shirer, *The Rise and Fall of the Third Reich*, 227)

You can see that such opinions and such an oath, one of unconditional obedience to a *man*, not to the law, would pretty much preclude moral disobedience. It was an oath that no thoughtfully courageous human being should in good conscience take. (Happily your own military obedience is strongly conditioned on the legality of an order, and that implies that it ultimately looks to the *law*, both institutional and moral, not to a person, except yourselves.) Once such an oath had been taken, however, along with a strong Lutheran sense of submission to the sovereign, an officer's Kantian conscience was, I imagine, paralyzed between two duties: the duty of oath-keeping loyalty and the dictates of human decency.

So that is a source of the perplexity concerning obedience that has remained vivid to me long after I ceased to think of myself as a refugee from the country of my birth and became a citizen in the country of my life.

Your profession is unusually full of dilemmas, many more than I've mentioned. Let me add a few: Military service is both a career that promises advancement and a service that asks for ultimate sacrifices. This fact was vividly brought home to me when a senior at my college invited me to his commissioning as a lieutenant in the Marine Corps. As we talked a little, I asked him—it was 1984, when esteem for the military was still low after Vietnam—what career opportunities and retirement benefits he was hoping for. He looked me straight in the eye and said, "I'm hoping to serve my country." So I'm supposing that you too have a somewhat self-contradictory double motive, career security and honorable service. Again, if you fly, you are expected to be good with your aircraft and good with your crew. I know from experience that the two talents don't naturally go together, since for years I sailed with a skipper who handled his little craft with superb skill, by the book and beyond, but whose mishandled crew would regularly jump ship at the first dock we tied up to, as I myself finally did. You are expected to be trim in body and acute in mind, when I know that big brains pretty often go together with big bellies; the best example is Thomas Aquinas, one of the three or four most mighty intellects I know of, who was so fat that a circular segment had to be cut out of the refectory table for him to fit into. Again, in a country where people are at liberty to dress and groom themselves as they like, even to the point of looking bizarre, you conform to detailed standing and daily orders concerning appearance in order to achieve uniformity. Members of a law firm might, to be sure, claim to be under a similar dress code, though many big firms recognize the anomaly of this imposition by having a "casual day"—jeans ᴏn Friday. This is all small stuff compared to the two great oppositions you live with, to which I have already alluded. The first and gravest arises from foregoing a right that Thomas Hobbes, who is in major respects the philosophical founder of this country, names in his *Leviathan* of 1651 as the primary "right of nature":

> The liberty each man hath, to use his own power, as he will himself, for the preservation of his own nature; that is to say, of his own life; . . . (Ch. XIV)

As human beings you are endowed with this right to life, and so the Declaration of Independence repeats. But you renounce and forego it in war; you have committed yourself to be put in harm's way, and though you are given the means to defend yourself, you may not use your own power as you will. For you are under orders. This is the terrific fact that gives warriors their dignity.

The commitment I want to consider, however, is the one that stands behind, though not above, the willingness to encounter deadly danger—the apparently self-contradictory choice inherent in a profession that commands and obeys: the free renunciation of most liberties to do as you will and to leave others at liberty to do likewise that belongs to a citizen of a free country.

When I was preparing this talk, your Professor Martin Cook told me of Mark Osiel's fine book, *Obeying Orders* (1999). It reflects on the canons of "due obedience," the warrior's most acute ethical problem, and describes the "oscillation of behaviors," a sort of unavoidable moral schizophrenia which is the practical result of the soldier's double life as a free, and therefore individually responsible, moral agent and as a member of the military obligated to obey another's orders. There are even writers, "who pride themselves on their critical faculties," as Osiel says tartly, who think that "obedience . . . has a mechanical brutish connotation that fits uneasily with our usual conceptions of moral responsibility" (Osiel, p. 60 and n. 64). This opinion is obtuse, but it's not so easy to say why it's obtuse.

Here's the point I want to make: Long before the moral responsibility of order-takers may become an excruciating issue in action, the dilemma of obedience is already present in the mere fact of having joined the service; to be committed to obedience is to be, *ipso facto*, in a morally ambiguous, double-edged situation.

I am, incidentally, assuming here that the following assertion of Alfred T. Mahan, the naval historian, still holds true at Colorado Springs, as it does at Annapolis and at West Point:

> The role of obedience is simply the expression of that one among the military values upon which all the others depend.

I found this quotation in a thoughtful article by your own General Mal Wakin titled "The Ethics of Leadership" (published in *Moral Dimensions of the Military Profession*, 1998. I had the pleasure of inviting Colonel Wakin, as he was then, to my own college for a lecture on Just War Theory, which was very well received because it gave our students a lot to think about).

The possible interest to you of an analysis of obedience is predicated on its centrality to your life now and as future officers, even if you scarcely ever think out consciously the meaning of the fact that the U.S. Uniform Code of Military Justice specifically prohibits disobeying a superior commissioned or non-commissioned officer or a standing order (Osiel, 1).

What, then, is obedience? It sometimes helps to listen for the original meaning in the etymology of a word. Obedience comes from a Latin verb *ob-audire*; you know the *audire* part from English words like "audible," which means "hearable." *Obaudire* means "to listen *to*" what is said, *to hear it with a will*. The word "obedience" is a sort of metaphor; it says "hear" where it means "attend." When parents say to children "Didn't you hear me? Can't you listen?" they aren't asking "Wasn't I audible?" but "Why don't you do as you're told?" To be obedient means hearing words in the specific, focused, responsive way called "listening to." My obedience to you means willing your words to become my motives and your intentions my actions. It is a readiness to let an outside voice into my head and take it for my own. "About face" says the voice, and I permit it to command my limbs, and I pivot around *as if* the maneuver were my idea.

If obeying means listening to a voice, it becomes important whose voice that is. Children listen to their parents because they are the children's protectors, at once benevolent and big. Adults, American citizens at least, by and large obey the laws of the land either because they understand and approve of them or because they face sanctions for breaking them. In the workplace, they also take orders from their supervisors, an obedience that is highly specific and restricted in time to their shift and their task.

And then there is that self-selected minority of people who join an order, say a religious community, where they live all their lives under an all-encompassing Rule. Let me read to you from the Holy Rule of St. Benedict (sixth century C.E.), which became the model for ordering monastic life in the West. The chapter "On Obedience" begins:

> The first degree of humility is obedience without delay. This is the virtue of those . . . who, because of the holy service they have professed . . . as soon as anything has been ordered by the Superior, receive it as a divine command and cannot suffer any delay in executing it. Of these the Lord says: "As soon as he heard, he obeyed Me. . . ."
>
> Such as these, therefore immediately leaving their own affairs and forsaking their own will . . . with the ready step of obedience follow up with deeds the voice of him who commands. (Ch. 5)

The Rule calls this life of obeying commands the "narrow way," by which

> not living according to their own choice nor obeying their own desires and pleasures but walking by another's judgment and commands, they live in monasteries. . . .

But, the Rule continues,

> This very obedience will be acceptable to God and pleasing to man only if what is commanded is done without hesitation, delay, lukewarmness, grumbling, or objection.

Now let me cite for you a description of military obedience, again quoted with approval by General Wakin in his article on the ethics of leadership. It comes from Samuel Huntington's *The Soldier and the State* of 1957 (which is why only men are mentioned):

> When the military man receives the legal order from an authorized superior, he does not argue, he does not hesitate, he does not substitute his own views; he obeys instantly.

You can't miss the similarities of monastic to military obedience: the insistence on prompt, non-argumentative action upon hearing the order of a superior. In fact, the military term "order" is not unrelated to the monastic term "order," meaning a community that lives under a Rule. A military order arises under an ordered command structure and the military code; it is the specific expression of the life of an *ordered* community.

But there are three enormous differences, all interdependent, between monastic and military obedience. First, the voice the religious hears is not really that of his Superior (spelled in the Order with a capital S), for he is considered to be only the mouthpiece for the voice of God; the voice of the military officer has merely human authority. Second, the purpose of monastic life is the salvation of the soul; that of the military, making war or keeping peace. And third, the monk obeys *every* order wholeheartedly; the soldier obeys only *legal* orders.

Why is that last qualification necessary? Not only because commanding officers are merely human and therefore their orders are sometimes badly judged and sometimes immoral, but even more so because it is not so clear who the ultimate voice is that a member of the Armed Services is bound to listen to.

So complex is that problem that higher officers in the field now often have a JAG (Judge Advocate General) officer with them to advise them on the lawfulness and morality of an order they intend to give. The lower order-givers and takers, however, are on their own in the field. As the trial of Lieutenant Calley, the officer directly responsible for the My Lai massacre in Vietnam, established (c. 1971), soldiers are required to disobey not only *prima facie* illegal orders but also ambiguously phrased though manifestly inhumane orders—in this case Captain Medina's incitement to slaughter innocents (Michael Walzer, *Just and Unjust Wars*, 1977, Ch. 19). I put this difficult obligation to myself in the following way: Civilians have a moral right to civil disobedience, meaning they gain respect by breaking demonstratively a particular law which they consider morally wrong while loyally submitting to the sanction of the law in general. The criterion that the disobedience was genuinely civil is that you present yourself for arrest. Civil disobedience is, then, a civilian *right*, but it is, remarkably, a military *duty*: A soldier is obligated to disobey a morally—*not* a tactically—bad order; military morality is more demanding than civic ethics.

In my terms, that means that warriors are to listen to a hierarchy of forces: first to their commanding officer, then to the military code of justice, then to the internationally accepted law of war, and above it all to a highest voice, an overriding Superior. Who or what is that final voice?

James Madison, the statesman who had the most practical political wisdom of any I know of, wrote the following remarkable words in a public document:

> Before any man can be considered as a member of Civil Society, he must be considered as a subject of the Governor of the Universe: And if a member of Civil Society, who enters into any subordinate association must always do it with a reservation of his duty to the General Authority, much more must every man who becomes a member of any particular Civil Society, do it with a reservation of his allegiance to the Universal Sovereign. ("A Memorial and Remonstrance," 1785)

Since Madison believed fervently that our relation to the divinity is a matter of private conscience, his words mean in effect that a human being, both as a citizen and as a member of an organization within society, is ultimately responsible to his conscience, where "responsible to" means "answerable to the voice of" an ultimate Superior who is *heard in each personal soul.* Since members of the armed forces are first and last citizens, and the military services are, in Madison's terms, "subordinate associations" imbedded in the civic—that is, the political—entity, that means that private conscience is the soldier's final commander-in-chief. It means: Obey your commanding officer promptly and without argument while reserving the possibility of personal, conscientious disobedience—of course, after making, if there is time, a reasonable and respectful argument. If that isn't a paradox, a deeply serious paradox, whatever could be!

In the list of hierarchy of voices, I have left out a chief level. Until you join and after you retire, you are civilian citizens; in this republic, even while you serve in uniform, your commander-in-chief is a civilian by Article II, Section 2 of our Constitution. Your private opinion of the president of the United States might be "Throw the bastard out!" and this opinion you'll express at the polls, but in public you owe him perfect loyalty and flawless respect. You have a curious duty to a sound-minded schizophrenia—"schizophrenia" is a Greek word meaning "split-mindedness"—which is one of this country's saving graces; I mean our military's ability to live as warriors and as citizens at once. Because of it we've never had one of those devastating military coups which betoken that the military has occupied its own country.

One of the first consequences of putting the military under civilian direction is that you, as members of the Armed Service, do not make but only carry out national policy. In other words, you become the last resort and most energetic tool of execution of a policy you have not set and of which you may not approve. I'm sure you all have in mind the most spectacular reassertion of this hierarchy of responsibility in our history, when our most brilliant soldier-statesman forgot the constitutional ordering of competences and put his own willful judgment above that of his very unbrilliant but far wiser commander-in-chief—expectably with devastating military results. When President Truman was finally driven simply to sack General MacArthur, that most popular general, he felt perfectly sanguine about the people's ultimate support for his defense of the Constitution, once a little bit of histrionically induced upheaval had subsided—and he turned out to be absolutely right. Incidentally, this plain citizen had himself been an exemplary officer, much beloved by his own Battery D, who was quite willing in combat flatly to disobey a stupid order; happily his colonel, to whom he reported himself, in analogy to an act of civil disobedience, was appreciative rather than vindictive, and Captain Truman got away with it (Merle Miller, *Plain Speaking: An Oral Biography of Harry S. Truman*, 1974, 97).

General MacArthur had listened to his own political judgment rather than to the voice of the civilian authority. That way of putting it raises the next question in line. The first question was: Whom do you engage to listen to when you sub-

mit yourself to a command structure? The answer was per-
plexing: a whole hierarchy of voices. If anything in your life
needs thinking out, it's that answer.

The next question then might be: What part of you sub-
mits? It seems to me that it is your will, your free will that cur-
tails, though it can never entirely abrogate, its own nature. For
to have a will means to make choices by oneself out of oneself,
that is, autonomously. You wouldn't want me here to attempt
to solve the problem of free will, which is this: How can we
be, when all is said and done, ultimate self-starters; how can
we explain moral boot-strapping, which is the M.O. (modus
operandi) of a conscience? I am simply assuming here that it is
part of our common humanity to be each separately capable of
deciding serious issues for ourselves. And one of these human
capabilities is to put our will in the service of someone or something else: Submission can be an act of freedom. I found a neat
corroboration of this thought in the writings of Maimonides,
the Jewish scholar of the twelfth century (who was court phy-
sician to Saladin in Cairo and wrote in Arabic—those were the
days!). As you probably know, the Israelites were the most law-
bound people of the West, bound by 613 rules (mostly found in
Leviticus) and living under dire threats of punishment for disobedience. Of listening to these divine commandments Maimonides says succinctly that Jewish Law would be as nothing
if obedience were not *given freely with open eyes* (*The Eight
Chapters*, Ch. 8). In other words, true obedience, as opposed
to the compelled submission of the very young, the enslaved,
and the domesticated animals, is not only an act but a *proof*
of human freedom. For it is a mark of the freedom of our will
that it can freely choose to curtail its freedom.

But your will could not be obedient in that genuine sense if
some part of it, of you, did not stand apart, reserve judgment
and monitor your agreement, in short, if you did not submit
your will self-consciously, guardedly. So self-awareness, ever

present and occasionally articulated among yourselves, would seem to be a necessary aspect of genuine obedience. As I said before: You need to talk *to each other* about such things.

And now a final question: What are the conditions of obedience? Here is a moment to return to the analogy of the military service to a religious order, since the main condition of obedience has the same name for both: faith, whose secular form is trust. I have read parts of your own Air Force Academy's *Little Blue Book*; I think these days it is referred to as *Core Values*. (I might say, incidentally, that I have a certain quarrel with what I've read: A manual on virtue should not have the tone of a bureaucratic directive; ignoble language cannot well induce noble conduct.) In this statement, the final element listed under the first virtue of a cadet, "Integrity," is humility, which, you may recall, happens to be the first virtue of a Benedictine monk as well, the one that obedience is specifically intended to foster, the renunciation of self-will. The final virtue, listed under "Service before Self" (whose nobler name would be self-sacrifice), is "faith in the system," that is a nonreligious faith or trust which you are expected to adopt. As leaders you are to "resist the temptation to doubt 'the system'." This moral rule seems to be a call to suppress your independent judgment. Can a thinking human being do that, perhaps even in the face of a rigidly stupid, meanly wrongheaded officer (such as even the Air Force must have) and his, or her, manifest mishandling of a situation?

Yes, I think trust is possible even in that case, for this secular faith is not placed in a person but, as *Core Values* says, in "the system," more humanly stated, in the military community, the fellowship of warriors and its standing orders.

The classical Greek historian Herodotus wrote of the great invasion of tiny Greece by mighty Persia and of the antecedent events. (Without having read Herodotus—I can't help interjecting—you can't know what it means to be of the West, and particularly, to be an American, for America is the West's very West.) Herodotus tells of the Spartan king called Demaratus whom the Spartans had exiled for certain transgressions and who had become an adviser to Xerxes, the Great King of the Persians.

As you know, Sparta was the most consummately military city of ancient Greece—I don't say "militaristic," because that term denigrates a handsome, organically shaped civil society which had its own sort of good life, though, to be sure, it also had its dark underside, as do all societies.

The exiled king is trying to tell the Persian king why an invasion of Greece is inadvisable. He says of these Spartans:

> For though they are free men, they are not in every way free. Law is the master they accept, and the master they fear more than your subjects fear you. Whatever it commands they do, and its standing orders are always the same: It forbids them to flee in battle, whatever the number of their foes and requires them to stand firm and either to conquer or die. (*Persian Wars*, VII 104)

The Spartan king makes the point that Spartan obedience is not to a royal slave master but to the Law. To obey Law is to obey a universal command, and what is universal has at least some affinity to reason; it is not *ad hoc* or *ad hominem*; even the worst law speaks, if it is truly a law, with the voice of patency and equity, which are among the marks of rationality.

What Demaratus says of the Spartans holds finally for you, too. In obeying one man's or woman's particular order, you are really submitting, as I said before, to a concrete appearance of the general military order which is geared to a military mission, namely, to serve, protect, and defend your country. In foregoing the normal exercise of free will in the interests of effectiveness, you are not abandoning yourself to arbitrary impositions but are abiding within the realm of reason, within which alone individual autonomy is possible. This thought goes some way toward resolving the paradox of obedience—but that is another long story to which I won't subject you tonight.

One last word about trust. Since we have, at the moment at least, no military draft, everyone in the Service is there voluntarily, but most of all you, who competed for and proudly accepted an appointment to the Air Force Academy. Presumably you had an idea of the mission and its system—though probably not a clear enough idea. Trust is very often and quite rightly first given in partial ignorance, from a general and cursory judgment, an intuition, that our loyalty will not be misplaced. Most marriages, for example, are entered into by that kind of leap of faith. But you have four years here to become knowledgeably faithful, and then the full condition for giving your life to the Service will be fulfilled. And once again the consequence of accepting that faith, which is a condition of sound obedience, is that you have some thinking to do.

So much for my very rudimentary inquiry into the nature of obedience. Let me end by reading to you a two-line memorial inscription written by the poet Simonides and recorded by Herodotus. It was set up in the place where fell almost all of the three hundred Spartans who were sent north to hold the pass of Thermopylae against hundreds of thousands of Persian invaders. It is plausibly imaginable that had they not slowed the Persian advance by their deaths, we would be speaking some derivative of Persian today, and the center of modern civilization—if modernity could even have come about—would be in Iran. I'll first read the inscription in Greek because it is beautiful:

Ó xeín', ángélleín Lakedaímonioís' hote teíde
  Keímetha toís keínón | rhémasĭ peíthomenoí.

O stranger, announce to the Spartans that in this place
  We lie, obedient to their standing orders.

I should tell you that the word I have translated as standing orders (*rhema* = *rhetra*) refers to the unwritten laws that ordered the Spartan community, and the word that means "obedient to" also means "having faith in," "trusting"—and that says it all.

And now, to co-opt an apt phrase, fire away!

THE EMPIRES OF
THE SUN
AND THE WEST

I shall begin with two sets of facts and dates. On or about August 8 of 1519 Hernán Cortés, a hidalgo, a knight, from Medellín in the Estremadura region of Spain, having sailed his expeditionary fleet from Cuba to win "vast and wealthy lands," set out from a city he called Villa Rica de la Vera Cruz on the Gulf of Mexico to march inland, west toward the capital of Anahuac, the empire of the Nahuatl-speaking Aztecs. The city was called Tenochtitlán and its lord, the emperor, was Montezuma II. Cortés knew of the place from the emperor's coastal vassals and from delegations Montezuma had sent loaded with presents to welcome—and to forestall—the invaders. The presents included many works of well-crafted gold.

Cortés had with him some 300 Spaniards,[1] including about forty crossbowmen and twenty arquebusiers, that is, men carrying heavy matchlock rifles. He probably had three front-loading cannons. His officers wore metal armor. There were

Friday Night Lecture, Homecoming, October 4, 2002, Annapolis, MD. This lecture is dedicated to my friend and fellow tutor William Darkey, who first introduced me to the book behind this lecture, William Prescott's *History of the Conquest of Mexico*.

fifteen horses for the captains and a pack of hunting dogs. (I might mention here that the Aztec dogs were a hairless type bred for food.) The band was accompanied by Indian porters and allies, a group that grew to about 1000 as they marched inland. Early in November they passed at 13,000 feet between the two volcanoes that guard the high Valley of Mexico. Some Spanish captains astounded the Indians by venturing to climb to the crater rim of the ominously smoking Popocatépetl. On November 8, Cortés was on the causeway to Tenochtitlan. On November 14, Montezuma, the ruler of a realm of 125,000 square miles, capable of putting in the field an army of 200,000 men with a highly trained officer corps, quietly surrendered his person to the custody of Cortés, declared himself a vassal of Emperor Charles V, and transferred his administration to the palace assigned to the Spaniards. He soon made them a present of the state treasure which they had discovered behind a plastered-over door in the palace aviary. Cortés's surmise that just to enter Tenochtitlan was to take Anahuac captive seemed to be justified.

On June 30, 1520, Cortés being absent, Montezuma was either murdered by the Spaniards or stoned to death by his own people as he appeared on the palace wall attempting to contain a rebellion. The latter account seems more plausible, since he appears to have been shielded by Spaniards to whom he was a valuable pawn and since some of his nobles were growing disgusted with his submissiveness. The uprising had been induced by the young captain whom Cortés had left in charge, who had massacred unarmed celebrants of the feast of Huitzilopóchtli, the city's chief god; this god both was and stood for the Sun.

The Mexican uprising culminated in the *noche triste*, the Sad Night, when the Spaniards were driven from the city with enormous loss of life. In June 1521 the Spanish situation looked desperate to them, as a vigorous, indomitable, eighteen-year-old emperor, Cuauhtémoc, Montezuma's second successor (the first having died of smallpox, probably brought to New Spain by one of Cortés's black porters), assumed the leadership of an Aztec army now better acquainted with these once apparently invincible invaders.

On August 15, 1521, just two years after his landing, Cortés's band, augmented by some new arrivals and an allied Indian army from Tenochtitlan's old enemy, Tlaxcála, fought its way, foot by foot, back into the city, with frightful losses on both sides. The Spaniards were supported by a flotilla of forty brigantines, light square-rigged sailing vessels that Cortés had ordered built and dragged overland to Lake Texcoco, the complex shallow water on which Tenochtitlan stood.—It was the first fleet of sailing ships to float on the lake.

I am still in the realm of fact when I say that within a few days this city, surpassing all cities then on earth in the beauty of its situation and the magic of its aspect, was completely razed. Within four years it was overlaid, under Cortés's supervision, by a complete Spanish city, whose cathedral, the Cathedral of Mexico City, was eventually built hard by the Great Temple of Tenochtitlan. In this total catastrophe the Spaniards had lost fewer than 100 men, the Aztecs or México about 100,000.

I have, of course, omitted myriads of gripping details, such as a novelist might hesitate to invent. But I shall now abbreviate an abbreviation: In August 1519 there was a large, powerful, highly civilized empire called Anahuac. By August 1521 it was gone; instead there was a new realm, a colony called New Spain; Spanish was replacing the native Nahuatl.

Now the second set of facts, even more curtailed. On May 13, 1532, Francisco Pizarro (like Cortés from the Estremadura and his distant relation) arrived at Tumbez, a port at the northern end of the Inca empire and of modern Peru. This empire was called by its people Tahuantinsúyu, meaning the Realm of the Four Quarters. Pizarro had 130 troopers, 40 cavalry and one small cannon. The Inca Atahualpa—Inca means Lord—had an army of 50,000 men. On November 16, 1533, the Inca came, at Pizarro's invitation, to meet him in the town plaza of Cajamara. There he was unintelligibly harangued by the chaplain of the expedition and given a breviary: the Inca scornfully threw the scribbles to the ground. Within 33 minutes, he having been seized, 4000 of his men had been massacred. Resistance and the empire itself fell apart with his capture. Atahualpa offered to fill his prison, a cell 22 × 10 feet, with gold to the height of his reach in exchange for his freedom. While the temples which were encrusted with gold were being denuded and the condition was being fulfilled, the Inca was condemned to death by burning. This sentence was commuted to strangulation when he agreed to be baptized. Pizarro soon took Cuzco, the capital, and installed a puppet Inca, Mánco Cápac, who mounted a rebellion; it was put down with great loss of life on the Inca's side in 1534. There followed a period of civil war among the conquerors. Again to summarize the summary: A tiny band of Spanish ruffians brought down, within two years, the most efficiently administered polity of its time. Quechua, the native language, was replaced by Spanish as the chief language.

It is thought that this second scenario was, on Pizarro's part, a reprise of Cortés's conquest. If so, it is a demonstration of the inferiority of imitations.

The kind of facts I have listed here are spectacular yet uncontested discontinuities in the stream of life. The dates, which tell us both the temporal order of these facts and their distance from us, serve to dramatize the discontinuity: About half a millennium ago there occurred, not very far south of us and close to each other in space and time, two mind-boggling events—the destruction by a very few Spaniards of two great civilizations.

We at this college have read or will read in Herodotus's *Persian Wars* how in July of 480 B.C. a band of 299 Spartans, the same in number as Cortés's original companions, died in holding the pass of Thermopylae against an Asian army of who knows how many hundreds of thousands, led by Xerxes, king of Persia. Their object was to give the Greeks time and courage to repel the invader. But the Spartans were defending their own land from a self-debilitating behemoth. The Spaniards' situation in Mesoamerica is just the inverse, except that in each case the few were the free. What, we may wonder, would our world be like if the Asians had prevailed in 480 B.C. or the Nahua in 1519 A.D.?

How could it happen? How did these American empires fall? Just as Herodotus drew conclusions about the nature of the Greeks from the Persian defeat, so one might wonder if illumination about the nature of our West might not be found in these catastrophes that mark the beginning of modern life. To put it straightforwardly: In reading about Mexico and Peru I began to wonder if there might be a clue in these events to the apparently irresistible potency of the West when *it* touches, be it insidiously or catastrophically, other worlds, be *they* receptive or resistant.

Let me explain the not altogether appropriate use of the term "the West" in my title, "The Empires of the Sun and the West." Our tradition—I mean the one whose works we study at this college—is usually called the "Western" tradition. It is thereby revealed as defining itself against the East, Near and Far, the Orient, the place where the sun rises. Our North American republic is in this sense the West's very West and its currently culminating expression. But, of course, the Aztecs— let me interrupt myself to say that the people of the imperial city of México-Tenochtitlan did not call themselves Aztecs but México and that they called those who spoke their language the Nahua and that the term Aztec was introduced to the English-speaking world by the aforementioned Prescott—these Mexica, then, of course thought of the invaders as being *from* the quarter of the rising sun, from the east. This turns out to be a significant fact. Columbus thought that he was "sailing not the usual way" but west—sailing west to reach the East,

Japan, China, India. It was for quite a while a very unwelcome discovery that the people whom the adventurers so hopefully called "Indians" (as I will continue to do here) inhabited a long continent which, although it contracted into a narrow isthmus in the middle, blocked the ocean route to the fabulous Orient. Thus Prescott calls Tenochtitlan "the great capital of the western world." So "West" is, strictly speaking, nonsense as used in this context, but I cling to it because it is the available shorthand for ourselves, for those living in the tradition that has its roots in Jerusalem and Athens, achieves its modernity in Europe, has come to its current culmination on this continent, and is spreading its effects all over the globe. What can be more necessary at this moment than to grapple with the being of this West?

As I read on it seemed to me often that the reasons given by historians for Anahuac's sudden collapse before the Spaniards might well be cumulatively necessary but could not be sufficient conditions. I mean that without their operation the Empires could not have fallen so quickly, but that altogether they did not so completely account for the fall as to make it seem unavoidable. It is true that the Spaniards brought horses into a land without draft animals, and so the cavaliers could run down the pedestrian Aztec warriors and frighten the Indians into seeing the Europeans as centaurs, four-footed monstrous men-horses. But these Indians soon learned that man and horse were separable and mortal; during their desperate and bloody defense of Tenochtitlan there appeared on the skull rack of a local temple, beneath 53 heads of Spaniards, the heads of a number of horses, of "Spanish deer," as they were now called. The crossbows and cannons may have delivered more swift and terrifying destruction than the Aztec javelin-throwers, the metal armor deflected the cuts of obsidian-studded wooden swords; the driving greed for that gold, which, as Cortés ironically represented to an Indian official, was the specific remedy for a disease that troubled the Spaniards, may have disoriented the people; the physical disease brought by the Spaniards, the smallpox, did more than decimate the uninoculated natives; Spanish luck at crucial junctures may have demoralized the caciques, the Indian chieftains; the harsh exactions and suppression of Montezuma's empire did indeed provide Cortés with Indian allies (though the 150,000 Indians that came with the now 900 Spaniards to retake Tenochtitlan were by their very numbers an encumbrance on the heavily defended causeways into the island city and by their excited hatred for their Mexica oppressors a danger to Cortés's prudent intentions); the crucifix may well, in Carlos Fuentes's words, "have made their minds collapse," as they saw how their own numerous gods demanded numerous sacrifices of *them*, while this one Christian god sacrificed one man, *himself*. Such factors or forces are called, in the categories in which history is conceptualized, technological, demographic, epidemiological, political, psychological, or what have you. Perhaps they were necessary to Spanish success. But a number of contemporaries thought that at various junctures it might well have gone otherwise. For example, the strong-minded king of Texcoco, Cacáma, said that all the Spaniards within Tenochtitlan could be killed in an hour; Cortés himself thought so. To me historical inevitability seems an *ex post facto* cause. It is the way a *fait accompli* presents itself, when passage has turned into past. I cannot quite tell whether my rejection of historical determinism should be reinforced or thrown into doubt by the fact that the Mexica themselves had given themselves over to fate, as I will tell. Perhaps that very self-surrender *was* a sufficient *condition*, the factor that makes the outcome practically certain. But that would only be half the *explanation*; for the other half one would have to look in the nature of the Europeans as well.

Before doing that, let me complete the apology for my title. In it I mention the two empires, though I will speak of one only, Anahuac. I mean no reflection on the Inca realm, that marvel of social administration and public works built with the most astounding masonry I've ever seen. But both of the Peruvian protagonists were like deteriorated copies of their Aztec templates. Pizarro was an intrepid thug, by all accounts, and Atahualpa a culpably and carelessly arrogant man with a violent history. Since it seemed to me that the pairs of chief actors in this drama not only were the main factors because both empires were autocracies, but were also in their very distinctive ways personally emblematic of their worlds, I chose the more humanly accessible, the more expressive duo, Montezuma and Cortés.

Finally, I refer to the Sun because the solar domination under which both these Precolumbian empires labored seemed to me more and more significant. The Incas called themselves the Children of the Sun; their great Sun Temple at Cuzco, the Coricáncha, was studded with gold, "the tears wept by the sun." So too the Mexica, who called their generals "the Lords of the Sun," had come into the marshes of Lake Texcoco, their place of destiny, led by priests who bore on their backs a twittering medicine bundle. It was Huitzilopochtli, who was reborn as a sun on the way at Teotihuacán, the birthplace of the gods, and later installed in Tenochtitlan in the Great Temple. There he was incessantly nourished with human blood. Of course, when I use the indicative mood in speaking of the Aztec gods, I am not reporting fact—I am telling what the Aztecs said and are thought to have believed. The most difficult thing, I have discovered, is for historians to find the right voice in speaking of alien gods, especially when they are many in number, fluid in function, and visible in many forms.

It is the Indians' relation to the sun that I have come to think of as symbolic of the whole debacle and even as its proximate cause. To anticipate my version of a common idea: The daily, annual and epochal returns of the heavenly body were to the Aztecs so fearsomely antic, so uncertain, that they burdened themselves, as their traditions taught them, with rituals and sacrifices. These were so demanding that they enfeebled both the Nahua empire and the Nahua's souls. The West's relation to the Sun was just the opposite.

In 1506, just about the time young Cortés came to the Indies, Copernicus was beginning to write *On the Revolutions of the Heavenly Spheres*. It is one of Western modernity's seminal works, which our sophomores study. In it he shows that the mathematical rationalization of the heavens is more economically accomplished and the celestial phenomena are better "saved" if the sun stands stably at the center of the world. But his motive is not only mathematical economy. "For who," he says, "would place this lamp of a very beautiful temple in another place than this, wherefrom it can illuminate everything at the same time?" Cortés was surely not a premature Copernican, but he acted out of a tradition in which one God controls the cosmos through the laws of nature. Since the deity is not capricious, celestial nature is ever-reliable, well-illuminated and confidence-inspiring. Nature's sun does not, in any case, respond to human propitiation and Nature's god prefers prayers to ritual sacrifices.

Let me append here a poignant incident told by Cortés. In the final days of the investment of Tenochtitlan, a delegation of parched and starving Mexica came to the barricades. They said that they held Cortés to be a child of the Sun, who could perform a circuit of the earth in a day and a night. Why would he not slay them in that time to end their suffering?

Let me hold off yet one more minute from my main task to tell you what motives drew me into a study so far from our Program. To begin with, there was the sheer enchantment of what proved to be a fragile civilization and the unburdened romance of comfortably un-current drama. All that romance I got from reading William Hickling Prescott's *Conquest of Mexico* of 1843, and his *Conquest of Peru* of 1847. Of the first book he himself wrote that it was conceived "not as a philosophical theme but as *an epic in prose*, a romance of chivalry." For this approach later historians, for whom demythification, deromanticization, and the dispersal of human deeds into forces and patterns is a professional requirement, despise him somewhat, and it took me a while to see what valuable lesson could be drawn from his telling. Prescott has it right; first the great tale, then the critical theory.

From the first I knew that I was reading the American Gibbon. We at St. John's used to read parts, particularly the notorious fifteenth chapter, of that English historian's monumental *Decline and Fall of the Roman Empire*, completed in 1788. To my taste the American is the finer of the two. Gibbon conceals in the magnificantly Latinate periods of his style the universal irony of the ultimately enlightened man. I do not fault him for sitting in judgment, for a non-judgmental historian is an incarnate contradiction and produces only an armature of facts without the musculature that gives it human shape. But I am put off by his judging as an Olympian enthroned on Olympus. In that fifteenth chapter, which treats the question "by what means the Christian faith obtained so remarkable a victory over the established religions of this earth?" (a question of the kind I am asking) he reflects with raised eyebrows in turn on the mortification of the flesh, pious chastity and divine providence, so as to come to a pretty secular answer, just as if Christianity were not first and last a faith. Surely when a faith conquers, its substance must be given some credit.

Prescott, on the other hand, who had in his youth privately critiqued Gibbon's style for its "tumid grandeur," writes with deliberate American plainness, though to this twenty-first-century ear, with a dignified elegance. What matters more to me is that he does his level best to enter into the feelings and thoughts of his alien world, finding much to admire in the Aztecs and much to blame in the Spaniards; for example he calls the massacre of the Indians in fateful Cholula a "dark stain" on Cortés's record. But for all his romantic pleasure in new marvels he never condescends to accept the horrifying elements of

Aztec civilization. He recognizes that these are not individual crimes but systemic evils that his Western liberal conscience cannot condone. One might say that he dignifies his subjects with his condemnation. For this candor he is, as you can imagine, belittled these days as naïve, culture-bound, and ethnocentric. I shall have a word to say on the sophisticated reverse bigotry of his belittlers.

His style, to add one more feature, is extraordinarily vivid; it compares to Gibbon's as a classical statue in all its original bright encaustic colors to one that has been dug up, now only bare white marble. This visual aliveness may be a "blind Homer" effect. When Prescott was a young student dining at the Harvard Commons, he was hit in the eye by a hard piece of bread during a food fight and was half-blind for the rest of his life. It is characteristic of this man that, although he knew whose missile had hit him, he never told the name. His enormous collection of sources was read to him and evidently richly illustrated in his imagination.

I might mention the other chief sources I read. (A longer bibliography, merging books read and those merely consulted, is attached.)

First for anyone interested in the actual course of the Conquest is Bernal Díaz del Castillo's *True History of New Spain* of 1555. This simply told, incident-rich account of the march on Tenochtitlan and what happened afterwards gains credence from the fact that the old trooper was disgruntled with his captain's assignment of rewards—the common condition of the Conquistador ranks; the poor devils got little for their endless exertions and wounds. In spite of his grievances, Díaz's love and admiration for Cortés unsuppressably dominates his story.

The Conquistadores are sometimes represented as having had eyes for nothing not made of gold. Here is the old soldier's recall of Tenochtitlan as he first glimpsed it, thirty-six years before, on a causeway leading toward the island city:

We were amazed and said that it was like the enchantments they tell of Amadis, on account of the great towers and *cues* (temples) rising from the water, and all built of masonry. And some of our soldiers even asked whether the things we saw were not a dream. It is not to be wondered that I here write it down in this manner, for there is so much to think over that I do not know how to describe it, seeing things, as we did, that have never been heard of or seen or even dreamed.

These men, some of them ruffians, but with medieval romances behind their eyes to help them see alien beauty, were evidently not altogether sick with gold greed. But those later writers who don't blame them for the one, accuse them of the other: they're either merely medieval knight-errants or merely mercantile expeditionaries. In fact, they seem to have been poignantly aware that they were seeing sights no European had ever seen before or could ever see after.

Here is what they saw: A city edged by flowering "floating gardens," the mud-anchored *chinampas*, lying on the shining flat waters of a shallow, irregular lake collected in a high valley guarded by the snowy peaks—even in August—of the two volcanoes; straight broad causeways connecting the city to the shore giving into straight broad avenues leading from the four directions of the winds to its sacred center, the center of the world, with its great, gleaming, colorfully decorated temple pyramid; a grid of smaller streets edged with bridged canals; a myriad of lesser temple pyramids, some smoking with sacrifices; palaces with stuccoed walls and patios polished to gleam like silver; sparkling pools; crowds of clean, orderly people going about their business, especially in the great market of Tlatelolco; gardens everywhere; and the white houses of the city's quarter million inhabitants with their flat roofs, the *azoteas* from which two years hence such a deadly shower of missiles would rain down on the returning Spaniards that the dwellings were demolished one by one.—All these features of the vision have been, incidentally, described with a poet's relish by William Carlos Williams:

> [T]he city spread its dark life upon the earth of a new world, sensitive to its richest beauty, but so completely removed from those foreign contacts that harden and protect, that at the very breath of conquest it vanished.

The mutual admiration of Indians and Spaniards was great—in the beginning. True, the Spaniards, whom Cortés's vigilance kept sleeping in their armor, stank in the nostrils of the much-bathing Indians, and the priests with their long, blood-matted hair in their gore-bespattered sanctuaries nauseated the Spaniards. (I omit here, for the moment, the Spaniards' response to the sacrifices themselves, which marked, on the Christians' side, the beginning of the end of amity.) The Spaniards were astonished by Indian craftsmanship. Díaz describes after decades a necklace made of golden crabs (others say crayfish) that Montezuma placed around Cortés's neck. Of course, Díaz described the golden gifts more often in terms of the pesos they weighed when melted down into bullion. I note here that the Aztecs did not, evidently, have scales and did not reduce objects to their universal stuff, ponderable mass (thus the Mexicans used natural items, quils of gold dust and cocoa beans, for currency, while the Spanish had the *peso d'oro*, the "gold weight," calibrated in fact to silver, to 42.29 grams of the pure substance); this intellectual device of universal quantification even those critics of the West who deplore it can hardly forego in the business of life. The Spaniards were astounded by, and perhaps a little envious of, the stately splendor of the cacique's accoutrements. The Indians, on their part, were amazed by the invaders' daring, tenacity, and endurance. They called them, as the Spanish heard it, *teules*, *téotl* being the Nahuatl word for god. The term seems to have been used somewhat as Homer uses *dios*, indicating sometimes just excellence and sometimes divinity. As we shall see, the Aztecs had a serious reason to call Cortés and his people gods. The Spanish, on their side, in their very horror of the frightful-looking Aztec god-images, paid them a certain respect in regarding them not as mere idols, deaf and dumb objects of stupid worship, but much as the Mexica themselves did: Sahagún, of whom I will shortly tell, records an Aztec ruler's admonitory speech in which he says: "For our lord seeth, heareth within wood, within stone." The god-representations were not masks of nothing to the Christians, but they were images of demons, of the Devil in various shapes. Thus in looking at the Nahuatl side in Sahagun's dual language text, I noticed that *diablo*, Devil, had become a Spanish loan word in Nahuatl— *one* new name for all the old divinities, to be abominated but also acknowledged.

The second eyewitness source is Cortés himself, who wrote to his sovereign, Charles V, five letters reporting on his activities. Of these *cartas de relación*, letters of report, all but one are extant in copies. They are not notes but voluminous, detailed accounts beginning with the first, pre-Cortés exploration of the Gulf Coast and ending with Cortés's own post-Conquest explorations; the second and third letter contain the material for this lecture. The English version conveys a flavor of studiedly plain elegance. These clearly literary works are charged by historians with being both subtly self-aggrandizing and consciously myth-making. To me it would seem strange if Cortés, in writing to his sovereign, on whom depended acknowledgements and rewards, did not portray his exertions most favorably. It might be said—I don't know whether in mitigation or exacerbation—that he was also willing to suppress a brave but irrepressible compañero's guilt: Nowhere have I found even a mention of Alvarado's culpability in the events leading to the *noche triste*. It is also said that Cortés invented the myth of an Aztec empire which rivaled Charles's own, to whet the Spanish emperor's interest in his new dominion. To me, the account itself, telling of tributes owed by the subject cities and of their chiefs obliged to be in attendance in Tenochtitlan, sounds more like information he was in fact given by proud Mexica officials or disaffected dependents.

Above all, Cortés fills his letters with myriads of meticulously noted detail—too thick and too vivid to be attributed to mere mendacious fantasizing. He would have had to have been a veritable Gabriel García Márquez to invent so magical a reality. For, he says, "we saw things so remarkable as not to be believed. We who saw them with our own eyes could not grasp them with our understanding." Cortés himself will appear in a moment.

The third source, the most exhaustive in scope and remarkable in method, is *The History of the Things of New Spain* by the before-mentioned Friar Bernadino de Sahagun. He had arrived as the forty-third of the religious that Cortés had requested in one of his letters to the emperor. The Conquistador needed them to carry on the task of conversion, because, as he said, the Indians had a great natural attraction to Christianity; indeed in the early post-Conquest years, Indians were baptized by the thousands a day. (The reasons that Cortés's observation is not implausible will be mentioned below.)

The name *New Spain* in Sahagun's title is, incidentally, Cortés's own for conquered Anahuac: "New Spain of the Ocean Sea." For the Conquistador it betokens a great colonial accession to old peninsular Spain and the emphasis is on "Spain." But later the accent shifts to "New," as the *criollos*, the Mexican-born Spaniards, rebel against the old country's domination. Eventually a nativist revival and a growing sense of nationhood leads to a rejection by the native-born Spaniards themselves of their Conquistador heritage, and when in 1821 the country achieves independence, it will be called by the old Nahua name for Tenochtitlan, *México* (now pronounced in the Spanish way, *Mehico*). Nativist Mexico's tutelary deity will be Quetzalcóatl, the dominating god of this lecture, of whom more in a moment.

Back to Sahagun. He learned Nahuatl himself and spent the rest of his life, with much untoward clerical interference, compiling the world's first inside ethnographic account. In his college he trained his own informants, Indian boys, often of noble descent, who could interview their living elders and obtain the information that Sahagun compiled in parallel columns, Spanish and Nahuatl. The work, in twelve volumes, is known as the *Florentine Corpus*. Lisa Richmond, our librarian, fulfilled my unexpectant hopes by buying the very expensive English edition for our library, and if one reader a decade finds the delight and illumination in it that I did, the investment will be well justified.

Sahagun begins with the gods and their births—for like Greek gods, these gods were born, at Teotihuacan, 33 miles northeast of Tenochtitlan. This sacred city was well over a millennium old when Anahuac was established, and in ruins. But there the Mexica came to worship, particularly at the great temple pyramid dedicated to Quetzalcoatl. What bound new Anahuac to old Teotihuacan—the name means City of the Gods—was their common era, that of the Fifth Sun, upon whose destruction the world would end.

Sahagun then records everything from the sacred rituals and binding omens to the set moral speeches (much more charming without failing to be scary than similar speeches made by our elders) down to the riddles people asked, such as "What drags its entrails through a gorge?" Answer: "A needle." The next to last book is an inventory of the "Earthly Things" of New Spain, its flora, fauna and minerals; the chapter on herbs begins with the plants "that perturb one, madden one," the hallucinogens. The twelfth book is Sahagun's own history of the Conquest.

Some say that the first bishop of New Spain, Zumárraga, conducted a huge *auto-da-fe*, a book burning of Aztec codices, those screenfold books composed in glyphs (stylized figures with fixed meanings) combined with lively pictures. Others say that those codices that weren't destroyed by the hostile Tlaxcalans or in the great conflagration of Tenochtitlan were spirited away by Indians. In any case, the art of illustration was still alive, and Sahagun used the talents of Indian painters to supplement his records in this visually delightful pre-alphabetic way.

Finally I want to mention the *History of the Indians of New Spain* by another Franciscan, affectionately named by his Indian parishioners *Motolinía*, Nahuatl for "Little Poor One," since he took his vow of poverty seriously. He reports the terrible post-Conquest sufferings undergone by the Indian population; worse than their cruel exploitation by the disappointed Conquistadores and colonists was the succession of European plagues (smallpox, bubonic plague, measles, for which the Indians reciprocated only with syphilis). I am impressed, over and over, with this pattern: that the inoculated West does most of its harm to other civilizations unintentionally, and I mean not only through their physical susceptibility but even more, through their spiritual and intellectual vulnerability. The reason we can cope with our dangerously developed, potent tradition is that we know how to fight back, how to subject our powers to constraining criticism and how to correct our aberrations by returns to sounder beginnings. *Critique* and *Renaissance* are the continual evidence of our self-inoculation, and we see right now the dangerous consequences of the Western invasion of souls not so protected.

But Motolinía also reports successes, not only in conversions, which were too stupendous in number and abrupt in spiritual terms to be always quite real. What is lovely to read about is not only his affection for the gentleness and dignified reticence of his boys but their quick intelligence and general talentedness; some learned enough Latin in a few years to correct the grammar—a tense but triumphant moment for their teacher—of a visiting dignitary. They sang liturgies like angels and easily learned to play European instruments. No wonder Mexico City was to become, in the eighteenth century, this hemisphere's greatest center of baroque music; its chief composer, Manuel de Zumaya, Chapel Master at the very Cathedral of Mexico City which replaced Huitzilopochtli's temple, was part-Indian.

I should also mention two more works written with great sympathy for the Indians: Bishop las Casas's *Short Account of the Destruction of the Indies* of 1542, a book of passionate accusation against the Spanish conquerors and colonists, and Cabesa de Vaca's *Relación*, the story of the tribulations of a discoverer of Florida, who was himself for a while enslaved by Indians.

By our contemporary historians the Aztecs are treated in almost comically opposite ways. Jacques Soustelle paints their daily life as an idyll of gentle, flower-loving, orderly culture, made poignant on occasion by the necessities of the ritual care and feeding of the gods. It is the myth of harmony and happiness the Mexica themselves encouraged in the revisionist accounts that succeeded the "book burning" by Itzcóatl, their first emperor. Inga Clendinnen, on the other hand, depicts a somberly severe, fear-ridden, God-encumbered society, whose sacrificial rituals, coruscating with whirling sights and penetrating musical noise, were, she says, "infused with the transcendent reality of the aesthetic." Hugh Thomas, the most recent grand historian of the Conquest, a sensible and thorough marshaller of thousands of facts, speaks similarly of "the astounding, often splendid, and sometimes beautiful barbarities" of Aztec ritual practice.

What astounds me is not the antithetical views of Aztec life, for these polarities seem to have been of the Aztec essence. What takes me aback is that my contemporaries seem to wish to appear as knowing what is beautiful but not what is wrong. There are of course exceptions, writers who feel insuperable moral unease over these alien customs they are by their professional bias bound to honor. The imaginary experiment that I, as an outsider and amateur, have devised for myself to put the profession in general to the test is this: When the Spaniards first came on the remains of ritual killings—later they saw the rituals themselves and eventually found the body parts of their own comrades—they broke into the holding pens where prisoners were being fattened and stormed the temples. Would the professors have done the same or would they have regarded the practice as protected by the mantra of "otherness"? I am assuming here that they do disapprove of human sacrifice in their own culture. For my part, I cannot tell what I would have had the courage to do, but I would have been forever ashamed if I had not shared in the revulsion, the reversal of an original appreciation that, for all their rapaciousness, the Christians had for the Indians—and I might add, for certain remarkable Indian women.

I have thus evolved for myself two categories of historians: non-condoners and condoners. The older writers tend to be non-condoners; they are not careful to cloak themselves in moral opacity; what they abhor at home they will not condone abroad, be it ever so indigenous and ever so splendid. One remarkable exception is the before-mentioned Bartolomé de Las Casas, who lays out the case for human sacrifice as being both natural—since men offer their god what they hold most excellent, their own kind—and also as being within our tradition—since Abraham was ready to sacrifice his son Isaac at God's bidding, and God himself sacrificed *his* son. The difficulty with this latter argument would seem to be that Abraham's sacrifice was called off, and God's sacrifice was unique, while Indian sacrifices were multitudinous.

Las Casas is the preceptor of Tzvetan Todorov, a European intellectual who, in his book *Conquest*, tries hard to come to grips with "the Other," with the Aztec non-West. He finally elevates the Other over his own: The Aztecs made sacrifices, the Spaniards committed massacres. And here the rational difficulty is that Aztec religion commanded these deaths and Christian religion forbade them, so that Todorov is comparing customs with crimes, an evil tradition with unsanctioned wrong-doing.

This enterprise of restricting universal morality in the interests of empathy with otherness puzzles me a lot. For if we are really and radically each other's Other, then those who leave their own side to enter into the Other will thereby also lose their footing as open-eyed contemplators. In any case, it seems to me that the non-condoning Prescott's grand narrative has done more for the memory of this bygone civilization than have the condoning contemporaries. For he induces what Virgil calls *lacrimae rerum*, tears for lost things—while they invite, in me at least, contrariness, resistance to their sanctimonious self-denial.

You can see that as I read on I developed an interest in historiography, the reflective study of historical accounting itself. For it seems to me of great current importance to consider a propensity of Western intellectuals, particularly pronounced in the social studies and expressive of a strength and its complementary weaknesses native to this tradition: knowledgeable self-criticism flipping into unthinking self-abasement before the non-West. I say this mindful of the moral quandary of pitting the humanly unacceptable, but, so to speak, innocent evils, the traditional practices of a whole civilization, against the crimes of individuals transgressing the laws of their own, crimes magnified by its superior power.

And now a final motive for this, my aberrant interest: We here on the Annapolis campus are only 200 miles further from Mexico City than from our other half in New Mexico; Incan Cuzco is nearly on our longitude of 76° W. Yet these pre-Columbian empires are hardly ever in our common consciousness, even less now than in the decades after Prescott's very popular book appeared. True, some of the skyscrapers of the

twenties and thirties intentionally recalled Mesoamerican pyramids. True, the Nahuatl words *chocolátl* and *tamálli* are in
our daily vocabulary, as is Nahua cooking, that is, Mexican
food, in our diets. The Aztecs had in fact a high cuisine; the
description of the emperor's daily service with its hundreds
of dishes—among which (lest we be tempted too much) there
may have been, as Díaz reports, the meat of little children,
boiled boy to put it bluntly—is staggering in its variety; indeed
there cannot ever have been a potentate more luxuriously or
elaborately served. Of all this we've adopted, through modern
Mexico, the low end, but where else do the Empires of the Sun
figure in our lives? This surprised sense of their missing influence made me engage in another one of those imagination-
experiments by which we see the world anew: What if, as King
Cacáma of Texcoco and some later historians thought possible, the Mexica had just killed Cortés and his band, so that the
Westernization of Anahuac had been held off for some centuries?—for it is not within my imagination that the West was
forever to be resisted. Suppose the unwitting extermination of
the Indians by disease had thus been prevented. (I might say
here that this huge demographic disaster, possibly among the
worst in history, is numerically unfixed. Some say Anahuac had
thirty million, some say it had four before Cortés. Some say by
the mid-fifteenth century this population had been reduced to
2.6 or 1.2 million, to be fully restored only much later.) Suppose, then, that the ravaged generation of the Conquest and
post-Conquest era had instead been preserved, and Nahua civilization with it. Suppose eventually North American jeans
and technology had drifted down and Aztec gorgeousness and
craftsmanship up the latitudes.—I might inject here that the
Peruvian novelist Mario Vargas Llosa, who has grappled seriously with such dreams, comes to the sad but realistic conclusion that the loss of native culture is worth the benefit to
ordinary people that these Northern imports bring.—Suppose moreover that our American English had absorbed some

of the suavely dignified classical Nahuatl, its urbane address, its poetic rephrasings, its expressive word-agglutinations; suppose as well that the speech of the Nahua had accepted some of our flamboyant informality. Suppose our clothing had been restyled by Aztec orchidaciousness and our manners had been a little improved by Aztec ceremoniousness. Suppose our political discourse had been informed by a neighboring monarchy against which we had never had to rebel. We can learn in our imagination whether such fine acquisitions could have come into our way of life without losing their hieratic heart. Would not one of the parties in this cultural exchange eventually turn out to contribute the core and the other the decoration? My provisional answer is that the West would assert itself as the substructure and the Empire of the Sun would become part of its recreation—they would be the pilgrims and we the tourists.

The Mexican writer Carlos Fuentes tells of a similar imagined reversal of history in the semi-historical story "The Two Shores." Here Aguilar, Cortés's first interpreter who had long lived with the Maya, speaks from the grave. He tells how even while in Cortés's employ he held with the Indians and, by always translating not what Cortés said but what he thought, caused trouble. He confesses that he was jealous of Malinche, the Nahuatl- and Mayan-speaking woman, whose Mayan Aguilar translated into Spanish. She soon became Cortés's mistress and learned Spanish; she was one of the central figures of the conquest, present and mediating on every great occasion; Aguilar was made redundant. But revenge is not his final passion. It is rather a plan to mount with his Mayans a reverse conquest, a successful invasion of Spain, and there to recall the defeated Moors and the expelled Jews, to inaugurate a darker-skinned, better-melded Europe, "a universe simultaneously new and recovered, permeable, complex, fertile," where "Sweet Mayan songs joined those of the Provencal troubadours. . . ." But Aguilar, as he dreams his impossible dream, is dead of the bubonic plague that did not attack only Indians.

So these imagination-experiments endorse the question raised by the facts with which I began: How can we understand what happened here, on this American continent, between 1519 and 1534? Can we compel the fortunes of war and the forces of history to show their human motive power?

To get at some sort of answer, I shall take up the four factors in the conquest of Mexico that seem to me most revealing: One is a god, Quetzalcoatl; one is a practice, human sacrifice; two are men, Montezuma and Cortés.

Quetzalcoatl, the most appealing of the Mesoamerican gods, is also most deeply implicated in the Mexican debacle. This is a complex figure, a god of human interiority and of the works of civilization, a searcher into the depth of hell and the guardian of terrestrial idylls, a priest king of Tula and the *deus absconditus* of Anahuac, an Indian Prometheus.

He was not the tribal god of the Mexica, having been in the country long before they arrived. Their god was Huitzilopochtli, the god of war and of the sun, or rather the Sun itself, who shared the great temple pyramid of Mexico-Tenochtitlan, the scene of so much of the drama in this tale, with Tlaloc, the god of rain; the god who floods the heavens is partner to the god who drenches the earth. When the Mexica were still Chichimeca (as the Nahua called the wandering semi-savages of the north), coming down from their mythical city of origin Aztlan (whence the name Aztec) in search of their appointed home, their priests carried on their backs, as I mentioned before, a twittering medicine bundle. This was Huitzilopochtli, reborn at Teotihuacan, the birthplace of the gods, as the Fifth Sun. His name means "Hummingbird On the Left" or "On the South," perhaps because he and his people went southwest to find their marshland home on Lake Texcoco, perhaps because the god-figure was half-bird, having a thin, feathered left leg. In effect their god was crippled. Cripples, dwarves, hunchbacks, albinos play a great role in Nahua history, partly because the valley people had an inexhaustible interest in the sports and varieties of nature: Montezuma's palace complex included besides an aviary, a zoo, an arboretum, a gallery of anomalous humans; but there may be something deeper to it, some sense of awe before the exceptional—I don't know.

The war god was a hummingbird because Aztec warriors who died in battle went not to the murky Hades of Mictlán but to a sunny Elysium where they flitted about feeding on flowery nectar—perfect examples of a dominant Aztec characteristic, the abrupt juxtaposing of or transiting from the brutal to the delicate.

Most of the Aztec gods seem to have had frightful aspects. There is a statue of Huitzilopochtli's mother Coatlicúe, a chunky monster with a necklace of human parts and a head like an oblong package made up from two compressed snakes springing from her neck. The tribal god himself must have looked inhumanly terrifying. Not so Quetzalcoatl. The Aztecs were very sensitive to human beauty—the ugliness of the gods is clearly deliberate—and this god was represented as beautiful, though in a way which, although not unique to him, is yet most remarkable.

Quetzalcoatl's name combines the word *quétzal*, a Mesoamerican bird that has precious green tailfeathers (the green of quetzal feathers and of jade was the color of the Mexica nobility), with *coatl*, meaning snake. So he is the bird-snake, or the Plumed Serpent, belonging both to the sky and the earth. And thus he is shown in some sculptures, with coils whose scales are lengthened into feathers neatly piled into a spiral. The fanged jaws are wide open and frame a handsome, spare young male face, with high-bridged nose, well-shaped eyes, thin-lipped mouth—the face, I imagine, of a young Aztec noble.

Is this face that of the god within a serpentine integument, or is the creature as a whole the god, or is it the god's priest in his ritual costume? It is not clear that it is even a permissible question. The Aztecs appear to have had the most flexible notions of their divinities. The gods amalgamate competences, share names, identify with their victims, and merge with their priests. As far as I can tell, this mode is neither confusion nor indeterminacy. It is rather a kind of conceptual fluidity which does become fixed in the very precisely promulgated rituals. The graphic art of the Aztecs expresses this multifarious melding by its complexly intertwined figures with their attributes all drawn indistinguishably on one plane and discriminable only to an expert in Aztec divinity.

But of Quetzalcoatl we know that he was indeed both god and man. As man he was then Lord of Tula, and as the Toltec lord he became fateful to the Mexica.

To me the most appealing characteristic of these newcomers, these recent Chichimeca, was their longing deference to a city of the past, Tula, a city forty miles north of their lake and overthrown more than 300 years before Montezuma's day. Tula was to Tenochtitlan what Athens has been to Europe and still is to us in Maryland and New Mexico: the source of wisdom, art, and ideals of life. The Toltecs were to the Mexica like gods, walking swiftly everywhere on blue sandals, wrapped in flowery fragrance. For them corn sprouted in enormous ears, precious cocoa beans—one of the Mexican currencies—were found in plenty, and cotton grew already dyed in rich colors. They made works of art so exemplary that the Aztecs gave their own craftsmen the generic name of *toltéca*, Tulans.

Over this earthly idyll Quetzalcoatl Topíltzin, Our Dear Lord Quetzalcoatl, ruled as priest and king, godlike but also all too human. I cannot tell you what then happened in all its tragicomic detail. But in brief, Huitzilopochtli and other gods arrived in the guise of mischief-making wizards. Never mind the disparity in dates. This is the story of a newer god of war undoing an older god of civilization, and, I suspect, the story of how Huitzilopochtli's people betrayed their assumed Toltec heritage. These wizards assaulted the Toltec lord, who had grown in some way neglectful, with portents and temptations. They tempted him with pulque, the wine made from the maguey cactus, the American aloe, whose consumption was fiercely regulated in Tenochtitlan. They raised indecent passions in princesses and induced civil wars that Quetzalcoatl had to win with his army of dwarves and cripples. They caused the Tolteca to sing and dance themselves to death. To these temptations the lord of Tula succumbed as a participant. Finally, however, they tried to force him to make human sacrifices. Here he balked and refused and was for that steadfastness driven from Tula. All this is told by Sahagun and other Indian sources. This is the moment to say once more what needs saying just because it seems too naïve for words: To report that Huitzilopochtli did this and Quetzalcoatl that is not to confer the status of existence on these divine figures. Indeed they became fateful to their people precisely because they were so vulnerable to non-existence proofs.

There is a stone head that shows the Dear Lord weeping, long clublike tears issuing straight from the god's eyes, probably those he wept as he went into exile. The same head shows him heavily bearded, an unusual feature in a young god, and among the Indians in general. He is also supposed to have been light-skinned.

Quetzalcoatl flees toward the east. He crosses, in space not time, the path of the Mexica's god going southwest, and he makes his way toward the east coast, there to embark with his loyal band on a raft of serpents and to drift into the rising sun—the very way Cortés, a white, bearded man, took in reverse going west and inland. Cortés comes this way in 1519, just as the year that in the Aztec calendrical cycle is Quetzalcoatl's birth and death year, *ce ácatl*, One Reed, had come round again. In this year the Dear Lord was destined to return by boat from his trans-oceanic exile. You can see the tragedy taking shape.

The biggest pyramid in America rose at Cholula to mark one of the god-man's stations of flight. There the old god failed his people when, on his way to Tenochtitlan, Cortés massacred more than a hundred unarmed Cholulan nobles in his temple precinct. Cortés thought he had uncovered a plot to betray his band to the Mexica. Perhaps he had, and perhaps the planned ambush would have been the end for him if he had not prevented it with his characteristic merciless decisiveness. That we shall never know, but we do know this: The Cholulans remembered an old prophecy that the god who had rested from his flight in their city would protect them, and that if they pulled a stone out of his pyramid, a flood of water would sweep the enemy away. With panicky energy they succeeded in wrenching out a stone—and got a cloud of dust.

The Plumed Serpent, briefly to finish his tale, was not permanently discredited, nor did he cease to occupy imaginations. He became the savior god of a resurrected Mexico. The friars who came at Cortés's request wanted a warrant for treating the Indians as aboriginal Christians; they saw in the wandering god St. Thomas, one of Jesus's twelve disciples who was his missionary to India. Quetzalcoatl was also the guardian god of the nativist movement in New Spain and Mexico, celebrated in murals and hymns by Mexican painters and intellectuals and even by that wandering Englishman D. H. Lawrence. His novel of 1926, *The Plumed Serpent*, is a repulsively fascinating, garishly proto-Nazi fantasy of the god's return in provincial Mexico, complete with the paraphernalia of Nuremberg: a charismatic god-representing leader, choreographed soldiery, Nazi-like salutes, and finally human sacrifice—all this so that the heroine, a manless ageing Irishwoman, might find a man who *is* a man, that is, who hardly ever talks. It is a travesty of the sorrowful Toltec divinity of civilization.

Human sacrifice was, I have learned to think, not really just a Mexican custom ascribable to "otherness." The Mexica knew the story just told of Quetzalcoatl. I cannot believe that some of them, especially their last emperor, did not reflect that they were co-opting the god into a practice he abhorred and over which he went into exile. Perhaps those priests of Huitzilopochtli, with their skull-decorated black gowns and blood-matted hair, were fanatics totally absorbed in their cultic task, but the educated nobles, admirers of Tula, so refined in their intimate habits and their social life, must have had qualms and doubts—unless there is *no* way to infer from ourselves to others.

The numbers are staggering. It is reported that at the inauguration of Huitzilopochtli's Great Temple in 1487, 20,000—by some readings 80,000—victims were lined up four abreast in queues stretching from the temple onto the city's causeways. (Is it altogether an ironical coincidence that these were about the numbers of Indians said to have presented themselves for conversion on certain days after the conquest?) And this killing went on, in smaller numbers, in the numerous minor temples of the city. Every twenty days, by the ritual calendar, there was a god's feast, requiring sometimes quite a few children, sometimes a woman, sometimes a specially prepared youth.

The operation itself is often shown in the codices. The victims march, mostly unassisted, to the top of the pyramid; there they are laid on a convex sacrificial stone, their limbs are held by four priests while a fifth chokes off his screams with a wooden yoke, the obsidian knife rips into the chest, the heart, still beating, is held up to the Sun and put in a wooden bowl, the "eagle dish." The victim is rolled down the steps to be dismembered and distributed for feasting according to a strict protocol. The victims are children bought from the poor, the pick of slaves for sale in the market (who are ritually bathed), beautiful young nobles prepared in a year of splendid living for their role as *ixíptlas*, god-impersonators. Evidently certain divinities, like the ever-present Tezcatlipóca, Lord of the Near and Nigh, who shared functions with the city god, were not only recipients of victims but were themselves sacrificed, albeit through their human incarnations—one noteworthy parallel to Christianity.

It seems to be true that these ritual killings were not sadistic in intention or demeaning to the victims. While there are reports of weeping family and frightened victims, the sacrificial human was evidently well co-opted into the performance. Moreover, the cactus button *péyotl* and the mushroom *teonanácatl*, "Flesh of the Gods," both hallucinogens, and the alcoholic pulque seem to have been administered to the sacrifices, who were, in any case, intoxicated with the ritual swirl and the musical stridor around them. For the prepared chosen at least this passage into a flowery next world was perhaps a high point of this life—though who knows how many victims, particularly the children, died experiencing extreme fear.

These frightful, somber, and splendid festivals were evidently thought to be truly necessary to the survival of the city and the continuing existence of its world. (There may even have been a more elemental need behind the ritual consumption of the sacred victim. In the absence in Anahuac of large animals like cattle, cannibalism may have been driven by protein-hunger; that, however, is a modern speculation.) Yet, as I said, the Aztec nobility, who were so finely attuned to right and wrong conduct (as their stock homilies, preserved by Sahagun, show), must have felt themselves to be living over a moral abyss, doing a balancing act in a threatening and fragile sacred world, which doomed them in their hearts for what they did and through their sacred duties for what they might omit to do.

I have neglected to mention the largest and most steady supply of victims, the prisoners.

The highest calling of Huitzilopochtli's people, the soldiers of the Sun, was war, and the object of war was to take captives, an even higher object than the subjugation of Anahuac's cities. Promotion in the army was strictly according to the number of prisoners taken. The warriors needed to take prisoners to rise in rank; the city needed prisoners for their flesh and blood, the sacrifices that would feed and maintain the good will of the gods. It was a tight circle of necessities.

This religious trap—I will call it that—had three devastating secular consequences. First, the Mexican army never learned, until it was too late, to fight to kill, to fight a war for survival in realest earnest. Second, Tenochtitlan trained up a deadly enemy for itself, the city of Tlaxcala, seated between itself and the eastern coast. There was a bizarre but logical institution in Anahuac, the so-called "flowery war," *xochi-yaóyotl*. The Triple Alliance of Anahuac, eventually dominated by Tenochtitlan and including Texcoco, had a mutual arrangement with three cities across the mountains, of which the aristocratic republic of Tlaxcala was the most independent. The agreement was to stage battles regularly for the sole purpose of obtaining from each other prisoners for sacrifice. This was a strange kind of ceremonious warfare, which required the high-born warriors skillfully to take their enemies alive, only to bring them back home to their delayed warriors' death. Meanwhile the Tlaxcalans remained free, in training, and full of hatred, and they became Cortés's most effective allies.

And third, the evidence and actual sight of human sacrifice turned the Spaniards' stomachs—as powerful a revulsion as the moral one, I imagine. So when, as I said, they saw the remains of their own people, an ineradicable repugnance seems to have turned their hearts, a disgust which became the pretext for much savagery of their own.

Montezuma was installed as *tlatoáni* of Mexico-Tenochtitlan in 1502. *Tlatoani* means "He Who Speaks," who has authority. Since Tenochtitlan was the secular and sacred center of the Aztec world, he was the speaker over the universe, the *úei-tlatoani*—usually rendered as "emperor." When he was killed in 1520 he was 52. His lineage was even shorter than the city's existence, whose founding date is 1345. The Anahuac empire was put together during the next century; Axayacatl, Montezuma's father, who died in 1481, was only the third emperor. As was the custom, the council that chose the new

lord did not go to the son but first to Axayacatl's two brothers. When Montezuma became the sixth emperor, Anahuac
was less than seventy years old. Historians disagree whether
objectively the empire was in a state of youthful vigor or in
the course of rigidified decline when Cortés came. But there
can be no doubt that Montezuma was a monarch who personally felt doom coming. Motolinia says (probably incorrectly)
that his very name—*nomen omen*—meant one who is sad and
serious, as well as one who inspires fear and respect.

As was necessary for the *tlatoani*, he had proved himself as
warrior and officer, but he was also a highly educated man.
The Mexica, like most high civilizations, were committed to a
well-defined and diversified plan of education for their young.
The set speeches, the traditional admonitions, that the ruling
nobles made to their boys and girls upon their having reached
the age of discretion are loving, somber, straitlaced, meticu-
lous—and full of Nahua charm. The one from which I will
read a sampling goes on for six of Sahagun's columns. It begins thus:

> Here art thou, thou who art my child, thou who art my precious
> necklace, thou who art my precious feather, thou who art my cre-
> ation, my offspring, my blood, my image.

And then the child is inducted into Aztec pessimism:

> Hear well, O my daughter, O my child. The earth is not a good
> place. It is not a place of joy; it is not a place of contentment.

Then the little girl is given rules of conduct, for example:

> At night hold vigil, arise promptly. Extend thy arms promptly,
> quickly leave thy soft bed, wash thy face, wash thy hands, wash
> thy mouth, seize the broom; be diligent with the sweeping; be not
> tepid, be not lukewarm.

> What wilt thou seize upon as thy womanly labors? . . . Look
> well to the drink, the food; how it is prepared, how it is made. . . .

Then the speech touches deep moral matters:

> May thou not covet carnal things. May thou not wish for experi-
> ence, as is said, in the excrement, in the refuse. And if thou truly
> art to change thyself, would thou become a goddess?

But there was also public education, a dual system. The
Young Men's (and Women's) House, the *telpochcálli*, was open
to the lower nobility and even to commoners. The boys' house
had features of our prep school. The emphasis was on physical
hardening and the performance of rough public service. A lot
of rowdy fun was overlooked; some of the older boys even took
mistresses, and, Sahagun reports, "they presumed to utter
light and ironic words and spoke with pride and temerity."

The second institution, the famous *calmécac*, was part
seminary, part cadet corps. Here went the high nobility and
commoners destined by talent to be priests. The daily rou-
tine was punishing; for example, sleep was often interrupted
when the boys were called to draw blood from their earlobes
and ankles with maguey spines. This self-sacrifice was said to
have been instituted by Quetzalcoatl, who was in fact the tutelary divinity, the super-tutor, of the calmécac. Discipline was
fierce. There were constant humiliations, and if a noble's son
was found even a little drunk on pulque he was secretly stran-
gled; a commoner was beaten to death.

The curriculum was rigid and rigorous. The boys learned
the revisionist Mexica version of Nahua history from painted
books that were expounded to them. They learned to speak
ceremoniously and to perform ritual songs and dances accurately. They learned, besides the sign and number count of the
360-day solar calendar with its five unfortunate "hollow" in-
tercalary days, the divinatory calendar. This was the "Sacred

Book of Days" by which the priest told the feast days of the gods, the personal destiny of a baby and the epochs of the world. This study was evidently the most effective initiation into the Aztec way of seeing the world. That is the reason why the friars, trying to extirpate Aztec worship, denounced this sacred calendar with particular vehemence as having cast loose from the natural heavenly revolutions and being an evil convention—as they said: "the fruit of a compact with the Devil."

The two calendars came together every 52 years, an era called the Bundling of the Years. Ominously, such an epoch evidently occurred in 1506, "One Rabbit," when just as many year-bundles had gone by as would make the setting of the Fifth Sun imminent, and with it the final destruction by earthquakes of Huitzilopochtli, his city, and the world whose center was Tenochtitlan. The year of 1519, moreover, was, as I said, *ce acatl*, "One Reed," the name of the year of Quetzalcoatl's birth, exile and prophesied return. A student of the calendar presumably knew himself to be living at once near doomsday and near delivery.

From this schooling and his experience in the field, Montezuma emerged as high priest, warrior and *tlatoani*: spiritually austere for all his palatial luxury, a severe father to his Mexica, rigidly religious, and, for all the self-abasement his set accession speech required, an autocratic and aristocratic ruler, the first to restrict high office to the nobility. He was inaccessible to the populace, stately and ceremonious with his nobles, reserved as to his person. When Cortés, as he himself tells, tried to hug him "in Spanish fashion," Montezuma's attendants stopped him; this was court etiquette but presumably also personal preference. But above all he was a burdened man, doom-ridden, half hopeful, self-doubtful. "What shall I do, where shall I hide? If only I could turn into stone, wood or some other earthly matter rather than suffer that which I dread!" he cried out, this victor of nine pitched battles, to his magicians who could not turn to good the omens of evil to come (and got severely punished for it). This was no coward's funk but a pious man's terror of a probably inevitable future—thus a self-fulfilling fear.

There was a city across the lake, Texcoco, a member of Tenochtitlan's Triple Alliance. It paralleled the Italian cities of the Renaissance in high culture; it was a Tula revived. In the fifteenth century it had a poet-king, Nezahualcóyotl, whose poetry has the fragrance that arises when the melancholy of existence melds with elegance of expression. Like a Nahua Lucretius he offers his bitter cup with the rim sweetened by honey. He speaks:

I, Nezahualcoyotl, ask this:
Is it true one really lives on the earth?
Not forever on earth,
only a little while here.
Though it be jade it falls apart,
though it be gold it wears away,
though it be quetzal plumage it is torn asunder.
Not forever on earth,
only a little while here.

This is beauty to console for the brevity of being, but in the Texcocan Renaissance prince it is without the panicky gloom of the Mexican Emperor of the late Fifth Sun. Nezahualcoyotl's underlying sense of life's inconstancy is the same, but Montezuma's was infected by the consciousness of a more starkly immediate doom.

I think that Montezuma was probably an overwrought exemplar of a Mexica noble: devout witness of constant bloody brutality; refined connoisseur of jade and feather work; watcher for imminent death and destruction; avid collector of fleeting things like birds and flowers; cruel lord and ever-courteous prince; liar of great ability and treacherous too, as the Tlaxcalans believed; high noble of candid and simple bearing: witness the poignant speech of submission he appears to have made to Cortés when he was still in his own palace, when he still believed in the Spanish savior. He said with a smile:

> You too have been told perhaps that I am a god, and dwell in palaces of gold and silver. But you see it is false. My houses, though large, are of stone and wood like those of others. And as to my body [here he threw open his cloak]—you see it is flesh and blood like yours.

Some see delicate irony in his words, particularly in the reference to the absence of gold. But to me his speech sounds heartfelt, and he was in fact submitting to men he thought might be *teules*, gods; Cortés's band, the *santa compañia*, the Holy Company, might indeed be bringing back Quetzalcoatl-Cortés, "the white hero of the break of day."

He had had some cause to be thus receptive, for in the decade before Cortés's arrival the omens had multiplied: the spontaneous combustion of Huitzilopochtli's temple, tongues of celestial fire, finally a bird found in Lake Texcoco bearing a black mirror in its head in which the emperor briefly glimpsed the strangers landing—Sahagun catalogues eight serious omens.

I think Montezuma became heartsick and started vacillating, now welcoming the Spaniard from afar with golden gifts, now holding him off or even arranging his ambush. In the end he was transfixed like a rabbit by a snake, truly a snake since Cortés played the role of the Plumed Serpent. So he sent the Spaniard Quetzalcoatl's regalia, since it was the year *ce acatl*, One Reed. Not all his nobles were pleased at the emperor's submissiveness; they wept when not much later they attended his litter to his place of custody, his father's palace.

Some historians think the omens were an *ex post facto* invention to make the catastrophe more palatable to simple people. But they sound very plausible; ominous events do occur in clusters before disasters (as Machiavelli observes in his *Discourses*), at least for those who have prophetic souls. The omens help explain Montezuma's fragility before the crisis. It was, I want to say, a type of fragility almost designed to highlight Cortés's robustness, as if Montezuma had found his fated match, the better to reveal the West to itself.

Once he had made his submission to the Spanish emperor and been taken into Spanish custody, another side of his character came out: He became receptive to new experiences, learned to shoot the crossbow, sailed Lake Texcoco on a brigantine, the first wind-driven vessel on those waters. —It is always the West's inventions, especially those that shoot far and go fast, that first beguile the non-West. He retained his exquisite courtesy and generosity; he became sociable and even affectionate with the Spaniards. It has been suggested that he was displaying the pathological bonding of a victim to his kidnappers. But by a concord with Cortés Montezuma was running his empire from Axayacatl's palace where he and the Spaniards were quartered, and he was free to indulge in his old pleasures like hunting. It is reported that if there was fun afoot he could dissolve in giggles.

But this priest-emperor never converted or gave up human sacrifice, although frequently subjected to Cortés's passionate theological harangues against the ritual on the grounds of human brotherhood. As Fuentes says, it was simply a more urgent question to him whether the sun would rise and the world go on than what the Spaniards did to him or his empire.

Nevertheless, I wonder if it ever came to him that his religious practices were, in the nature of things, futile, that the Christians had a sun that moved reliably and stably in its heavenly orbit (and would soon even stand still at the world's center) precisely because it was *not* a god and therefore not amenable to human exertion and sacrifice. Octavio Paz says in his *Labyrinth of Solitude* that the Aztecs committed suicide because they were betrayed by their gods. I think they were, speaking more precisely, betrayed by their trust in their visible and palpable gods, who (as I think in contrast to the early invaders, who acknowledged them as devils) did nothing and were nothing and absconded more crassly than could an invisible deity or one less abjectly served—a truth I have, strangely enough, *never* found enunciated by the historians I have read.

Cortés, finally, the Conquistador, seems to me a man as emblematic of the conquering West as Montezuma was of the empire of the doomed Sun. Cortés was a hidalgo from an old, turbulent, moderately situated family. Having gotten into various scrapes, he chose to come to the Indies in 1504 when he was nineteen—an age more often given over to wanderlust than to acquisitiveness. In 1519 he began to subdue Anahuac, whose chiefs became, as he put it, somewhat equivocally, to his sovereign, "Your Majesty's vassals, and obey my commands." No sooner had he conquered Mexico for Spain than he was beset by endless *audiencias* and *residencias*, tribunals and inquiries, conducted by officials whose rectitude was apparently not much greater than his own and whose daring was considerably less. Nevertheless, by 1529 he was Marquess of the Oaxaca Valley and Captain-General of New Spain, empowered to discover further lands and to colonize them. (In fact following Mexico he discovered and named California after a queen in one of those medieval romances.) He died in 1547, and his bones have undergone grotesque removals paralleling his downward course in Mexican history, during which Quetzalcoatl was raised to a national hero while his unwitting impersonator was suppressed by the descendants of the Conquest.

The story of his and his Holy Company's march toward Tenochtitlan in 1519, his first peaceful entrance into the sacred and magical city, his expulsion, near-annihilation and devastating re-entry have lately been retold in all its fiction-defying detail by Hugh Thomas in *Conquest*. He lands on Anahuac's eastern shore with his little fleet of "water houses," as the natives described his three-masted square-riggers, of the type called *naos*. When they first saw them, they reported on them as "mountain ranges floating on water." His boldest first stroke is to dismantle his ships before he marches inland. Now the thirty-four-year-old sailor emerges as a man of many devices and deceits, a bold man of faith—and greed-inspired audacity—albeit *somewhat* more devoted to the salvation of his soul than to the amassing of gold; a resilient man well acquainted with suffering and depression; a man of self- and other-punishing endurance and scary tenacity, who seems to live on little sleep; cruel and charming, careful of his companions and demanding their utmost; prudent and daring; circumspect and lightning-quick; generous and grasping; kind and manipulative; and always an adventurer and a wanderer—as complex a man in his way as Montezuma. Prescott says in his personal memoranda, in which he details for himself the oppositions of Cortés's character:

> The great feature of his character was constancy of purpose. . . . He was inexhaustible in resources, and when all outward means were withdrawn, seemed to find sufficient to sustain him, in his own bosom.

Now listen to the beginning of Homer's *Odyssey*:

> Tell me, O Muse, of the man of many twists who wandered so much when he had sacked the sacred city of Troy. He saw the towns of many men and knew their mind, and suffered much on the sea, seeking to save his soul and the return of his companions.

No two men could be more alike; if I were to inventory the characters of the two adventurers nearly every feature in one list would turn up quite recognizably in the other, including the bouts of depression. And this happy circumstance tells me that Cortés was *not* primarily a man of his time: not just a medieval knight-errant or a mercantile-minded gold prospector, or a hard-to-control vassal of the Spanish crown, or a fierce competitor for the rights of first conquest.—He was certainly all these, and it was because he returned to the Gulf Coast to intercept his Spanish pursuers that he first lost Tenochtitlan. But before these and more fundamentally he was a man who in his intense individuality expressed an ancient and enduring type of the West, Odysseus the self-sufficient, who talks to his own heart, who has many twists and devices, who is blunt and tactful, who can be driven to extreme cruelty and engage in gratuitous acts of kindness, who lies but not ignobly, and above all, who can, in a pinch, rely on his virgin goddess, Athena, *because he relies on himself.*

In Cortés that ancient pagan character type seems to have comfortably accommodated, or better, absorbed the God from the other root of the Western tradition, though Cortés was particularly devoted to the Virgin. Hugh Thomas says that he became more God-fearing as the expedition went on— who wouldn't? His flagship sailed under a banner he had inscribed with the saying: "Friends, let us follow the Cross and if we only have faith in this sign we shall conquer." He was citing the legend under which the Emperor Constantine fought the battle that in 312 turned the Roman Empire Christian. Cortés's Christianity is a debated subject, but to me it seems unquestionable. One kind of evidence is that this prudent commander several times put his expedition at risk because of his religious impetuousness and had to be restrained by Bartolomé de Olmeda, the wise and patient friar with the expedition, a man who while practicing prudence also thought of the Indians' feelings—so unlike Pizarro's fatal chaplain. On one memorable occasion, the emperor, at Cortés's request, invited him with some of his captains to come up the Great Pyramid of Huitzilopochtli. Montezuma himself was, as usual, carried to the top, but Cortés insisted on marching up all 113 steep narrow steps and declared to the solicitous emperor waiting for him that "Spaniards are never weary;" indeed, as I mentioned, Cortés slept little when on campaign. Montezuma then obtained permission from the priests for Cortés, who was clearly already in the Christian conqueror mode, to enter the sanctuary. This reeking place so disgusted him that he asked Montezuma with a smile—not a charming one, I imagine—how so wise a prince could put his faith in a representation of the Devil. He offered to install in this temple, as he had on other pyramids, a cross and an image of the Virgin, before which the false gods would shrink into oblivion. Montezuma was deeply shocked and said—here is irony—that these were the gods that had ever led the Mexica to victory. Cortés, perhaps nudged by Friar Olmeda, apologized. But it was a dangerous moment. Montezuma had to stay behind to expiate the sacrilege. This action, which could have meant the early end of Montezuma's policy of submission, was certainly impolitic and clearly inspired by pure if untimely Christian fervor. In his own account Cortés naturally suppresses this incident in favor of what must have been a later occasion, when he did actually topple the idol down the pyramid steps, and, as he claims, stop the sacrifices.

Cortés became de facto emperor of Anahuac close to the time, namely 1513, that Machiavelli's *Prince* appeared. So I looked Cortés up, as it were. I have often wondered for whom this manual on rulership is meant, since natural princes already know it all and untalented rulers will simply use it as permission for misconduct. Cortés, it turns out, knows most of Machiavelli's lessons: how to fight both like a fox and a lion, for he was proud of his "cunning stratagems" and fierce even when wounded and unarmed; how not to be good on occasion, for he could be brutal; how to get credit for every exploit, for his letters take care that he should; how to rule more by love than fear, as his trooper Diaz attests; how, finally, to be lucky, and—a Machiavellian or Odyssean trait of his own—how to lie royally without being commonly dishonest.

But there were many more things that he did not do by this book but did rather against its explicit advice: he relied heavily on auxiliaries, fought with an amateur's improvisation, and did not study eminent predecessors—for there were none. But above all, Machiavelli doesn't seem to know, or at least to enunciate, the one thing most needful to an imperial conquistador: faith—in Cortés's case, Christian faith, but faith also in a more expansive sense, as I will try to show.

Both rulers made mistakes. Montezuma should not have sent gold to greet the "Holy Company," though how was he to know? He should not have quartered the Spaniards in Axayacatl's palace where the state treasure was hidden—and so on. But the chief mistake was to believe the prophecies and to submit to the omens, and so to the bearded white men coming over the water. Some of his nobles seem indeed to have realized this, but they were themselves used to submitting to their lord, and so they wept silently.

Cortés's errors were those of a nervous yet decisive aggressor. At Cholula he stained his name with a possibly preventable massacre. At Tenochtitlan, when he hastened to the coast to repel his pursuers, he left in charge a valorous young brute, Pedro d'Alvarado, whom the Indians called *Tonatíuh*, the Sun, because he was blond and beautiful. He proved worse to them than their own doomed Fifth Sun, for as he was edgy, eager and without judgment, he unleashed a massacre on the unarmed celebrants of Huitzilopochtli's festival which ended every chance of peaceful dominion and brought on that Sad Night. This was the night when the Spaniards, their Indian allies, and the Spanish women fighting desperately alongside their men, were driven from the city and nearly exterminated.

Above all, he razed Tenochtitlan, the finest city in the world. Was it a mistake, a crime? Here is what he himself says in his account of the recapture of the city from the Mexica, who under the young Emperor Cuauhtémoc, Montezuma's nephew, had learned the Spanish skills: to fight to kill, to fight at night, to fight from the water. The passage is from the third letter to Emperor Charles V:

> All I had seen forced me to two conclusions, the one that we should regain little of the treasure the Mexicans had taken from us; the other that they would force us to destroy and kill them all and this last weighed on my soul. I began to wonder how I could terrify them and bring them to a sense of their error. It could only be done by burning and destroying their houses and towers of the idols. . . .

Of course, the letter explains first things first: why the Emperor isn't getting his customary fifth of treasure. Of course, it assumes that the Mexica are legally in rebellion. But it also reveals a certain travail of spirit, a conscience, a care for a people whose intelligence Cortés admired and whose fate he pitied, albeit he was its cause. On Cortés's premise the destruction was a necessity, but was the premise itself necessary? For my part, I simply cannot judge. It is true, however, that once he was master of Anahuac he looked carefully after his realm and probably did it more good in the long run than it ever was in Montezuma's power to do: He spent his own resources in rebuilding the country, introduced new plants and draft animals, condemned the enslavement of the Indians and recorded in his will his deep misgivings of conscience about the institution of slavery itself, and tried to mitigate the treatment of the natives by the colonists. And, of course, he abolished human sacrifice. All in all, his dubious deeds had the effect of relegating Anahuac to the past; his good deeds gave Mexico a future. And, pressed to think in these terms about the Conquest itself, I suppose with the Peruvian writer Mario Llosa that it belongs in the long run to the credit side of something, call it human welfare.

But the question I proposed was how and why it could happen. So let me try to come to some sort of conclusion. Two worlds clashed (here the cliché tells the simple truth), and the leaders happened to be emblematic of their worlds. Let me first compare the divinities that led the leaders.

We have an alumnus, Peter Nabokov, the stepson of the man to whom this lecture is dedicated, William Darkey. He is an expert on Indian sacred life and its sacred space. When he heard that I was reading on this subject he sent me a large box of books from his private library. In one of these books I found an article containing an antithetical listing of Aztec and Christian religiosity.

On the left, the Nahua side, is listed (I select for brevity's sake) Symmetry, Autonomy, Interchangeability, and Cyclicality. On the right, the Spanish side, is listed Hierarchy, Centralization, Fixity, and Linearity. This right side is in fact recognizable as a checklist of features condemned *in* the West as evils *of* the West, a compendium of the self-critique of the West such as was current in the later part of the last century.

I also recognize the left side of the list, and it does appear to me to be descriptive of Aztec religion. But notice this strange effect: how each characteristic of that religion induced an *opposite effect* on the Aztec polity. The complexly related Symmetries of divine functions make for a draining tangle of rituals; the Autonomy of the deities—as many as 1600—leads to a burdensome multiplicity of services; the Interchangeability of identities leads to dependence on priestly interpreters; and the Cyclicality leads to a sense of inescapable doom. In fact it was Anahuac that most tended toward social Hierarchy, administrative Centralization and rigid Fixity of protocol. The Spanish side, on the other hand, gave its real-life practitioners one supreme God, reliable in his operations, author of a stable creation, progressing hopefully into a new day. And so it was the Spaniards who could afford to be free, flexible, energetic, and self-reliant: When God permits them to be defeated it is, Cortés says, on account of their own sins, a deserved punishment, not a divine antic.

But, a student of Aztec religion might argue, the similarities to Christianity are remarkably exact and numerous, so why would religion make the difference? To give a sampling of the parallelisms: The Indians had the symbol of the cross, a Maltese type, that turns up frequently in their visual art. They had absolution by confession, though it could be undergone only once in a lifetime. They had a form of baptism, ritual fasting, even an invisible god. Above all, they had the ritual ingestion of their god's blood: the victim's or their own blood was kneaded into loaves of amaranth seeds that were god-images and were then eaten. This last practice, the analogue of Christian communion, is most interesting to me, because some scholars represent this Christian sacrament as a form of cannibalism that brings Christianity closer to the Aztec feasting on flesh. But, of course, the blood partaken of during the Christian Eucharist is precisely *not* the blood of a living human being. Even a very untheoretical Christian knows that it is a mystery which is accompanied by a complex rational theology. Communicants understand, if vaguely, that the wafer and wine are neither merely symbolic nor brutely real—the nature of their transformation is open to rational questioning: For example, have they undergone *transubstantiation*, so that the substance itself, the bread and the wine, are to be regarded as now the body and blood of Christ, or have they achieved *consubstantiation*, such that they present a duality of visible properties and invisible essence?

I may be allowed to dismiss the beguiling but bizarre notion of the friars that the Indians were lapsed Christians, baptized a millennium and a half ago by Quetzalcoatl/St. Thomas; at any rate, they themselves were always afraid that the willing conversions of the Indians were perhaps rather shallow and masked the survival of the old similar-seeming worship. It remains a problem, requiring really deep investigation by people who know *not only* the methods of comparative ethnography but the ways of faith, whether such similarities betoken pure coincidence, or are features belonging to some general human religiosity, and whether such all-human phenomena have a deep or shallow common root. To me it seems, judging only at first glance, that a religion supported by many disparate narratives, whose meaning, being a matter of memory, is uncircumventably in the hands of trained priests, is simply incommensurable with a religion that has one master story whose ever-new interpretations, carried on by priests, theologians, and laymen alike, strive for coherence. Let me make my point brusquely and minimally: Such a religion, Christianity in the present case, seems to me simply more energizing. To wit: Cortés liked to read, as he said, when he had time, and he knew some theology which, in turn, gave him the self-confidence to harangue an emperor. He went to mass in the morning without fail and was ready for the day. In defense, Montezuma could only tell divine stories—myths to us—and insist on his gods' past services, which he had to keep securing by spending every day much time and many resources on arduous cultic performances.

Moreover, Cortés's Holy Company could rely on their God who, being invisible—though having one and only one human incarnation—was therefore impervious to sudden toppling. This God, a god mysterious but not capricious, made nature according to laws and left it largely alone. Thus God's created nature was open to the self-reliant inventiveness of human beings. This natural realm, being amenable to human rationality, invited initiative, for its God had himself engaged in radical innovation when he created the world and when he irrupted into history in human form.

I have been engaged by this puzzle: We know that the Indians had wheeled toys; why did Anahuac wait for Cortés to introduce wagons? It seems to me that it is not generally true that necessity is the mother of invention, but rather than inventions develop necessities: We see a convenience and we need it. Anahuac, to be sure, had no draft animals and enough slaves and

commoners with tumplines to drag its building stones anywhere. But why didn't someone think of the splendor of rolling
in stately carriages over the waiting causeways of Tenochtitlan? By my premise it was not lack of need but something
else, at which I am guessing: the Aztecs were close and loving
onlookers and clever users of nature, but they were not on the
lookout to go her one better, to whirl rather than to walk over
her terrain. Perhaps the wheel isn't the most convincing general example, since it seems to have come to the Western world
not as an original invention but by diffusion, probably from
Mesopotamia, but to me its absence in Anahuac does seem testimony to Aztec invention-inertia.

Theology, the laws of nature, interpretative accessibility,
and inventiveness—these are great but they are not the only
advantages that these Westerners who came out of the East
carried with them. Others have been intimated: the fraternal
equality of human beings insofar as they are ensouled creatures that Cortés preached to the Aztec nobles, whereas Anahuac was caste-ridden; the ensuing closeness of the leader to
his men that made Cortés listen to the complaints and sometimes—never at crucial moments—heed the advice of his companions, whereas Montezuma was deliberately remote—his
subjects had to avert their eyes when he passed—and autocratic; the project of propagating to all the world a truth felt to
be universal that unquestionably drove Cortés if not the "Holy
Company"—the name was first given ironically—whereas the
Mexica rather collected the gods of other cities, ever more of
them, so that Montezuma even established a sort of all-Ana-
huac pantheon for them; and, for our times, above all, the
tenacity of the Christians in holding on to life, whereas the
Aztecs seemed somehow—I'm far from understanding it—to
surrender themselves more readily to the thought of death and
to death itself.

Of course, the Conquistadores' Christianity was intertwined with that other root of our West, pagan antiquity, par-

ticularly the intellectual taproot, the Greek one. From this dual root stems, it seems to me, that faith in a more comprehensive sense I mentioned before, the faith that underlies a daily life free for confident projects: the trust in the stable motions of nature combined with a contemplative care for transcendence, the faith in "the Laws of Nature and of Nature's God," to cite our founding charter.

All of us here know—or will learn in the next four years—how much the Christian and post-Christian West owes to the Greek science of celestial nature and the philosophical account of its divinity. But I want to recur to the human model that is exemplified with such spectacular accuracy by Cortés, the Homeric Odysseus, the first mature Western man (for Achilles, though in years the same age in the *Iliad* as was Cortés in 1519, is constitutionally a youth). This antique man, a soldier and sailor too, is free, self-reliant, inventive, a discoverer of new lands, be it of the world or the soul, and, I nearly omitted to say, the lover of women of stature. Cortés, too, like Odysseus, who had his semi-goddesses abroad and his Penelope at home, had in his life two royal daughters of Montezuma and two Spanish wives, but above all his comrade, his advisor and interpreter, Malinali or Malinche, the Mexican princess christened Doña Marina. It was his partnership with her that gave him his Nahua nickname—the Indians addressed him as "Malinche;" if it was meant in derision, it was a misplaced scorn. She and Cortés were, like Odysseus and Penelope, one in their wily works, and they had a son, Don Martin Cortés (named after the Conquistador's father), a son to whom he was as attached as Odysseus was to his Telemachus.

I cannot pretend to understand how this distinctive species of Odyssean individualists is propagated down the ages, nor can I quite figure out whether the type produces the tradition or the tradition generates the type. In other words, to me this question seems askable and therefore pursuable: Whatever may be the case for the rest of the human world, is our

West ultimately more a civilization or a kind of human being? I tend toward the latter, but for the moment I will take the safe though weasly way and say that together, type and tradition in tangled reciprocity, they are responsible for the West's apparently irresistible expansiveness. The Empires of the Sun, on the other hand, fell so fast into ruin because they and their leaders displayed characteristics that were, so to speak, the fateful complement, the matched antithesis, of the men and machines of the West.

The lessons learned in thinking about a problem amount more often to collateral insights than direct solutions. So I want to end with two such lessons I believe I learned: first, that we really must come to grips with this actual expansiveness of the West and if, on thoughtful consideration, it proves necessary, consider candidly its possible superiority—superiority, that is, in the scope it gives to individual human nature by the universality of its conceptions. And second, that we, as conscious representatives of that tradition, owe those overrun and extinguished civilizations, with all their irreplaceable strange beauty, a respectful remembrance—not merely as projects for research but as objects of human regard.

Books Read and Books Consulted

Baldwin, Neil. 1998. *Legends of the Plumed Serpent: Biography of a Mexican God*. New York: Public Affairs.

Boone, Elizabeth Hill. 1994. *The Aztec World*. Washington, D.C.: Smithsonian Books.

Broda, Johanna, Davíd Carrasco, and Eduardo Moctezuma. 1987. *The Great Temple of Tenochtitlan: Center and Periphery of the Aztec World*. Berkeley: University of California Press.

Cabeza de Vaca, Alvar Núñez. 1542. *The Account: Alvar Núñez Cabeza de Vaca's Relación*. Translated by Martin A. Favata and José B. Fernández. Houston: Arte Público Press (1993).

Carmack, Robert M., Janine Gasco, and Gary H. Gossen. 1996. *The Legacy of Mesoamerica: History and Culture of Native American Civilization*. Upper Saddle River, N.J.: Prentice Hall.

Carrasco, Davíd. 1982. *Quetzalcoatl and the Irony of Empire: Myths and Prophecies in the Aztec Tradition*. Chicago: The University of Chicago Press.

Clendinnen, Inga. 1991. *Aztecs: An Interpretation*. Cambridge: Cambridge University Press.

Columbus, Christopher. 1492–1504. *The Four Voyages of Christopher Columbus*. Edited and translated by J. M. Cohen. Baltimore: Penguin Books (1969).

Conrad, Geoffrey, and Arthur A. Demarest. 1988. *Religion and Empire: The Dynamics of Aztec and Inca Expansionism*. Cambridge: Cambridge University.

Copernicus, Nicolaus. 1543. *On the Revolutions of the Heavenly Spheres*. Translated by Charles Glenn-Wallace. Great Books of the Western World, no. 16: Ptolemy, Copernicus, Kepler. Chicago: Encyclopedia Britannica, Inc. (1952).

Cortés, Hernán. 1520's. *Hernán Cortés, Letters from Mexico*. Translated by Anthony Pagden. Oxford: Oxford University Press (1986).

Diamond, Jared. 1999. *Guns, Germs, and Steel: The Fates of Human Societies*. New York: W. W. Norton.

Díaz del Castillo, Bernal. 1555. *The Discovery and Conquest of Mexico*. Translated by A. P. Maudslay. New York: Farrar, Straus and Giroux (1956).

Díaz, Gisele and Alan Rodgers. c. 1500. *The Codex Borgia: A Full-Color Restauration of the Ancient Mexican Manuscript*. New York: Dover Publications (1993).

Florescano, Enrique. 1999. *The Myth of Quetzalcoatl*. Translated by Lysa Hochroth. Baltimore: The Johns Hopkins University Press.

Fuentes, Carlos. 1998. "The Two Shores." In *Clashes of Culture*. Chicago: The Great Books Foundation.

Galeano, Eduardo. 1985. *Memory of Fire: 1. Genesis: Part One of a Trilogy*. Translated by Cedric Belfrage. New York: Pantheon Books.

Gibbon, Edward. 1788. *The Decline and Fall of the Roman Empire*, Vol. I. New York: The Modern Library.

Jennings, Gary. 1980. *Aztec*. New York: A Tom Doherty Associates Book (1997).

Kadir, Djelal. 1992. *Columbus and the Ends of the Earth: Europe's Prophetic Rhetoric as Conquering Ideology*. Berkeley: University of California Press.

Klor de Alva, J. Jorge. 1999. "Religious Rationalization and the Conversion of the Nahuas: Social Organization and Colonial Epistemology." In *Aztec Ceremonial Landscapes*. Edited by Davíd Carrasco. Niwot, CO: University Press of Colorado.

Lafaye, Jacques. 1976. *Quetzalcóatl and Guadalupe: The Formation of Mexican National Consciousness, 1531–1813*. Translated by Benjamin

Keen. Foreword by Octavio Paz. Chicago: The University of Chicago Press.

Las Casas, Bartolomé de. 1542. *A Short Account of the Destruction of the Indies.* Translated by Nigel Griffin. London: Penguin Books (1992).

Lawrence, D. H. 1926. *The Plumed Serpent [Quetzalcoatl].* New York: Vintage Books (1992).

Le Clézio, J. M. G. 1993. *The Mexican Dream: Or, The Interrupted Thought of Amerindian Civilizations.* Translated by Teresa Lavender Fagan. Chicago: The University of Chicago Press.

Leon-Portilla, Miguel, editor. 1969. *The Broken Spears: The Aztec Account of the Conquest of Mexico.* Boston: Beacon Press.

———, editor. 1980. *Native Mesoamerican Spirituality: Ancient Myths, Discourses, Stories, Doctrines, Hymns, Poems from the Aztec, Yucatec, Quiche-Maya and Other Sacred Traditions.* Mahwah, N.J.: Paulist Press.

Llosa, Mario Vargas. 1990. "Questions of Conquest," *Harper's Magazine* (December):45–53.

———. 1989. *The Storyteller.* Translated by Helen Lane. New York: Farrar, Straus and Giroux.

Machiavelli, Niccolò. 1513. *The Prince and The Discourses.* Translated by Luigi Ricci. New York: Modern Library (1950).

"Motolinía" (Fray Toribio de Benavente). c. 1541. *History of the Indians of New Spain.* Translated by Francis Borgia Steck, O.F.M. Richmond, VA: William Byrd Press (1951).

Naipaul, V. S. 1969. *The Loss of El Dorado: A History.* New York: Penguin Books (1981).

Paz, Octavio. 1985. *The Labyrinth of Solitude and The Other Mexico; Return to the Labyrinth of Solitude; Mexico and the United States; The Philanthropic Ogre.* Translated by Lysander Kemp, Yara Milos, and Rachel Phillips Belash. New York: Grove Press.

Pearce, Colin D. 1997. "Prescott's Conquests: Anthropophagy, Auto-da-Fe and Eternal Return." *Interpretation,* Vol. 24, 3 (Spring):339–361.

Peck, Harry Thurston. 1905. *William Hickling Prescott.* Port Washington, N.Y.: Kennikat Press (1968).

Prescott, William Hickling. 1843, 1847. *History of the Conquest of Mexico and History of the Conquest of Peru.* New York: The Modern Library.

———. *History of the Conquest of Mexico.* Introduction by James Lockhart. New York: Modern Library (2001).

———. 1823–1858. *The Literary Memoranda of William Hickling Prescott,* Vols. I, II. Edited by C. Harvey Gardiner. Norman: The University of Oklahoma Press (1961).

Ricard, Robert. 1933. *The Spiritual Conquest of Mexico: An Essay on the Apostolate and Evangelizing Methods of the Mendicant Orders in New Spain: 1523–1572.* Berkeley: University of California Press (1982).

Sahagún, Fray Bernadíno de. 1547–1579. *General History of the Things of New Spain (Florentine Codex*, 12 Books). Translated by Arthur J. O. Anderson and Charles Dibble. Published in thirteen parts: Santa Fe, N.M.: The School of American Research and The University of Utah (1953–1982).

———. 1585. *Conquest of New Spain: 1585 Revision.* Translated by Howard F. Cline. Salt Lake City: University of Utah Press (1989).

Séjourné, Laurette. 1976. *Burning Water: Thought and Religion in Ancient Mexico.* Berkeley: Shambala.

Soustelle, Jacques. 1955. *The Daily Life of the Aztecs on the Eve of the Spanish Conquest.* Translated by Patrick O'Brian. Stanford: Stanford University Press (1970).

Thomas, Hugh. 1993. *Conquest: Montezuma, Cortés, and the Fall of Old Mexico.* New York: Simon and Schuster.

Todorov, Tzvetan. 1984. *The Conquest of America: The Question of the Other.* Translated by Richard Howard. New York: HarperPerennial (1992).

Townsend, Richard F., editor. 1992. *The Ancient Americas: Art from Sacred Landscapes.* Chicago: The Art Institute of Chicago.

Von Hagen, Victor W. 1957. *Realm of the Incas.* New York: Mentor Books.

Walker, Ronald G. 1978. *Infernal Paradise: Mexico and the Modern English Novel.* Berkeley: The University of California Press.

Williams, William Carlos. 1925. "The Destruction of Tenochtitlan: Cortez and Montezuma." In *In the American Grain: Essays by William Carlos Williams.* New York: New Directions Books (1956).

Wolf, Eric. 1959. *Sons of the Shaking Earth.* Chicago: University of Chicago Press.

Notes

Mile-High Meditation:
My Take on How to Think and How to Be

1. It's wonderful how, once you've set out on an inquiry, everything speaks to you. The following comes from Heidegger, *Being and Time* (p. 299). He says that when human being (*Dasein*) is properly itself, it is aboriginally equally in truth and untruth; in its truth it appropriates untruth properly to itself. He means (I think) that human being is from birth enmeshed in a world of care that distracts it from its proper being; from this uncircumventable untruth it must recover itself in its truth—which is to understand itself as a project of finite possibilities—but even that resolutely free human being is still dependent on and falls back into the distracting world of its birth, though now with understanding.

I make note of this find because it does remind me that my thoughts are neither new nor ought to be—just mine, and probably not even that; I've read too many books. This I know: that waxing original is perilously close to concocting.

In any case, the passage isn't quite in tune with the apprehension that I'm trying to articulate: that there is a compaction of truth and falsity not only in human apprehension but in all there is.

2. Again, it is Plotinus who turns out to know things I need: He has an ontological scheme, deeper than my attempt to find a this-worldly place for wrongness, for folding badness into the large whole that encompasses the visible cosmos, the universe of intellect, and its Beyond. If the Good as the One and the First governs All by letting its goodness flow out and down, then the Last, the remote edge, must, for the sake of completeness, be acknowledged, though it be the ultimate fall-off from unity and good: limitless and bad. And so, in degrees, throughout the whole: Not-good is both

functional and necessary to give goodness its matter so that its forms may take shape.

3. Plato says in his *Seventh Letter* that there are certain matters he never put into writing because they cannot be learned that way (341c); they require being together, face-to-face over time.

4. In preparing to read Shakespeare sonnets with my graduate students, I came on this passionately proposed hermeneutic mode, "a pluralistically committed way": It decries "the debilitating effects of insisting that anything that is true must be exclusively true" and recommends that almost all of a reader's responses should be simultaneously maintained (Stephen Booth, *Shakespeare's Sonnets*, pp. 507 ff.). The justification for the abnegation of choice is, implicitly, that the poem can really support (because the poet really intended) mutually jostling readings and, explicitly, that while decisions really change real-life events, no judgment alters a recorded poem. This view is attractive except for its psychological dangers: A mind long inflated with a multitude of equi-valent possibilities tends to go flabby. From within this, my meditation, a pluralistically readable poem poses an exercise: to find that meaning of the poem whose internal determinations the alternative readings articulate. In fancy terms: I'm for disambiguating ambiguity; *yes* and *no* can, even must, coexist, but not coordinately.

5. I remember now that Socrates (my teacher in questions if not in answers) calls himself a lifelong lover of this way of inquiry which, he says, is wonder-full; he speaks of "the wonders of the one and many"(*Philebus* 14). It seems so to me, too.

6. Plotinus, Plato's executor, so to speak, puts it this way in his essay *On Beauty*: Beauty is *shapeliness*, being visibly well-formed through participation in, being like in looks, to that "invisible look" (*eidos*) that is a Platonic Form (*Ennead* I 6).

7. Wouldn't it have been convenient to have known back then that one Numenius called Plato an "Attic-speaking Moses" (*Moyses attikizon*)? This hypothesis, that Greek wisdom is orient-derived, was taken up again, now in the spirit of political correctness, in the last century by Martin Bernal.

8. I've long been persuaded that the time-space sensibility of Kant's Subject is a humanization of Newton's divine sensory receptivity.

Madison's "Memorial and Remonstrance":
A Model of American Eloquence

This study was written under a Mellon Foundation Grant for Individual Study. Reprinted with slight alteration from *The St. John's Review* 32 (1981): 55–73.

1. James Madison, *The Papers of James Madison*, vol. 8, *1784–1786*, ed. Robert A. Rutland and William M. E. Rachal (Chicago: University of Chicago Press, 1973), 295–306. I know of no detailed study of the Memorial.

2. "In this masterly paper, he discussed the question of an establishment of religion by law from every point of view—of natural right, the inherent limitations of the civil power, the interests of religion itself, the genius and precepts of Christianity, the warning lessons of history, the dictates of a wise and sober policy,—and treated them all with a consummate power of reasoning, and a force of appeal to the understandings and hearts of people, that bore down every opposing prejudice and precluded reply. This noble production of the mind and heart of Mr. Madison" is, Rives concluded this perfectly just appreciation, a triumphant plea in the great cause of religious liberty, "never surpassed in power or eloquence by any which its stirring interests have called forth." William Cabell Rives, *A History of the Life and Times of James Madison* (Boston: Little, Brown, 1859), 632.

3. Neal Riemer, *James Madison* (New York, 1968), 12–13. Riemer does not rate Madison's rhetorical gifts very high, particularly when compared to those of Jefferson and of Paine. He describes the style as earnest, forthright, simple, unadorned, quiet. "His writings convince but do not take fire." I think his estimate too much reduces rhetoric to oratory.

4. *Papers*, 8: 295–98; "Madison's 'Detached Memoranda,'" ed. Elizabeth Fleet, *William and Mary Quarterly*, 3rd Series, 3 (October, 1946): 555–56; Irving Brant, *James Madison*, vol. 2, *The Nationalist: 1780–1787* (Indianapolis: Bobbs-Merrill, 1948), 343–55; Charles F. James, *Documentary History of the Struggle for Religious Liberty* (New York: Da Capo Press, 1971), 128–41; Ralph Ketcham, *James Madison* (New York: Macmillan, 1971), 162–68; Anson Phelps Stokes, *Church and State in the United States*, Vol. I (New York: Harper, 1950), 339–45; Manfred Zipperer, *Thomas Jefferson's "Act for Establishing Religious Freedom in Virginia" vom 16. Januar 1786*, Dissertation (Erlangen, 1967), 24–28.

5. James, 129.

6. The speeches are extant in the form of notes; see *Papers*, 8:195–99.

7. Galliard Hunt, "Madison and Religious Liberty," *Annual Report of the American Historical Association* (1901), Vol. I, 168.

8. Rives, 631.

9. "Detached Memoranda," 555–556.

10. *Papers*, 8:473.

11. *Papers*, 8:298.

12. To display the bare bones of the argumentation I have stripped it of Madison's diction and added connectives.

1. Because of the unconditional priority of religious duties over civil obligations, religion is wholly exempt from any secular direction.
2. So much more so is it exempt from governmental interference.
3. Therefore even the smallest infringement of religious liberty constitutes an insupportable breach of the limitations on government.
4. Governmental aid to religion is necessarily discriminatory and therefore violates the basic principle of equality.

5. Furthermore it constitutes officials the judges of orthodoxy and enables them to use religion politically.
6. At the same time it weakens Christianity by making it depend on secular support.
7. Moreover, such aid contaminates the purity of Christianity.
8. Above all, it is unnecessary to the security of a free government; indeed it is dangerous.
9. It discourages immigration by signalling possible persecution.
10. And it encourages emigration of dissenting citizens.
11. It encourages violent animosity among the sects.
12. In thus hindering free movement it in fact restricts the spread of Christianity.
13. The attempt to enforce so unpopular a law will undermine social stability.
14. Therefore before the bill is enacted into law the will of the majority should be fairly ascertained and represented in the legislature.
15. Ultimately, however, religious liberty being coequal with the other natural rights, the legislature has in any case no authority to abridge it, unless it is granted to have unlimited power to take away all rights.

13. Since the texture of the Memorial will sometimes be best brought out by comparison with Madison's other writings on religious liberty, that dearest of his causes, a list of his chief expressions on the subject is subjoined. I want to observe here that while Madison's language soon acquires a certain canonical quality, it never becomes formulaic. Iteration does not wear away its warmth.

1. 1773–75. A series of youthful letters addressed to his friend from Princeton, William Bradford. These were written when Madison was in his early twenties and express in youthfully vigorous language his disgusted preoccupation with evidences of religious persecution in Orange County and in Virginia as a whole.
2. 1776. His first small but important contribution as a lawmaker, his amendment of George Mason's draft of Article XVI for the Virginia Declaration of Rights. Also his own rejected version.
3. 1785. The "Memorial and Remonstrance," his most extensive writing on the subject.
4. 1788. A note on the value of a multiplicity of sects, meant for the Virginia Convention.
5. 1789. An early version and the final form of the first article of the Federal Bill of Rights, the First Amendment.
6. 1792. Essay "On Property," expressing a theory of rights, and particularly religious rights, as constituting personal property.
7. 1811. Presidential Veto Message, against the incorporation of the Episcopal Church.
8. 1811, 1813. Presidential Thanksgiving Messages, with caveats about publicly ordered prayer.

9. 1819–1822. Letters demonstrating that state support is not necessary to the religious sects.

10. 1823. Letter to Edward Everett, on the secular university.

11. "Detached Memoranda" (fragmentary essays separated from his main works in the nineteenth century), containing historical notes and exhortations concerning religious liberty, and an account of the events around the Memorial.

12. 1832. A late letter to the Rev. Jasper Adams giving proofs from American history that Christianity is not in need of state support.

The sources for these texts are: (1) James Madison, *The Papers of James Madison*, vol. I *1751–1779*, ed. William T. Hutchinson and William M. E. Rachal (Chicago: University of Chicago Press, 1962) 100–161 passim; (2) *Ibid.*, 174; (3) *Papers*, 8: 298–304; (4) James Madison, *The Forging of American Federalism*, ed. Saul K. Padover (New York: Harper and Row, 1965), 306; (5) Stokes, 345; (6) *Ibid.*, 551; (7) *Forging*, 307; (8) Adrienne Koch, *Madison's "Advice to My County"* (Princeton: Princeton University Press, 1966), 33–34; (9) *Forging*, 308–310; (10) Stokes, 348; (11) *William and Mary Quarterly*, 554–562; (12) Galliard Hunt, ed., *The Writings of James Madison*, vol. 9, *1819–1836* (New York: Putnam, 1910), 484–88.

14. George Campbell, *The Philosophy of Rhetoric* (1776), ed. Lloyd F. Blitzer (Carbondale, IL: Southern Illinois University Press, 1963), 365.

15. *Papers*, 1:38.

16. Frank Swancara, *Thomas Jefferson vs. Religious Oppression* (New York: University Books, 1969), 124.

17. Samuel Stanhope Smith sent him a disquisition "on that knotty question of liberty and necessity," for light on which Madison had "frequently attacked" (i.e. approached) him. Madison's response is lost, but Smith observes in a later letter: "I have read over your *theoretical* objections against the doctrine of moral liberty; for *practically* you seem to be one of its disciples." *Papers*, 1:194, 253). For Madison's theory of human nature in general, see Ralph L. Ketcham, "James Madison and the Nature of Man," *Journal of the History of Ideas*, 19 (1958): 62–76.

18. "Detached Memoranda," 556.

19. Wilber G. Katz and Harold Southerland, "Religious Pluralism and the Supreme Court," *Religion in America*, ed. William C. Mclaughlin and Robert N. Bellah (Boston: Houghton Mifflin, 1968), 273.

20. Alexander Landi, "Madison's Political Theory," *The Political Science Reviewer*, Vol. 6 (Fall 1976), 77–79.

21. John Wise in *Vindication of the Government of New England Churches* (1717), quoted in Sidney E. Mead, "The 'Nation with the Soul of a Church'," *American Civil Religion*, ed. Russell E. Richey and Donald G. Jones (New York: Harper and Row, 1974), 53 ff.

22. On Madison's views of the problems of majoritarian rule, see above all *Federalist*, no. 10; also Landi, 84 ff.

23. *Papers*, Vol. 8, 297.

24. See Jefferson's Letter to the Danbury Baptists, 1802; on Roger Williams, see Loren Beth, *The American Theory of Church and State* (Gainesville: University of Florida Press, 1958), 65. The American author of the separation doctrine was Roger Williams, with whose ideas Madison was probably acquainted through his connection with the Baptists of his county.

25. John Adams's entry in his diary shows how the Boston Tea Party caught the imagination as a beginning: "This is the most magnificent Movement of all. There is a Dignity, a Majesty, a Sublimity, in this last Effort of the Patriots, that I greatly admire. . . . I can't but consider it as an Epocha in History" (December 17, 1773).

26. "Detached Memoranda," 557.

27. John Locke, *The Second Treatise of Government and A Letter Concerning Toleration*, ed. J. W. Gough (Oxford: Basil Blackwell, 1976), 149.

28. Swancara, 123–32; "Detached Memoranda," 556.

29. To Mordecai M. Noah, 1818; to Jacob de la Motta, 1820.

30. "Detached Memoranda," 555.

31. Koch, 33; cf. "Detached Memoranda," 560–61.

32. *Papers*, 1:172–75.

33. For example, in the Declaration of Independence there is "Nature's God," man's "Creator," "the Supreme Judge of the World." In his law Jefferson used one designation that pleased the devout, "holy author of our religion," the very one employed by the Baptists in their resolution against the assessment bill (James, 138).

34. See *Papers*, 1:170 ff.

35. See Hunt, "James Madison and Religious Liberty," *op. cit.*, 166.

36. Stokes, 22–26.

37. Letter to Edward Livingston, 1822; to Rev. Jasper Adams, 1832.

38. Locke started writing on toleration in the decade before Spinoza's *Treatise*, which appeared in 1670, though the *Letter* postdated it (1683–1684). For Locke's lack of interest in Spinoza see Leo Strauss, *Natural Right and History* (Chicago: University of Chicago Press, 1974), 211.

39. See, for example, the theological catalogue for the library of the University of Virginia, which he hastily tossed off at Jefferson's urgent request, listing an astonishing number of church writers of the first five Christian centuries (Rives, 641–644).

40. Landi, 80–84.

41. John Milton, *Selected Prose*, ed. C. A. Patrides (Baltimore, MD: Penguin, 1974), 316.

42. Letter to Rev. Jasper Adams, 1832. The opinion here expressed seems to have been current. For example, just the preceding year Tocqueville had asked a Catholic priest whom he had met in his travels through the Michigan Territory this very question: "Do you think that the sup-

port of the civil power is useful to religion?"—and had received the same answer Madison was to give Rev. Adams, a decided negative. See George Wilson Pierson, *Tocqueville in America*, ed. Dudley C. Lunt (Gloucester, 1969), 203.

43. Evidence for such a long-term decline in the second half of this century is given in Rodney Stark and Charles Y. Glock, *American Piety: The Nature of Religious Commitment*, Vol. I (Berkeley: University of California Press, 1970), 204 ff. Of course, the question would become moot, should a massive religious revival refute the sociological projections. Addendum in 2010: Just such a revival has indeed occurred.

44. "Detached Memoranda," 554.

45. "Detached Memoranda," 556–57.

46. Beth, 66. Madison's own church allegiance was so vanishingly weak a factor in his opinions about religious liberty that it can be relegated to a footnote. He was, in fact, a born Episcopalian with strong Presbyterian associations from his Princeton days, apparently a communicant of no church, who displayed unfailing respect for the faiths of the sects.

47. Stokes, 551. The starting point of the essay appears to be Locke's definition of property as life, liberty and estate in the *Second Treatise of Government*, Ch. 9.

48. *Notes on the State of Virginia*, Query XVII.

49. Madison liked to quote Voltaire's Article on "Tolerance" in the *Philosophical Dictionary*. "If one religion only were allowed in England, the government would possibly become arbitrary; if there were but two, the people would cut each other's throats; but as there are such a multitude, they all live happy and in peace." See Koch, 76.

50. Jefferson, too, had complained of the underrepresentation in both houses of the middle and upper counties, and of the arms-bearing population in general.

51. "Detached Memoranda," 554.

52. *Forging*, 36.

53. Campbell, *The Philosophy of Rhetoric*, 215–16, 285, 35. I. A. Richards, for example, in his *Philosophy of Rhetoric* (New York: Oxford University Press, 1965), 70, decries the use of just such terms as "misleading and unprofitable."

54. Rives, 25, n. 1. It is the spirit of Swift's definitions which I. A. Richards's rhetoric is intended to oppose.

55. *Papers*, 1:32–42.

56. *Papers*, 1:18–19.

57. Microfilm, Princeton University Library.

58. "James Madison's Autobiography," ed. Douglas Adair, *William and Mary Quarterly*, Third Series, 2, no. 2, 202, 207. See also Robert A. Rutland, "Madison's Bookish Habits," *The Quarterly Journal of the Library of Congress*, 37, 2 (Spring 1980), 176–91.

59. Sources: Irving Brant, *The Bill of Rights, Its Origin and Meaning* (New York: New American Library, 1967), 400–18; *The Supreme Court and Education, Classics in Education* No. 4, ed. David Fellman (New York: Teachers College Press, 1976), Pt. 1, 3–124.

60. Stokes, 26–30, gives a history of the term. The contemporary political use of the phrase "The Establishment" is, of course, quite different, since it has no reference to legal confirmation.

61. Letter to Rev. Jasper Adams, 1832.

62. "Detached Memoranda," 558–60; Letter to Edward Livingston, 1822.

63. *Religion in America*, 275; "Detached Memoranda," 559.

64. An example is his reply to Rev. Adams, 1832.

65. For the definition of secularism, see Stokes, 30–31. Just this year, the secular religion issue has again been raised in *Seagraves v. State of California*. [1980—Ed.]

A Reading of Lincoln's "Gettysburg Address"

All page references to Lincoln's speeches are to *The Collected Works of Abraham Lincoln*, ed. Roy P. Basler (New Brunswick, 1953–1955).

1. For a description of the events of the Gettysburg dedication and a collection of commentaries on the speeches see Carl Sandburg, *Abraham Lincoln, The War Years* (New York, 1939) II, pp. 452–477.

2. For an annotated collection of the various versions see *Collected Works*, VII, pp. 17–23.

3. *Abraham Lincoln: His Speeches and Writings*, ed. R. P. Basler (New York, 1962), p. 47. Hereafter cited as *Speeches and Writings*.

4. Edward Everett, *Orations and Speeches* (Boston, 1892), IV, pp. 622–659.

5. See Harold Zyskind, "A Rhetorical Analysis of the Gettysburg Address," *Journal of General Education*, IV (1950), pp. 202–212.

6. For an analysis which does justice to the tremendous implications of the speech see Harry V. Jaffa, *Crisis of the House Divided* (Garden City, N.Y., 1959), pp. 183–232.

7. In thinking out these paragraphs I received much help from the doctoral dissertation (Chicago, 1964) by George Anastaplo, "Notes on the First Amendment to the Constitution of the United States," Appendix I, 6, p. 600 ff.

8. Cf. *Speeches and Writings*, p. 216.

9. From a speech indirectly reported in *Herndon's Lincoln* (Chicago, 1890) II, p. 415.

10. See Carl L Becker, *The Declaration of Independence* (New York, 1958), p. 142.

11. Cf. *Speeches and Writings*, p. 538.

12. *Op. cit.* p. 45. Addendum in 2010: Stephen Booth, in *Precious Nonsense* (Berkeley: University of California Press, 1998), argues in his chapter on the Gettysburg Address that the speech contains "undelivered sense" and also "plain nonsense" and that both potentiate its pregnant vitality. On rereading my essay, it seems to me an argument before the fact that neither preciousness nor nonsense was a Lincolnian mode.

The Paradox of Obedience

1. This lecture was delivered shortly after a sexual harassment scandal occurred at the Academy.

The Empires of the Sun and the West

1. I can't help noticing that the number of the Spanish conquerors of Mexico, pitted against a huge indigenous army, is exactly the same as the number of Spartan defenders of Greece, pitted against an immense invading army; see end of previous lecture and below in this one.